Bilinguality
and Literacy

2nd Edition

Bilinguality and Literacy

Principles and Practice

2nd Edition

Edited by
Manjula Datta

With a Foreword by
Colin Baker

continuum

Continuum
The Tower Building
11 York Road
London SE1 7NX

80 Maiden Lane, Suite 704
New York
NY 10038

First edition published by Continuum, 2000
This second edition © Manjula Datta 2007

British Library Cataloguing-in-Publication Data
A catalogue record for this book is available from the British Library.

ISBN:
978-08264-93293 (hardback)
978-08264-93309 (paperback)

Library of Congress Cataloging-in-Publication Data
A catalog record for this book is available from the Library of Congress.

Typeset by Free Range Book Design & Production Limited
Printed and bound in Great Britain by Athenaeum Press, Gateshead, Tyne and Wear

Contents

In memory of my father
Sri Kedar Nath Dutt
who understood children's minds so well.

Acknowledgements

My thanks go to all those who have supported me in writing this second edition. Many colleagues at London Metropolitan University, particularly Alayne Ozturk and Cathy Pomphrey, and Raymonde Sneddon of the University of East London, read drafts at various stages and their comments have been very helpful. My thanks also to Jenny Lovel, my editor, for her interest in the linguistic skills of bilingual children and continuous support.

Once again my special thanks go to all the children who continue to provide me with the opportunity to work with them and the pleasure this affords. I warmly appreciate the efforts of many schools in facilitating and supporting my work, as well as the headteachers, staff and student-teachers, who have shown much interest in their children's development and enthusiasm to share their understanding with me.

I am grateful to all my friends and family, my husband Peter, and daughter Tanya, for their ongoing support.

Preface to the Second Edition

In writing this second edition I have reflected on colleague, teacher and student feedback on how they used the book, especially what to them were the most significant points in the book. This, together with my own teaching, observations and further research has led me to argue strongly that in multilingual, multicultural classrooms bilingual children's language and literacy development is necessarily an intercultural experience. The bilingual mind works interculturally in processing and constructing meaning, and any language learning by definition is an intercultural experience. Additionally, reflecting on the range of abilities demonstrated by the bilingual learners situated in the book I have used the term 'multi-ability' rather than 'mixed ability' in this edition, the latter somehow suggests a fixed status quo. This I feel better expresses the dynamic nature of learning and potential development in an intercultural collaborative setting, in that when offered the opportunity to learn at a *personal level* using their funds of cognitive and cultural resources, bilingual children demonstrate greater language and literacy learning ability. Many children in my study from 'low ability' settings in class demonstrated significant potential to learn, responding to sociocultural approaches to learning, and working with teachers with shared knowledge and understanding of how the bilingual mind works. This is exemplified in children's work throughout the book.

Manjula Datta
London
February 2007

Foreword

Colin Baker

There are few themes of such contemporary cross-disciplinary interest as bilingualism and literacy. As we move forward in a new millennium, as an information-led society, global trade, travel and technology make internationalism and intercultural communication increasingly possible and preferred, languages and literacy become truly international topics.

The themes of bilingualism and literacy contain some stark contrasts: the plight of endangered languages set against the increase in bilingualism and multilingualism for business, international government and global communications; the frequently impoverished nature of language minorities sometimes based in inner-city areas, other times in poor scattered rural communities contrasts with international business executives whose income is greatly aided by fluency in several languages; the urgent need to preserve the rich oral and written traditions of the smaller languages of the world, compared with the fast-moving rise of international languages, particularly English, Spanish and Mandarin, that foster the future of the global village. The study of bilingualism and literacy thus contains contrasts and tensions, dilemmas and debates.

The themes of bilingualism and literacy are enacted in such varied human settings, encapsulating the experience of natives, refugees and emigrants; rich Cuban-Americans and poor Colombians; the Chinese diaspora and local Calcutta experience; sometimes intimidating schools and intimate families; the loneliness of immigrants and the collaborativeness of language communities. At our peril we forget the considerable variety of experience and the diversity of construction of meaning that is owned by bilinguals and multilinguals.

This book celebrates such variety and diversity by portraying the rich linguistic and cognitive resources that bilinguals bring into classrooms. Such resources both enable and extend learning beyond what is often thought necessary. The book shows how, in a variety of contexts, teaching strategies that integrate meanings from both languages and cultures in school learning lead to high achievement. When two or more languages and cultures are present across the curriculum, international research suggests that there is value-addedness in attainment, and standards in classrooms rise.

The educational use of two or more languages and cultures requires activation at different levels of decision-making: classroom practice, school provision and policies at classroom, departmental, school, Local Authority and national level. When such policies are positive to bilingualism and cultural diversity, they create a powerful learning resource for bilinguals not only at the cognitive level, but also for personal, social and economic self-fulfilment.

The beauty in the cultural diversity of our world is well encapsulated in varied local literacy practices. To our global advantage, we reproduce and maintain such diversity. *We do this not for the sake of literacy or language, but for the sake of children.*

It is in the richest interests of child development that minority language literacy and biliteracy is supported by parents, teachers, communities and advocates (of whom academics are one important voice). There are so many advantages for children who become bilingual and especially biliterate:

- communication advantages with the nuclear and extended family, in language communities and internationally;
- cultural advantages in gaining a deeper enculturation, a wider multiculturalism, and different worlds of experience that are most authentically encapsulated in literary practices in different languages;
- the potential of greater tolerance and less racism due to a wider vision of society and recognition of equality in diversity;
- the cognitive advantages of being bilingual and biliterate, such that bilingual children develop increased creativity, sensitivity to communication and metalinguistic awareness;
- the character advantages of becoming thoroughly bilingual and bicultural through raised self-esteem and an increased security in identity;
- the curriculum advantages that seem to particularly relate to biliteracy, where children who are thoroughly biliterate tend to attain higher standards throughout the curriculum;
- the growing research which suggests that bilinguals learn third and successive languages easier than monolinguals;
- the economic and employment benefits that are increasingly shared by bilinguals and biliterates, whose linguistic advantages over monolinguals give them not only value-addedness but also increasingly a critical advantage in language minority niche economies, in jobs that require a multilingual customer interface, and in international careers in trade, government and communication.

Such are the advantages of bilingualism and biliteracy that monolinguals must increasingly be seen as deprived. We disadvantage monolinguals and monoliterates at two levels. First, at the individual level, we deny monolinguals equality of opportunity by depriving them of the communication, cultural, cognitive, character, curriculum, cash and career advantages shared by many bilinguals and biliterates. Second, at the societal level, we deny the past and impoverish the future if we fail to retain the richness of linguistic, cultural and literary diversity. Internationalism best means retaining colourful language and cultural variety, not moving to monochrome standardization. *We do this not for the sake of the people of the past, but for the sake of all children of the future.*

Professor Colin Baker

Notes on Authors

Manjula Datta was educated in Nairobi, Calcutta, Bristol and London. She is a Senior Lecturer in Bilingualism and Language Education at London Metropolitan University. She has published her work in books, journals and in the educational press and has acted as consultant on several bilingual education projects. For five years, she was an active member of the ESOL and TESOL Review Board at Trinity College, London. Her work has been quoted in a number of government guidance documents on minority language children's learning and achievement. She is the co-author of *A World of Languages: Developing Children's Love of Languages*, CILT, 2004.

Peter Cunningham is a Senior Lecturer at London Metropolitan University (Department of Education and Institute for Policy Studies in Education). He serves as a member of the Refugee Teachers' Task Force (Employability Forum) and on the Executive Committee of CiCe (Children's Identity and Citizenship in Europe).

Ian Menter holds the Chair of Teacher Education at the University of Glasgow. He has worked at the University of Paisley and was previously Head of the School of Education at the University of North London. He has led projects for the Economic and Social Research Council and the Scottish Executive.

Azar Sheibani is the Head of the Refugee Assessment and Guidance Unit (RAGU) based in the Department of Applied Social Sciences, London Metropolitan University. Over the past 15 years she has researched and worked on refugee issues in various capacities at national and transnational level.

Maggie Ross is Headteacher at the Dorothy Gardner Nursery School, Westminster, London. She has extensive experience working with bilingual children and their families in early years settings. Previously she was a Senior Lecturer in Early Childhood Studies at the University of North London.

My Language Story

Manjula Datta

I began my teaching career in Loreto Day School in Calcutta. I taught languages – English, Hindi and Bengali – as a first, second and third language to middle school pupils. In every region in India children learn three languages in school; these include a regional language, for example Bengali in Calcutta, Hindi as the national language, and English. The pupils in my class shared all my languages, and although in an English medium school, it was not their native language. However, within the class population there were those of Anglo-Indian origin for many of whom English was their native tongue. Likewise in Bengali and Hindi medium schools, the medium of instruction was Bengali and Hindi, but language policy remained trilingual. Moreover, if there were large groups of other language speakers in any region, for example Gujarati or Tamil in Calcutta, it was a normal practice to include the language in the school curriculum. Multilingual education was and still is the norm in India.

It was not until I came to England that I became 'aware' of being a multilingual. I must say I found it hard to relate to the term, because not only did I think multilingualism was the norm but until then I had not thought of my languages as different or separate entities. Growing up and educated multilingually, all my languages, Bengali, Punjabi, Hindi, English, served different social functions (I will return to the subject below). In other words, my languages arose 'out of social functions. Language is defined for the child by its uses: it is something that serves his set of needs' (Halliday, 1975, p. 17).

However, when I started teaching in London in 1976, I became aware of the perception and status of bilingualism or multilingualism of children in schools. I went through an enormous culture shock, my whole world of education and schema of multingualism was in turmoil. It was very different from my own experience of multilingualism, learning as well as teaching. In classrooms I found children's bilinguality equated with 'low ability' and their first language was regarded as a 'barrier' to excellence in education. In most cases parents were told to use English at home, and this significantly affected parent–child communication and children's identity. In reality the affect factor, or the emotional aspect of language, was totally ignored or overlooked. There was no opportunity for bilinguals to learn their first language academically even in schools where most children spoke a minority language. I was confused and quite disturbed to see bilingual children withdrawn from class to be given facile exercises in English grammar and vocabulary rather than learning the whole language through the curriculum alongside their peers. Evidence shows that children learn 'more language and language behaviour' from their peer group (Duley et al., 1982, p. 30). I was saddened to see that bilingual children felt uncomfortable about their bilinguality, and that they were embarrassed by their first language and wanted to hide it in school. Most lacked motivation or positive self-concept to learn English energetically and many teachers believed that children's bilinguality was a handicap to learning and low achievement was inevitable. I read later in the Bullock Report, *A Language for Life* (1975, Ch. 20), that the cause of low achievement in minority-language children was deeper than the ability to scan print: 'No child should be expected to cast off his [sic] language as he enters the threshold of school', that their low achievement was due to unavailability of reading resources that reflected minority children's identity: 'books do a great deal to shape children's attitudes' (ibid.). (I will return to misconceptions in Chapter 2.)

Throughout my teaching I have been looking into ways of how bilingual children might best be supported to achieve their full potential in learning and literacy in English. Writing this book gave me the opportunity to reflect on my own language history explicitly. I was born and brought up in Nairobi, cosmopolitan capital city of multilingual Kenya. One could hear the sounds of many languages: native Swahili, Kikuyu, some Asian languages (mostly Punjabi and Gujarati), and European languages, especially English, used in many contexts and for many purposes. Both my parents were Bengali speakers from Calcutta and I grew up speaking Bengali at home with my parents and my brothers and sisters. Punjabi was my 'friendship language' which I learned to speak fluently while playing with friends both in my neighbourhood and at school. My school languages were Hindi and English. Bengali was not offered as a mainstream school language as there was only a small population of Bengalis, mostly from Calcutta, settled in Nairobi. I learned to read and write in Bengali at home and in my Sunday community language school.

I did not go to school until I was seven. My mother taught me, along with my brothers and sisters, to read and write in Bengali, Hindi and English at home, almost simultaneously. Looking back on it, it was not an insurmountable task for my mother, nor were we prodigious children.

How did I learn to be literate in three languages at the same time?

Certain underlying factors made it possible. Although the writing systems were different, transferability of skills between these languages was quite transparent to me, and could be attributed to my bi/multilingual mind or ways of thinking, synthesizing similarities and identifying differences and wanting to learn new rules to negotiate these. It helped me to develop a flexible mind.

All Indian languages have a common lexis and grammatical rules derived from Sanskrit. For example, in Bengali the alphabet is divided into two sets: a set of 40 consonants and a set of 12 vowels. English has 26 letters in the alphabet (21 consonants and five vowels), but there are 44 phonemes. Unlike English where one vowel can represent many sounds or phonemes – for example, *a* in c*a*b, *a*rm, r*a*te – in Indian languages there are no such irregularities and each phoneme is pronounced as it is written. Moreover, digraphs such as *ch*, *th*, *sh* and *ph* are represented by individual consonants as well. There are no grapheme–phoneme irregularities at any level, there is internal and external consistency, and words are pronounced as they are written.

My mother taught me to decode text in Bengali very early using phonic skills. As I was already a competent speaker of Bengali I was able to operate on the semantic and syntactic level with ease. Reading in Bengali made sense to me. My literacy development in Hindi was interesting, linguistically speaking. It demonstrated clearly how knowledge and skills are transferable between languages. Bengali and Hindi share a common lexis and syntax, although there are some differences in script and pronunciation and the grammatical use of the operative verb. But learning to apply a different rule was not a problem, as my spoken fluency in Punjabi aided me in this process. Hindi and Punjabi are what one may call 'sister languages' and share common use of the operative verb, and therefore my fluency in Hindi was helped by the 'sounds' of the operative verb in Punjabi in my head. My mother used the same processes and principles as with Bengali to teach me Hindi. As Hindi shared a common lexis with my other languages it was not difficult for me to extend my vocabulary in Hindi; decoding words in Hindi made sense to me.

The story of my learning to read in English (which was my third language at this stage) may look quite simple at one level. Learning the alphabet followed a singsong pattern of vowel practice – for example, *the cat sat on the mat* – to decode simple words. My mother used the same method of teaching me the grapho-phonic principles in English as she had in Bengali and Hindi. I felt secure in the process. I remember that learning and applying these skills, albeit differently, was not a problem at all. In school we read *Primary Readers* to practise reading skills. I was able to decode English words fluently but was neither excited nor motivated to read in English. School reading was an academic exercise of skills and it left me 'empty' inside. All through my initial literacy learning in Bengali, Hindi and English there was a *fluid interchange* of knowledge, concepts and skills between my three languages. I learned early in my life that languages work with each other.

However, acquiring these reading and writing skills is only one thread of my language history. These skills alone did not make me a reader. I remember the significance of stories from a variety of sources in my wanting to read, to become a reader in these languages. In Bengali the stories were mostly fables from *Panchatantra* (Five tantras or stories), *Thakumar Jhulee* (Grandmother's Pouch), endless *chhaura* (*chh* is strongly aspirated) or rhymes and poems. I learnt to make meaning in other ways as well. My mother taught us Tagore's music and an aunt taught us Indian dance, which we performed at cultural concerts in our community school. I learned different ways of representing meaning from my childhood. Memorizing significant poems was a cultural ritual. To this day I remember reciting Tagore's 'Birpurush' (Brave Man) at a concert with the passion of a young child determined to guard her mother from the highwaymen; my translation of the poem is given below:

> *Mother, imagine you are with me*
> *On a long journey visiting foreign lands*
> *You are sitting in a palanquin*
> *With the doors slightly ajar*
> *And I am riding a red horse*
> *Galloping beside you*
> *Kicking a cloud of red dust . . .*
> *Suddenly I hear the war cries –*
> *Haa- rey- rey- rey- rey- rey . . .*

The poem goes on to depict how Birpurush saves his mother from village dacoits. I still carry the sounds of the poem in my head and the vividness of the images has stayed with me over the years; I can almost taste the red dust kicked up as Birpurush fights to save his mother. I also remember 'Ultadanga' or 'Upside-down Land', a humorous poem, and how it gave me enormous pleasure to recite the sounds and recall the images. Alongside these poems were ceaseless stories from the two Indian epic poems, *Ramayana* and *Mahabharata*. I remember how I revisited these stories and verses in different forms, repeated to me by countless 'visiting' aunts in gatherings at home and elsewhere. This rich 'listening input' (Duley et al., 1982) helped me develop an awareness of cultural values, use of different linguistic styles and a love for literature. I recited the poems and verses from the two epic poems to my daughter who became an avid reader of mythologies, Indian, Greek, Roman, Norse and Irish by the age of ten.

My motivation to read in Hindi came from elsewhere. It was influenced and sustained by the sound and sight of the language in the moving images on the big screen, endearingly known as Bollywood films. It was through these films I was introduced to oratorical and rhetorical speech. I recall how awe-inspiring the experience was. It was the enactment of the whole speech event, booming as well as celestial voices seemed to be coming from heaven accompanied by awesome images with rich and lavish costumes and high powered drama on an epic scale, an awesome feast to a child's eyes and ears. I experienced the magical as well as terrifying power of language, of words, and my hunger for literature grew.

My source of emotion and energy in developing literacy in English was provided by my father. I fondly remember that when I read to my father in English how he would *bring the text alive* by embellishing it with his own stories. He would pick out some key words from the text and share his knowledge of certain content words, as well as sharing some of his childhood stories around those words. I developed a tremendous appetite for these stories and always was very keen to read to my father. Also it was comforting to know that father was once young and that he too was mischievous. To this day I remember stories about 'flying kites on the terrace', 'a laughing parrot', 'the lioness that took Mr Kelly by the arm from a hunting camp as he had killed her cub', 'sailing in a stormy sea', and 'ponds and ghosts'.

My father grew up in a house in Calcutta surrounded by ponds. He told me how my grandmother used to keep an eye on him and his five brothers and sisters by warning them about the dangers of ponds with all kinds of stories. Apparently these ponds belonged to an ogress, and at midday when the sun was at its height she would stretch out her bony hands to snatch any child who happened to be there. She told them how some children were taken to a world beneath the ponds, never to return. In the evening the ponds became the playing fields for ghosts. No sooner was it dusk and the sun was setting behind the horizon than you could hear the sounds of a million ghosts whistling whoooooooooo … whooooooooooooshshsh … around the ponds, over the ponds, across the ponds, some went under the ponds – they could do anything, take on white shapeless forms floating and flying in the wind: whooooooooooooooooooooooo. Sometimes you'd hear a big splash in the water; that was when a ghost abducted a child and took it to the underworld, *'Come away, Oh human child / to the waters and the wild'* (Yeats, 'The Stolen Child').

Amidst these stories my father also read me interesting stories from newspapers. For example, the story of the African elephant which wandered out of the jungle one day and saw a parked jeep with two blaring headlights. Mistaking it for a beast perhaps, the elephant attacked the jeep. He made two pronged, three pronged, and all round attacks on the jeep again and again until it was reduced to a heap of squashed metal. After this mammoth feat the elephant was seen walking away from the scene swinging his tail with careless abandon! Stories like these initiated me to the magical power of words in English. My appetite for stories in English in many forms grew steadily stronger. Later I became a voracious reader of English classics.

We went back to India when I was twelve. In Calcutta it was my parents' choice to admit me to an English medium school as my home literacy in Bengali did not have academic rigour. Bengali and Hindi became my curriculum subjects, and English became the medium of learning the curriculum. My sisters immersed themselves in Tagore's music and alongside this the world of Tagore's poetry was unfolded to me by aunts and cousins, who sometimes recited the various poems across the courtyard. I enrolled in a dance school to learn Indian classical dance, *Katthak*, rooted in story-telling with hands, feet and body movements synchronized with appropriate facial expressions and *talas* or rhythm. I also became interested in listening to radio plays in all languages as well as cricket and tennis commentary in English with my father.

Simultaneously, being in an English medium school I was formally introduced to the world of English literature. I have fond memories of my teacher's love for literature. I recall vividly Ms Saldanah's facial gestures, tone and intonation; her engagement with text and felicity with words was total – emotional, intellectual and passionate! I can hear her booming voice resonating the sounds of Tennyson's poem 'The Charge of the Light Brigade':

Theirs not to make reply,
Theirs not to reason why,
Theirs but to do and die:
Into the valley of Death
Rode the six hundred

Both the form and the content had a profound influence on me. I also remember sitting in a classroom in the middle of Calcutta, surrounded by an incessant flow of serpentine traffic on the streets outside, and how the sounds of Wordsworth's 'The Solitary Reaper' came floating to my ears.

Behold her single in the field
Reaping and singing by herself

With these words Ms Saldanah located us in the quiet pastoral Hebridean scene to be at one with the mood and atmosphere of the poem, and to experience and appreciate the form and content of Wordsworth's poem. The sweltering heat of Calcutta summer didn't matter. In my imagination I was transported to the distant Hebrides and heard the solitary reaper singing. She left us with the profound line, '*Will no one tell me what she sings?*' Memorizing significant poems was a part of the school curriculum. I found it a valuable experience, especially when the poems were presented with such profound feelings and images; the sounds became easily memorizable. For days I stayed with the solitary reaper, '*The music in my heart I bore / Long after it was heard no more*'. I memorized the poem to invoke at my leisure the sounds that created such poignant images. I pursued my interest in literature and went on to read English as my first and second degree at Calcutta University. To this day I remember the mammoth Coffee House in College Street. It was the hub of student life, buzzing with sounds of literary discussion in different languages and the debating of passionately held views. It was all very energizing. Apart from pursuing my academic interest I passed an audition test to take part in radio plays produced in Hindi by All India Radio, Calcutta. Soon after, I joined *Calling All Children* as a story reader and story-teller in English.

After graduating I started teaching at Loreto Day School which is where this chapter begins. Under a very supportive and imaginative Irish Principal, Sister Eithne, I enjoyed teaching very much and taught English, Hindi and Bengali to middle school pupils as their first, second and third language. But the time came for me to move on. Before leaving I asked Sister Eithne if there was anything I should be aware of before coming to London, '*Not very much except there won't be any coolies at the airport to carry your baggage. You'll have to push your own trolley.*'

I qualified with the PGCE from Redland College, Bristol. I enjoyed the training, especially learning about 'meaningful' ways of teaching children to make connections with new concepts, the importance of their personal experiences in school learning and the ways children make sense of the environment – in short, about how young children learn. I remember having exclaimed in a maths session one day: 'If this is learning, give me more!' I also remember how on my first practice I came in contact with a different use of English, in a class of eight- and nine-year-olds.

'*Could you distribute these books please?*' I asked a young girl. She stared at me for some time and replied,
'*Say that again.*' I repeated my request to which another girl said, '*Yes, give them out, give them out.*'

The two young girls were unaware of how they activated my ears to informal use of English in the classroom. However, I feel teachers need to switch between informal and formal use of English to enable young children to 'tune into' the formal style.

When I started my first teaching job in an inner London mutilingual school with its multitude of languages and varieties of English, the linguistic boundary of my formal use of English was challenged further. For the first time I was spoken to in Cockney, a London dialect of English, my only previous experience of it being from the film *My Fair Lady*. I remember how in Calcutta we used to copy the accent and have fun creating those sounds! But in my very first class, nine-year-old Johnny looked uncomfortable when I asked him to repeat his request, *'Can I ge' a drink o' wa'er Miss?'* Still quite confused about what exactly he wanted to drink and out of sheer desperation, I said *'yes!'* Some of the other uses I came across were, *'I ain't going to come'*, *'I brang my library book back'*, *'I didn't do nothing'*, and *'you learnt me it'* which reminded me of Shakespeare's Caliban, *'you learnt me your language!'* Then a completely new style of using words in speech came from the 'Brixton boys' of African-Caribbean origin. All the children in my class started to say *'wicked!'* which was a particular way of saying *'good'* and was accompanied by a ceremonious shake of the right hand. The latest is the usage of 'cool' in a variety of contexts in an appreciative sense.

In many ways, since my arrival at Heathrow Airport I feel I am still pushing a trolley, trying to get it right. The journey has not been smooth, although the direction has always been focused on providing the best educational opportunities for bilingual children, indeed for *all* children. This book forms a part of that journey and I hope it will help other educators to reflect on the best strategies for responding to the complex cognitive, linguistic and literacy knowledge and skills that bilingual children bring to school learning. I hope also that it will help in identifying and addressing the children's specific needs so as to make learning in an additional language a rewarding experience for every child, and, at the same time, make teaching an equally rewarding experience for oneself. This book exemplifies this in a number of case studies.

Throughout my research I have been in continuous dialogue with teachers and listened to their perceptions of bilingual children's strengths and needs in their literacy development, as well as listening to children. These comments are shared in different chapters. I would like to add that these were the comments from teachers dedicated to teaching in multilingual classrooms and reflected their genuine concerns. They also expressed their concern at the current overload of 'required' teaching which left very little time to devote to raising the quality of bilinguals' literacy learning. They felt that bilingual children needed sustained literary encounters, and more time, space and opportunities to internalize language and learning.

Listening to children, who shared Arabic, Bengali, Chinese, Punjabi, Hindi and Urdu amongst them, I found that many of them explicitly or implicitly suffered from 'language anxiety' of some kind. Sometimes it was an intangible grasp of cultural meanings embedded in language and literature in English. *'Why don't they write in normal language?'* I was very disturbed to learn that many older bilinguals were avoiding writing stories, as they thought they *'wouldn't get good marks'*. Some said *'You write a good story and they [examiners] might say "Oh! this is rubbish"'*, which may indicate a cultural difference in looking at ways of making a good story. To this end my research outcomes indicate it is crucial that bilinguals' languages and cultures are kept together in teaching and learning approaches to language and literacy learning in English, since this is their natural world. Talking to younger bilinguals, many of them seemed ambivalent and did not seem to have a view except that their English was 'OK' or 'all right', but both groups of children thought that spelling was *'easy-peasy'*.

The above issues formed the central thesis of my research and are the main focus of this book.

I must add that I have always found teaching bilingual children exciting. I believe the English language is 'enriched' by their sometimes 'unique creative expressions' or ways of looking at meaning and experiences. This to me is the most important aspect of multilingualism and multiculturalism: 'The development of academic skills in English depends not just on exposure to English . . . but equally on the knowledge and concepts that the children have inside their heads that help them make sense of English' (Cummins, 1996, pp. 111–12).

This book is about the concept or phenomenon of bilinguality, the knowledge and concepts and skills that bilingual children bring to classroom learning, rather than 'visible' use of their languages in classroom learning. Hamers and Blanc (1989, p. 265) define 'bilinguality' as 'a psychological state of the individual who has access to more than one linguistic code as a means of social communication'. However, bilingual education is desirable for every bilingual child; as Colin Baker claims in his Foreword to this book, schools with a substantial number of children sharing one minority language must consider providing bilingual education for children so as to achieve maximum educational gains as well as a deep learning of English.

In keeping with the focus of the book I have used the term 'bilingual' rather than 'multilingual' as well as 'first language' and 'second language' for clarity and accessibility to a wider range of readers. The term 'code' in general refers to different languages as well as varieties of the same language, and styles within a language, but I have referred to 'code' as a language in the book.

My research, though not exclusively, focuses on Asian bilinguals for two reasons. It was sheer pragmatics. I thought my knowledge and spoken fluency in the many Asian languages in London, together with my observations of children's cultural experiences in a variety of contexts outside school, would allow me to look closely at the possibilities of relating their linguistic and cultural experiences to school learning. From my personal experience I knew this would enhance their quality of learning; moreover, knowledge, understanding and practice are transferable between languages and teaching contexts. On a wider map, as an educator from a minority community I felt it was essential to bridge the gap between bilinguals' home and school life and learning, that their personal meanings must inform and enhance their meaning-making capacity, and interpretation skills in school learning. I observed bilingual learners very closely in many contexts: as speakers, meaning-makers using their languages and other forms of communication, for example singing and dancing, as readers and as writers. I used video and audio-cassettes to record some of these observations. The outcomes are presented mostly as case studies so that colleagues can reflect on what is best practice for bilingual children between three and eleven years of age in varying learning contexts. The final message of this second edition of this book is that bilingualism is an asset and that children's bilinguality is an active and fluid force in their schema which makes further meaning-making possible.

A brief description of the chapters in the book is given below.

Chapter 1 descibes my experience as a bilingual/multilingual person and shows how English was located in the continuum of all my languages, and within this the significant contribution made by my parents and English teacher to my literacy development in these languages. My English teacher's affirmation of my learner-identity was crucial to my motivation to read English at a higher level.

Chapter 2 looks at some of the attributes of 'being bilingual' and argues that bilingual children's literacy learning in English is necessarily an intercultural process, that bilingual children engage in deeper literacy meanings interacting with both their learning worlds. It highlights bilingual children's literacy experiences at home and argues for validating these as useful and rich resources for further literacy development in English. It explores the relevance of *sociocultural* approaches to teaching and learning at home and in school. To that end, it strongly argues for an 'intercultural literate community of learners' in class as well as adequate training for trainee-teachers and practising teachers to enable and empower them to equalize learning opportunities for *all* children.

Chapter 3 gives us snapshots of the fluidity of the bilingual mind and language behaviour in a nursery setting switching between languages and cultures to communicate and learn. This is reflected in the parents as well in communicating with their children and others, thus keeping both their *languages and cultures close* to each other.

Chapter 4 looks at the *centrality of rhythm* in language learning, the foundation of which starts at home. It shows how rhythm in language triggers rhythmic thinking in bilingual children's responses to literacy in early childhood settings and helps develop an emotional relationship with English and school learning.

Chapter 5 presents a range of case studies of bilingual readers and looks closely at the learning attributes of each child and how these are developed strongly by 'significant others' with intercultural orientation to literacy development and affirmation of bilingual learner-identities. It highlights the importance of every child's entitlement to maximize their potential to learn.

Chapter 6 looks closely at bilinguals' potential to write vigorously by uniting their cultural literacies in their English compositions. It argues for situating bilingual writers in the collaborative intercultural literate community of writers where meanings and best topics are exchanged fluently in personal advancement of learning. We will encounter some samples of children's writing with unique blends of images and linguistic expressions and artifacts. Keeping their languages and cultures together affects bilinguals' ability to think deeply and coherently in developing stages.

Chapter 7 develops the above approach further by looking closely at text as a model for bilinguals' literacy development at a higher level. To this end it argues for *imagination* as a tool for 'dialogic' thinking to *unite* both their literacy worlds, to enable them to 'read beyond the literal'. The fluidity of the process juxtaposed with 'reading like a writer' strengthens their conceptual development and creates a strong motivated relationship with English literary language, as suggested by the review of the process by the children.

Chapter 8 argues for a rethinking of policy and practice so as to recognize schools as communities that are an integral part of multilingual and multicultural Britain, and playing a vital role in the making of future citizens. It argues for appropriate and active language policy to reflect the demographic changes in school populations, and raises issues of social justice.

Chapter 9 draws our attention to the cultural and language experiences of refugee children in the classroom and suggests ways of addressing these in policy and practice. It emphasizes the importance of listening to the voices of refugee children and parents, and supporting their integration and aspirations.

Chapter 10 summarizes the underlying factors that affect high learning outcomes for bilingual children. Looking ahead, it advocates bilingualism for all children, so that children living in multilingual and multicultural Britain are equipped to take their place in an era of globalization.

Bilinguality, Literacy and Principles

Manjula Datta

'likhaai, padaayi nahi sikhogi,
tow gadhey ki tarhey rahogi'
['If you don't learn to write or read,
you'll live the life of a donkey']

In every society literacy carries a 'power status' and is perceived as enhancing economic, social and political opportunities for the individual. That literacy is valued in all cultures can be gauged by some of the popular sayings that are prevalent in different cultures to warn young people of what may befall them if they are not literate. For example, the above saying in Hindi is shaped as a rhyme for children to remember. I have heard many Hindi-speaking parents in Britain use the same metaphor to remind their children of the importance of learning to read and write.

Many parents desire their children to be biliterate and consider ways of supporting this outside school, but others accept literacy in English as the only outcome in British schools. Bourdieu defines literacy as a form of 'cultural capital' (Bourdieu and Passeron, 1977), however non-recognition of minority language literacy practices and skills in most mainstream schools consequently withholds 'cultural capital' from owners of these literacies. These children are disadvantaged at the point of entry into their school learning, which is contrary to that suggested by the Bullock Report, *A Language for Life* (1975). In England the lack of central government policy on any form of bilingual education (Gundara et al., 1986) has created a chasm in bilingual children's ability to maximize their learning potential. It has also given rise to tension in language minority homes. This is echoed in Li Wei's statement:

> '[O]ne of the main concerns ethnic minority communities have is to help their British-born children to learn the non-English mother tongue. Maintaining the mother tongue is an important issue to them, because there is a real need for everyday communication within the family and within the community.' (2000)

By excluding children's languages and cultures from classroom learning, we are excluding one of the most important issues in education, that is, to develop young children's thinking skills. The National Curriculum for teachers in England (see QCA/DfEE, 1999) states: 'By using thinking skills pupils can focus on "knowing how" as well as "knowing what" – learning how to learn' (p. 22). To that effect it promotes the development of a range of thinking skills embedded in curriculum learning: information-processing skills; reasoning skills; enquiry skills; creative thinking skills; evaluation skills (ibid.).

In the bilingual context these skills develop best when children's cultural literacies are seen as a rich resource, and situated positively in classroom learning. Central to this is the understanding of children's bilingual identity or *how the bilingual mind processes and constructs meaning*. The bilingual mind is most active and productive when the teaching and learning approaches create a 'dialogue' in the bilingual mind, which enables them to use their personal knowledge and literacy meanings from *both* their learning worlds, home and school, to process or construct meaning. The evidence in different chapters of this book underpins this as the foundation for bilingual children's learning and literacy development. This would require teaching professionals to be adequately knowledgeable about bilingualism and have an understanding of 'bilingual' learner-identity to inform their classroom practice. A recent TTA (Teacher Training Agency, renamed Teacher Development Agency) survey (2004) showed that only 25 per cent of trainee teachers considered their preparation for teaching pupils with English as an additional language (EAL) was 'good' or 'very good'. This compares with 84 per cent who rated the *overall* quality of training as 'good' or 'very good'.

The aim of this chapter is to look at some underlying principles in literacy learning that inform best practice in multilingual classrooms:

- knowledge and understanding of bilingualism;
- knowledge and understanding of the 'joined-up' relationship between language, culture and cognition, and how the bilingual mind works;
- being knowledgeable about bilingual children's wealth of cultural literacy developed in sociocultural contexts, and the significance of these literacies in their lives and for curriculum learning in school;
- developing intercultural and collaborative approaches to literacy teaching and learning in multilingual classrooms

There are as many definitions of bilingualism as there are types of it. (For a fuller discussion of various definitions of bilingualism, see Baker and Prys Jones, 1998.) But for the purposes of this book, childhood bilingualism is considered distinguishable from adolescent or adult bilingualism. The second language is referred to as English in this context.

Part 1: About children's bilinguality

Childhood bilingualism may be simultaneous or consecutive. When a child develops 'two mother tongues from the onset of language'. The child grows up, for example, in a family where the parents speak two different first languages, and aspire to bring up their child bilingually. This child is deemed to develop simultaneous bilinguality. On the other hand, consecutive bilingualism occurs mostly when the language minority child first attends school or pre-school care centres, and is exposed to the second language formally as a medium of education and informally through social relationships in these environments.

However, within the category of consecutive bilingualism there are many variations. These occur, for example, in language minority homes where the first language is the major language in the family, but communication between siblings tends to switch between their two languages. A large number of second-generation bilinguals in British schools fall into this category of 'fluent speakers' of their first language. There is strong evidence from my research to suggest that children's spoken fluency also affects their cognitive development. If and when used appropriately, for example developing different literacy concepts such as narratives, poems, plays, characters, setting, dialogues, it allows positive transfer of literacy knowledge and skills to make deeper meanings, and accelerates literacy learning in English. This is most visible in schools which have a positive attitude to children's bilinguality. Also, literacy in the first language is actively encouraged in these families and children come to school with varying degrees of reading and writing skills.

In some other language minority homes, young bilinguals mostly use English but their parents almost always speak and respond to them in the first language. Hearing as well as seeing the first language being used in their day-to-day life gives these bilinguals a sound understanding of their first language and the cultural nuances of words and images. Evidence suggests they use this knowledge to their best advantage in extended familial, cultural and religious contexts. Theoretically they are known as 'passive bilinguals'.

Another variation relates to bilingual homes where parents are fluent bilinguals, and switch between languages in specific contexts. The first language is used mainly to express familial, emotional, religious or cultural meanings, whereas English is spoken in educational and wider cultural contexts. Thus, young bilinguals listen to and participate in a range of language use in both languages and are known to use this knowledge intelligently in appropriate contexts.

However, a child's degree of bilinguality can be charted on a continuum which is not static at any given time. It has been widely observed that many second-generation bilinguals from different communities in Britain are learning their first language in their adult life after formal education, while many others are learning through visits to their root countries, mainly to develop stronger familial ties.

In all the above variations children are also exposed to a range of cultural experiences – heritage literature, mythology, art, religion and music. Their cultural experiences are rich, and their voice is strong. Language transmits culture. This is discussed later in the chapter.

Unfortunately, there are widespread *misconceptions* about minority children's home language and literacy experiences in relation to school learning. 'One of the major problems has been that educators have taken the view that any child that speaks differently is deficient in language ability' (Goodman, 1982, p. xxxvi), despite the fact that linguistic study reveals that all languages and dialects have 'systematic phonology, grammatical structure and vocabulary' (ibid.). In addition, teaching literacy in the second language to a culturally diverse population has its own complex dimensions. Teacher awareness of the possibility of different literacy practices in different cultures is important. Open-ended classroom talk provides the best source of information for this. I first became aware of this when a colleague, concerned about a seven-year-old bilingual child's reading development, made an offhand comment: *'Well, she doesn't even get a bedtime story, what do you expect?'* The statement made me sit up

Loan Receipt
Liverpool John Moores University
Library Services

Borrower Name: Griffiths,Charlotte
Borrower ID: ********

Bilinguality and literacy :
31111012135917
Due Date: 08/11/2016 23:59

Total Items: 1
01/11/2016 12:40

Please keep your receipt in case of
dispute.

in consternation and muse to myself, 'I too did not have a bedtime story', yet my childhood was immersed in the world of stories at home, oral and written in three languages (see Chapter 1). Although well meaning, my colleague had perceived the child's underachievement as 'cultural deprivation' from a majority-culture point of view. Such assumptions or reductive views lead to low expectations and seriously impede children's potential to achieve. Commenting on compensatory education programmes for pre-school children in America, Bernstein (1972, p. 137) noted:

> If children are labelled *culturally deprived*, then it follows that the spontaneous realization of their culture, its images and symbolic representations, are of reduced value and significance. Teachers will have lower expectations of children, which the children will undoubtedly fulfil.

Devaluing children's culture devalues their essential literacy skills or symbolic representations associated with it, depriving them from using these resources to develop literacy in English strongly. We must also note that it is vital to map children's underachievement or lack of motivation (see, for example, Kasi in Chapter 5) against a wider background of learning rather than lack of knowledge, skills or ability. 'If teachers can listen to their pupils and their families without prejudice, they too may learn to move more easily and confidently between language worlds and cultures. This is, after all, what schooling demands of many of these young children' (Whitehead, 1990, p. 84). We need to understand that in a culturally diverse class the 'mainstream norm' is not necessarily the minority norm, and conversely, minority children should not be expected to respond to mainstream culture as the only cultural norm.

Another *misconception* closely associated with the above has persisted over time, namely that children's bilinguality is a 'barrier' to excellence in education, which is quite contrary to international research evidence, including this book. Even today parents are asked to talk to their children in English at home. This is not only damaging to parent–child and wider relationships in the community: it reduces the value of family literacies at a variety of levels, such as family anecdotes, stories in home languages, seeing language being enacted in many moods (sad, happy, angry) and in different ways – persuasion, recall, instructions, commands, debates. It works against the most important theoretical concept that language and literacy skills are transferable between languages.

Some educators hold a *misconceived* view that they are unable to support a bilingual child's learning strongly without being able to speak the child's home language and as such their role has limited impact on the child's learning. This demonstrates 'inadequate' knowledge and understanding of bi/multilingualism on the part of teaching professionals as the above-mentioned TTA survey showed. Most importantly, teachers must understand how languages interact and work with each other to make meaning, rather than operating against each other or functioning as separate entities. This was my experience as recounted in Chapter 1. However, the above concern is genuine and must be addressed in designing an appropriate curriculum for Teacher Education courses to empower teaching professionals in a diverse society. Europe, including Britain, is becoming increasingly multilingual, and most classrooms in different parts of the country will have new entrants from a variety of minority language backgrounds./Developing knowledge and understanding of bilingualism and how bilingual children think and learn is as crucial as learning about the teaching and learning objectives in the language and literacy curriculum. Teachers must be empowered to address equality or 'inclusion' issues of minority-language children's education in schools (QCA/DfEE, 1999, pp. 37–8).

Conversational and academic language

In many multilingual classrooms bilingual children's spoken fluency in English is misconstrued as academic language proficiency. Ofsted (Office for Standards in Education) draw attention to this misconception in their statement that 'pupils who have English as an additional language (EAL) need extra support *long after they become fluent speakers* [my emphasis]' (Ofsted, 2003, March). This relates to Cummins' BICS and CALP development theory (1981, 1984, 1996, 2000). He proposes that bilingual children acquire Basic Interpersonal Communicative Skills (BICS) or one-to-one conversational fluency in English within two years and without much stress. However, they need to develop knowledge of how English is used for cognitive development or academic purposes. This he terms as Cognitive Academic Language Proficiency (CALP). These are higher level linguistic skills (1996, pp.57–9), for example the ability to recall, interpret, infer, deduct, analyse, synthesize and evaluate meanings, by using 'language itself' or just words. Evidence shows that it takes a minimum of five to seven years to develop academic proficiency in a new language (Collier, 1997; Cummins, 1981, 1984). However, the evidence from my work suggests that the process could be accelerated by appropriate teaching and learning strategies that include and integrate both their learning and literary worlds. This is evident throughout the book.

We must also note that in our everyday conversations in spoken language or dialect we use many of the skills associated with CALP, such as recalling stories or events, interpreting meanings, evaluating situations or favourite television programmes, inferring meanings from cultural use of language, idiom, metaphor, etc. However, these conversations are supported by shared contexts of interest, culture and the two-way participatory nature of conversations, which is further supported by extra linguistic communication of meaning – gestures, tone/intonation and facial expressions. To be able to move from the immediacy of conversational speech to 'disembodied' use of language at an abstract level in academic contexts is a crucial cognitive leap, requiring an integrative strategy to build on children's experiences of using language at a personal level rather than taught as a new concept. Also, evidence shows that the development of reading and writing skills in the first language accelerates this process (Cummins, 1996, 2000).

The importance of 'exploratory talk' as well as 'reporting back' was emphasized by the Bullock Report *A Language for Life* (1975). These two modes of oral language demand context-related linguistic and literacy skills. Exploratory talk involves exploring the possibilities of solving a problem at personal and group level. The language used in exploratory talk is close to spoken or conversational language, being tentative, mostly in phrases, including false starts, or 'dead-ends in thinking' and may be repetitive. On the other hand, the process of 'reporting back' demands semantic and syntactic clarity to represent meaning. However, without exploratory talk, reporting back becomes a poor language and learning experience: 'the two activities should be related, the one arising from the other in a purposeful way' (Bullock et al., 1975, p. 146). Evidence of group talk at all levels – reading, listening, recalling and retelling stories, interpreting, evaluating or reconstructing text using their entire linguistic and cognitive repertoire – is of significance for bilinguals to develop academic language proficiency. This may involve crossing linguistic and cultural boundaries. Talk creates multilayered and multidirectional thinking and learning development in multilingual classrooms; this is evident throughout the book. In Chapter 5 we see Nadia very comfortably talking to her friends about the pictures and the text in a very animated way; however, when she is asked to 'recall' what she had read she shows 'insecurity' in her range of appropriate vocabulary and meaning structures (semantic and syntax). We will see how Nadia develops this representational language, or uses language for ordering and sequencing thoughts at an abstract level, in Chapter 5.

An American colleague put it very succinctly,

The greatest failure of contemporary education has been precisely its inability to help teachers understand the ethnolinguistic complexity of children, classrooms, speech communities, and society, in such a way as to enable them to make informed decisions about language and culture in the classroom. (Garcia, 1996, p. vii)

Some of these complexities are discussed in this chapter and further addressed in other chapters throughout the book.

Multilingual classrooms are made up of different speech communities and although the classroom language is common, 'A common language is not enough to make a common speech community' (Phillips, 1972, p. liv). Heath's (1983) ethnography of three English-speaking communities in America, with different cultural orientations to literacy learning and literacy events at home, contributed significantly to this debate. Sociolinguists find the word 'language' inadequate to describe people's use of language and prefer to use the term 'speech community' (Aitchison, 1992, p. 104), which they define as 'any group of people who consider that they speak the same language' (ibid.). Hymes (1972, p. xxii) distinguishes between two language functions: 'referential', or the formal unit structures of a language, and 'social', or how language is used in different contexts. He claims that 'meaningfulness of language is interwoven of [these] two kinds of meaning'. It is very important that the two functions are clearly understood in language education. Social constructs of meaning or interpretation of cultural artifacts in English literature presuppose shared meaning and behaviour of any particular culture – this must be recognized and clearly understood by teachers to make literature in English accessible to bilinguals. Strategies for teaching literature are explored in Chapter 7.

Moreover, children from some cultural backgrounds may find it difficult to engage in whole-class discourse or give personal opinions since to do so might be perceived as 'boastfulness'. Small-group talk and learning or peer observation is essential to develop these skills. When teaching a culturally diverse class of children teachers need to observe closely and 'carefully as they first step into the classroom' (Gregory, 1996, p. 23). *Peer-group* learning is very productive in gaining access to mainstream cultural practices, in that exchanging their own cultural practices, meanings and ways with words helps to develop confidence in bilinguals to become active class members. Equally there is strong evidence to suggest that these cognitive and cultural exchanges not only open the minds of majority-language speakers (English in the UK), but also encourage a heightened awareness of their own ethnicity, as well as an understanding of how people's languages are intimately related to their cultures (Genesee, 1987; Lambert, 1984; Swain and Lapkin, 1982).

The bilingual mind and cognitive flexibility

Language is our most important instrument for forming concepts. It is the tool that the individual uses when she handles her surroundings, in order to be able to take the world to herself, to grasp it, to comprehend it. (Skutnabb-Kangas, 1981, p. 3)

We begin with the premise that minority language children entering school already have a well-developed language. According to Chomsky, 'anyone who knows a language must have internalized a set of rules which specify the sequences permitted in their language' (in Aitchison, 1992, p. 26). Their experience in and understanding of the first language acts as a *cognitive sponge* to absorb and make sense of the second language. Evidence from current research (Bialystok, 1991; Collier, 1997; Cummins, 1988, 1996, 2000; Wong, 1991) suggests that bilinguals' *languages are interdependent*, in that linguistic skills are transferable from one language to another. Verhoeven's (1994) research indicates 'positive transfer between languages in literacy skills, sound systems (phonology) and communication skills'. *Transferability* of knowledge and skills from one language to another appears to play a critical role in bilinguals' learning.

There is also wide-ranging empirical evidence to suggest that bilingualism leads to greater *cognitive flexibility* as well as greater understanding of language as a symbolic and rule-governed system. These are essential tools for academic success. From their personal experience, bilinguals understand that all languages have a different phonology, vocabulary or word order and understand the social aspect of language use well. It is easier for bilinguals to understand the arbitrariness of the naming system in different languages. We see three-year-old Nitya, a fluent Hindi speaker, newly arrived from India, engaging in linguistic pattern making after three weeks in the nursery: '*Tota maney (means) parrot, bandar maney monkey, baagh maney tiger, shaer maney lion ...*' Nitya is playing the game of pairing the names of animals in Hindi and English. This is a satisfying knowledge for her in that objects are named differently in different languages. Nitya's play demonstrates the development of a bilingual mind in that she has a heightened awareness of how languages work. This is also known as metalinguistic skill. She is also developing an awareness of social contexts for language use, or sociolinguistic skills: '*Papa, hum nursery mei English boltei hain*' [Papa we speak in English in the nursery] '*aur hum ghur mei Hindi boltei hain*' [and at home we speak in Hindi] '*leikin hum English bhi boltei hain*' [but we speak in English as well].

In Chapter 4 we see five-year-old Raki demonstrating her metalinguistic awareness in experimenting with her knowledge about the writing system in three languages: Bengali, English and Arabic. She understands that all her languages have an alphabet, although some may have different orientations, and they are used as tools for reading and writing. It would appear in her continuum of thinking that she understands ways of using different writing systems can *converge* in some ways but may *diverge* in others. Bilinguals also understand that a content word may have a different signification or could be interpreted differently in different cultures, for example, 'wedding', 'prayer', 'food'. Language carries cultural reality. This experience develops a greater capacity for 'disembeddedness' or the ability to 'separate out individual words from meaningful sentences' (Bialystok, 1991) and identifying word boundaries with ease in the written language. These cognitive skills are considered to give bilinguals an advantage in relating to symbolic systems, such as reading (Donaldson, 1978).

Bilinguals' metalinguistic skills are also demonstrated in their speech acts, in that switching languages is a natural pattern in the language behaviour of bilinguals. Bilinguals' *code-switching* is described as 'the use of more than one language in the course of a single speech act' (Gumperz, 1982, p. 59). Bilinguals have two sets of language sounds in their head, and their use depends on particular contexts and purposes for talk as well as a shared language between participants. For bilinguals, their two languages are not two different entities (see Chapter 1); metalinguistically they are on the same language continuum and they use them interchangeably in appropriate contexts. 'An infant bilingual spontaneously translates for two adults each of whom speaks one of his languages thus establishing equivalences between his two languages' (Swain and Wesche, 1973). This is a common practice that teachers in multilingual schools are aware of. Children in my research used this behaviour in peer- and friendship-talk, as well as to clarify teacher instructions between themselves. Bilingual teachers often use both languages to give instruction where needed, as well as to emphasize or clarify teaching points. Evidence shows that most code-switching is 'unconscious' or natural language behaviour. The following conversation between five-year-old bilinguals makes this point succinctly:

> *Safia*: 'I talk in Bengali when I go to Bengali shops and I talk in English when I go to English shops.'
> *Farhana*: 'I know Bengali, English, India, Pakistan, Hindi and Urdu [Farhana is obviously mixing up the names of countries with the names of languages] . . . I talk in English to the doctor, in hospital, in school.'
> *Me*: 'Where did you learn Hindi?'
> *Farhana*: 'From [Hindi] video films . . .'
> *Sabina*: 'I talk to the Chinese in English.'

Bilinguals constantly 'monitor what is the appropriate language in which to respond'. This is also known as *communicative sensitivity* (Ben-Zeev in Baker, 2006, p. 161), which demonstrates their heightened awareness of how language is used with different people. Sabina (see above) makes a strong cognitive inference from her experience of switching languages, that switches occur only when speakers share a language; 'bilinguals need to be aware which language to speak in which situation' (ibid.). Sabina understands that the Chinese have a different language, and as she does not speak Chinese, she must speak to them in English, as everyone living in Britain will know English. Linguistically it parallels the stylistic variations or the use of regional varieties of English, for example Cockney in London, and Standard English. It is also comparable with the use of registers by monolinguals. The difference lies only in the choice of different linguistic symbols or language for bilinguals. 'This "language reflects context" paradigm is built on the well established foundation that we have speech (and also non-verbal) repertoires from which we can select to meet the normative demands of situations' (Giles and Coupland, 1991, p. 3).

We may conclude from the above discussion that young bilinguals are skilled language users. It is clear that they bring an array of linguistic and cognitive skills which can be positively integrated to learn a second language deeply, for example, English. In all contexts school language should be an 'additional tool', in that it should be added to rather than replace the first language. 'When a second language and culture have been acquired with little or no pressure to replace or reduce the first language, an additive form of bilingualism may occur' (Lambert, 1974). Current research in second-language teaching indicates that teachers should take adequate account of students' first language and culture as cognitive tools for developing effective teaching tools for high learning outcomes. This is discussed later in the chapter.

Bilingual children, second-language acquisition and affective variables

There are several factors that influence successful acquisition of a second language, of which 'classroom language environment' (Krashen, 1982, p. 13) is of paramount importance as a social context for speaking and listening. 'The language environment encompasses everything the language learner hears and sees in the new language' (ibid.). A second language is learned interactively and in context. Communication of meaning and understanding messages is crucial to teaching and learning a new language.

The language that learners hear and see in naturally occurring contexts or around learning activities in the classroom enables second-language learners to access meaning. Speaking about a child's everyday experience of language, Halliday (1975, p. 20) said, 'what he encounters is "text" or language in use: sequences of language articulated each within itself and with the situation in which it occurs. Such sequences are purposive – though very varied in purpose – and have an evident social significance.' Social meaningfulness in bilinguals' second-language learning is essential.

Playing with the second language and acting out different moods and modes of the language in a variety of contexts (see Chapter 4), including playing with colloquial, idiomatic, proverbial and formal use of English, are all part of bilinguals' developing knowledge and understanding of the second language. Through repetition and rehearsal they internalize new vocabulary and meaning structures and, like first-language learners, generate more. They learn that language is dynamic, purposive and fun.

Bilinguals' acquisition of their second language is seriously affected when they are confined to 'inactive' learning; for example completing worksheets, answering multiple-choice questions or responding to 'closed' comprehension questions. An interactive and stress-free language environment and 'comprehensible input' (Krashen, 1982, p. 13) that is cognitively demanding offers bilinguals optimum learning potential. Bilingual children learn best in collaborative learning environments and in peer-learning situations. Children need high context support in the early stages of learning the second language to support their understanding (Cummins, 1984, 1996). They progress to low context support or the ability to use abstract language with more experience and maturity. But in all contexts learning should be cognitively demanding.

However, on entering a new language environment minority language children go through a *'silent period'* during which they go through a process of 'tuning into' the sound system of the new language and 'seeing' how the new language works, how it is enacted. This is essential for beginner bilinguals, and although called a 'silent' period, cognitively it is the most active period in bilinguals' learning process, when the bilingual mind is constantly seeking to make sense of the new language as well as making linguistic and cultural links with their experience of the first language. The process is helped and accelerated by what they know about language already – tone, intonation, facial expressions, gestures and other extra-linguistic communications.

The role of affective variables in learning English as an additional language

In many studies of second-language acquisition 'emotions are seen as vital' (Johnstone, 1993, p. 139). Some of the factors identified as playing a primary role in the second-language acquisition process are known as 'affective variables' – 'those emotionally relevant characteristics of the individual that influence how she/he will respond to any situation' (Gardner and MacIntyre, 1993, p. 1). Evidence shows that where teachers are seen to use 'the control functions of ... questions in the classroom . . . they rarely express their own feelings, beliefs, interpretations or opinions' (Olsen and Torrance, 1981, pp. 239–40), and provide poor models of language to bilingual children. Moreover, the practice of teaching from worksheets gives children experience of using language for informational purposes only.

One of these variables is *motivation*, which is known as the 'prime indicator of language learning process . . . and it co-relates significantly with achievement in the second language' (Gardner and MacIntyre, 1993, p. 3). Minority-language children are highly motivated to learn the second language for social, educational and personal aspirations. They are strongly supported by their parents to succeed, especially to work towards higher economic goals and to establish themselves as citizens with rights and obligations. However, the motivation of a child may be negatively affected in school. One such factor is language anxiety. In the second-language learning environment this is defined as 'a learned emotional response' (ibid., p. 6) to learners' attitudes towards the teacher and teaching strategies. This is reflected in their self-perception, beliefs, feelings and behaviour. It is critically important that bilinguals are located positively in class and supported by strategies that help develop a voice in their new language.

The teacher–learner relationship with shared knowledge, understanding and objectives is another major variable in bilingual children's learning. This leads us to consider the relationship between teaching and learning approaches that affect the outcomes of bilingual children's language and literacy learning in English positively and strongly.

Part 2: Teaching and learning approaches

In all cultures young children are guided into developing cultural literacies as well as a sense of self through participating in cooperative and collaborative cultural 'doings' with experienced members in the family. Cooperatively achieved learning underpins the foundations of learning and development.

In any given environment or culture, collaborative or shared talk is central to learning development.

Learning development as a social activity

According to Vygotsky, learning 'awakens' a variety of thought processes or 'internal developmental processes that are able to operate only when the child is interacting with people...' (1978, p. 90). He believed that consciousness or concept forming was the end product of socialization in a variety of social settings, for example, interactions at home, in the community and school, as well as the wider social networks. Evidence from my research strongly suggests that for bilinguals learning development is essentially a 'sociocultural' process within the classroom and beyond.

These social interactions enable the bilingual child to make connection with learning at a personal and cultural level; they further make it possible to internalize learning and use it to their advantage. These two levels – from social to personal – are crucial in children's learning – one without the other makes a poor mode of learning.

Most of what is taught in school is 'declarative' type of knowledge (Anderson, 1985) using formal language. Children are taught the procedures about how to use this knowledge formally; 'disembedded' from real life experiences; collaborative talk helps them to make personal connections with learning, with new concepts. Most children find it difficult to internalize formal teaching of knowledge, and fail to make it a part of their language repertoire to use it fluidly, to manipulate meaning for higher learning outcomes. My research children demonstrated deep language anxiety despite having a sound conceptual understanding of narrative structure (see children's comments in Chapter 7). A sociocultural approach to learning helps bridge the gap between curriculum subject knowledge and cultural or personal knowledge and motivates learners to cross linguistic and cultural boundaries to negotiate or construct literacy meanings deeply, and at *personal levels*. A social construction of learning helps develop multi-ability children to learn in the zone of proximal development (ZPD) with ease. The zone is described as the distance between a child's 'actual developmental level as determined by independent problem solving' *and* the higher level of 'potential development as determined through problem solving under adult guidance or in collaboration with more capable peers' (Vygotsky, 1978, p. 86). A 'shared understanding' between a more competent or knowledgeable adult and learning subjects – Bruner's 'consciousness for two' (1986, p. 74) – is critical for guiding learners into the higher zone. This makes learning a cumulative process for the bilingual child, where a more knowledgeable adult 'remains forever on the growing edge of the child's competence' (ibid., p. 77). We encounter many images of these teachers throughout the book: we see knowledgeable practitioners, nursery nurses and student-teachers in early childhood settings supporting children's learning and literacy development with sensitivity in Chapters 3 and 4; we see Samia in the role of a competent peer collaborating with Nadia's immediate needs in her reading development, with the researcher as the 'significant other' with knowledge and understanding of how the bilingual mind works to support her wider development as an independent reader; we see Ian and Karen, two student-teachers collaborating with Zaida and Kasi's reading and identity development; we see a class teacher as the 'significant other' in collaborating with ten-year-old Salina for developing critical reading skills, in Chapter 5. Whereas in Chapters 6 and 7 we see the researcher in a similar role of 'consciousness for two', that is, being knowledgeable about their current achievement and future learning potential using the personal wealth of cultural resources and guided instructions to write strongly in literary language in English. This learning occurs in *collaborative learning* situations, where children's identities are strong and negotiated further through their learning. 'Good teaching does not require us to internalize an endless list of instructional techniques. Much more fundamental is the recognition that human relationships are central to effective instructions' (Cummins, 1996, p. 73). Most important in this relationship is teacher knowledge of bilingual children's cultural literacy experiences and how these might be used in their literacy learning to develop their reading and writing strongly in English, and beyond the literal level. It is only by being involved actively and creatively in the meaning-making processes with significant others that bilinguals learn 'how to construct themselves as readers' (Wilks, 1998, p. 144) or writers. The bilingual voice is strong and learning is multidirectional when they construct knowledge collaboratively at a personal level. It is a strong affect-creating factor in their learning development. *Teacher–learner relationship* plays a major role in affecting learners' motivation, self-confidence and aspiration for high learning outcomes in this mode of learning.

> This is true for all students, but particularly so in the case of second language learners who may be trying to find their way in the borderlands between cultures ... For students to invest their sense of self, their identity, in acquiring new language and participating actively in their new culture, they must experience positive and affirming interactions with members of that culture. (Cummins, 1996, p. 73)

Another important affect creating variable is the type of *feedback* that teachers give to children's speech, reading or writing. One type is approval or positive feedback, another is correction, but 'research has produced a rather discouraging view of the effect correction has on learners' errors' (Krashen, 1982, p. 35). While teachers need to provide good models of English and meaningful contexts for English use, they must also understand that making errors is a natural aspect of any language-learning process. In gaining a sense of their new language, bilinguals should be encouraged to take risks, and making errors is a part of this process.

Language awareness work in multilingual classrooms is valuable not only in creating positive self-esteem for the minority language child but also in making the learning environment intellectually stimulating and linguistically alive. This is discussed further later in the chapter.

Language, culture and cognition

Language, culture and cognition are inextricably bound up with each other. In all cultures children learn to make sense of life and the environment around them through shared cultural activities. Language is not just a naming system. It is not a 'culture-free code, distinct from the way people think and behave, but rather it plays a major role in the perpetuation of culture...' (Kramsch, 1998, p. 8). The significance of people's way of life is interpreted culturally and the named things in any language are products of its culture. For example, the universal concept of marriage has different names in different cultures and has different cultural significance and interpretations. Language 'symbolizes cultural reality' (ibid.). When children learn to use language for communication they acquire the membership of a particular system of meanings that help them to make sense of the world around them. Language, culture and cognition are interrelated. 'All definitions of language agree that it is an important part of culture. There is a consensus that culture is a complex entity which comprises a set of symbolic systems, including knowledge, norms, values, beliefs, language, art and customs, as well as habits and skills learned by individuals as members of a given society' (Tylor, discussed in Hamers and Blanc, 1989, p. 115). These symbolic systems act as cognitive devices for the 'internal organization and shaping of experience' (Bruner, 1965) that make further meaning-making possible. Culture is not just a product but also a process of making meaning (Floria-Ruane, 2001). This was evident in my work with bilinguals from an early age. In the snapshot below we see the emerging process in five-year-old Dipesh using his cultural 'symbol' as a cognitive device to negotiate meaning. Following the good practice in some schools, Sinead O'Sullivan, a student-teacher, encouraged her children to say 'good morning' in their own languages. She started it off by saying, 'dia ghuit' used for good morning in Irish. Dipesh looked uncomfortable, and when asked why, he replied:

'We don't say good morning in Gujarati. [There's an equivalent expression in Gujarati but it is very formal.] *We say, "keim chho?"* [chh is aspirated], *How are you? "saru chhey," I'm well.'* He went on to say, *'Miss, you've got to say, "Dipesh, keim chho?" And I'll say, "saru chhey".'*

Following this exchange Sinead suggested they choose the way to *greet* one another. The above dialogue between Dipesh and his teacher awakened issues of learning development in multilingual classrooms at many levels. First, the 'inclusive' ethos or culture in the class enabled Dipesh to enter into an intercultural dialogue with his teacher, which also indicates how the bilingual mind works. Concurrently, his teacher became sensitive to language use in multilingual, multicultural classrooms and replaced 'good morning' with a more 'universal' term of *greeting*. The other children perhaps concurred with or learned through Dipesh possibilities of alternative ways of communicating a common message in different cultures. Such intercultural learning is a multidirectional meaning-making process; this will be explored more closely below by looking at the nature of children's cultural literacy learning at home. For bilingual children, literacy learning in English is necessarily an intercultural meaning-making process and they are best situated in a model of intercultural literate communities of learners in school settings.

Sociocultural learning contexts at home

Skutnabb-Kangas (1981, pp. 1–3) describes language as a 'tie' and a 'tool'. 'Language is what binds us to others, both in the historical perspective (vertically) and in the present (horizontally).' The young child growing up in a family develops a sense of self through these perspectives by participating in familial activities including family tales and anecdotes, heritage stories, religious songs, etc., which are handed down from generation to generation – language transmits culture. In all cultures significant 'others' share responsibility to accomplish the task of sharing and imparting cultural knowledge and skills to their children to help them develop a sense of self – parents, siblings, grandparents are all part of this process. Sometimes this learning is non-verbal in that children learn by observing more experienced adults in joint participation, responding to prompts or encouragement. Rogoff (1990) terms such teaching and learning as 'guided participation' (p. 191), where children look, listen, participate and learn, and feel free to ask questions.

In bilingual homes, children are surrounded by songs, rhymes and heritage stories to fulfil their emotional needs and develop a sense of self, as the following vignettes of two Bengali families suggest: here we see Samia (aged six) and Nadia (five) demonstrating their identity of 'being bilinguals' (or multilingual in Nadia's case) in their particular ways. Samia engages in fluent translation of Islamic religious stories from English to Bengali for her grandmother, whereas Nadia incorporates personal linguistic and cultural choices into her pathways to multiliteracy.

Samia's mother said:

'Samia could recite a whole book of Bangla rhymes before she was two and knew her English alphabets. Now at home she reads stories from Islamic books in English, which she translates for her grandmother in Bangla . . . she loves buying books . . . she is learning Arabic at home and we'll soon start teaching her to read in Bangla . . . she doesn't have a bedtime story but takes a book to bed every night . . . she has got books in her bedroom.'

Nadia's mother told me:

'[A]s a child she [Nadia] loved funny rhymes, and now she has an insatiable appetite for stories. She loves stories about anything – a bird sitting on the window ledge, injections, her relatives in Bangladesh or folk-tales, the ones that I grew up with . . . her favourite time for stories is when I'm cooking.' She also told me that Nadia enjoys 'acting and singing English and Hindi pop songs ... everyday after school she goes to her mosque school to learn Arabic, to read the Qur'ān, and on Saturday to her Bengali school – "as a Bengali girl she should know her own mother tongue". At home Nadia's older sister and father help[ed] her to read English text. It is a cultural norm that older siblings, both girls and boys, are expected to pass on knowledge to younger ones.'

In Chapter 5 we will see how Nadia uses this wealth of knowledge and learner identity as the driving force behind her development as an avid reader in English in a short period of time.

In most homes, letters in different community languages travel long distances, bringing good or bad tidings. Adults read them and share the news with the children, perhaps relaying some ongoing family chronicles. Newspapers are eagerly read and major happenings create a 'buzz' in the community. Children participate in these talks if considered appropriate, or are just 'active listeners'. Four-year-old Anwar's (see Chapter 4) pictorial representation of a tragic boat accident in Sylhet in which 25 people died bears testimony to the importance of these communications in young children's lives.

Cultural literacy and transferable skills

'She danced like a flickering flame'

Throughout the book we have evidence of a strong co-relationship between children's cultural literacy knowledge and skills and the development of deep literacy learning in English. One of the objectives of my study was to look specifically at some evidence of minority children's personal or cultural lives outside school and how it affected their literacy skills in English, specifically their writing abilities. To this effect, I observed a group of fluent Hindi-English bilinguals over a period of time, and saw them often switching fluently between languages and cultures at home, dancing, singing and play-acting in Hindi as well as English. All the children were avid watchers of Bollywood films and diligently copied the popular songs and dances, but when they talked about these films they normally switched into English, evaluating the story line, best acting, best dialogues, etc. Talking about dialogues, they were seen to switch back into Hindi, enjoying quoting the dialogues. They also took their favourite songs to parties. My intention of working with the children was welcomed by all the families. I have presented some selected episodes that show how bilinguals learn literacy skills from both their languages and cultures, from their simultaneous worlds.

At the time of this study Namita and Nirmala were nine and six years old. The sisters had two close friends: Sanjay, aged five, and Parul, aged eight. In our first session the children talked about many things, including their recent visits to India. Among other familial matters Namita and Nirmala were very excited in telling me about a new film, *Raja Hindustani*, that they had seen in India, but they informed me that it had yet to be released in England. Namita talked about how hot the sun was in India and how she 'got sunburnt'. Nirmala talked about how cows wander about in the street and walk in and out of people's *angan* (courtyards). Apparently a cow had eaten her grandmother's plants in the garden. Parul excitedly explained how she played *Holi*, the spring festival of colour, by spraying and splashing friends and passers-by with *gulal* (vegetable dye). She also informed me that people wear old rags to prepare for a good drenching! Sanjay talked about seeing a film about Hanuman, the monkey god in the epic poem, *Ramayana*, who could 'fly like the wind'. There was a lot of laughter, giggles and excitement, and a lot of head-nodding. I either joined in the talk or asked helpful questions to enable further elaboration and talk. I was also keen to identify possible topics for writing.

Bollywood films and cultural literacy

Life on the Bollywood screen is always larger than life. Bombay films offer simple choices between good and evil alongside catchy, foot-tapping songs that go a long way to achieving their popularity. There is a vibrancy to this genre of films that is invariably uplifting, and the plot-line always takes recourse to high drama as it unfolds. Each film is a moral allegory, and 'difficult' situations are always finally resolved to fit in with society's mores. The most successful films include a range of hit songs and eye-catching and highly choreographed dances, which are then imitated with enthusiasm by many Asian children.

I had a variety of talks with the children to explore their understanding of metaphorical use of language in Bollywood songs (following teachers' comment that 'bilingual children can't read beyond the literal'). I videoed most of my talk with the children. Given below are three extracts taken from video clips, with English translations in brackets.

The first song we talked about was:

> 'sholaa jo bherkei' (just as the flickering flame) 'mera mun dherkei' (my heart is beating).
> 'What does it mean and how will you dance to it?'
> 'Shola means flame' said Namita, and got up to demonstrate a shaking, leaping, spiky and excited dance. On further questioning about why the dancer's feelings were compared with a 'flickering flame', the responses were varied:
> 'She was frightened', said six-year-old Nirmala.
> 'Was there a real flame?' I asked.
> 'No', said Namita and Parul in unison.
> 'She was excited', said Parul.
> 'She was excited like the flickering flame, she danced like a flickering flame, perhaps something exciting was going to happen' said Namita excitedly with a flickering hand gesture.

The next song was:

> 'mere naina saavan bhado . . .' (my eyes are like saavan and bhado [the two monsoon months in India when it rains heavily])
> 'Why are the heroine's eyes compared with saavan and bhado?' I asked.
> 'Saavan is when it rains', said Namita. 'What's bhado?' she asked.
> 'It's the other monsoon month', I replied.
> 'Oh that means she was crying . . . she was crying because she was sad', she said thoughtfully.
> 'Yes, she was', repeated Nirmala, lost in her thoughts.
> 'Yes she was crying buckets', said Parul, giggling.

Their favourite songs were from *Raja Hindustani*. No sooner was it mentioned than they started singing, swaying their heads from side to side. Sanjay joined in as well. I tried to explore the first line of the song: '*aai ho mere zindegi mei tum bahaar bunkei*' (you have come to my life like blossoms of spring).

> 'What does "bahaar" [blossoms of spring] mean?' I asked.
> 'Outside', replied Nirmala.
> 'What kind of outside?' I asked.
> 'Happy outside', said Nirmala, and then the older sister, Namita, took over to say rather impatiently, 'The boy says that the girl is like beautiful spring flowers to him, that he loves her . . . he's happy to be with the girl', with a mischievous smile.
> 'Shall we do the dance?'

Nirmala and Namita sang and danced with grace and felicity, synchronizing their eyes, hands, feet and moving rhythmically to music. Indian traditional dance is a form of story-telling, and Indian film songs follow a rich lyric-writing tradition of rhymes with vivid imagery, saturated with metaphors and other literary devices. Looking at their poems (presented later in the chapter), it would seem that activating their cultural awareness influenced their mode of poetry-writing.

Unforeseen familial forces sometimes seem to be at work. For example, Namita, a Hindi-English bilingual, wrote a poem in Hindi using the Roman script when she was nine years old.

'ek panchi'

ek panchi ura pare per
ek panchi ura pare per
usay maalum nahi kaun hai vo
vo panchi pare pare per gaya
usay koi nahi milaa
urr urr ker vo panchi
mur gaya

Here is Namita's translation of her poem:

'One bird'

One bird flew to the tree
One bird flew to the tree
She didn't know what she was
That bird flew from tree to tree
But she found no one

Flying flying that bird
Died

When asked why she repeated some lines or phrases in her poem, Namita's simple answer was, *'they all do it'*. Namita's father enjoyed writing poems and read them at 'kavi sammelan' (poets' gathering), where Namita noted this characteristic. He always took his family with him. Poetry reading is a shared activity in the Indian culture in that the audience joins in with the choral lines or phrases, interspersed with exclamations of 'vah bai vah!', implying 'how beautiful!'.

Poetry-writing and transferable skills: home and school

Namita, Parul and Sanjay loved writing poems. They had many things to write about. They were all deeply personal experiences and events which they enjoyed sharing with their friends in the community and school. The idea of a real audience was greeted with excitement. But before that we talked about poetry as a form of writing.

> 'How's poetry different from other writings?' I asked.
> 'Poetry is different from other writings, because it rhymes . . . but it cannot rhyme also . . .
>   you write it however you like', replied Namita.
> 'You can have long lines or short lines . . . you can repeat lines . . . you can say things
>   differently . . . I like funny poems', added Parul.
> 'I like poems . . . because they write nice poems . . .', said six-year-old Nirmala.
> 'What makes "nice poems"?' I asked.
> 'Nice words', she replied promptly.
> Five-year-old Sanjay nodded to confirm.

It is clear that the children had developed a deep understanding of poetry from school literacy learning: *'you can say things differently'*, *'you write it however you like'* indicate awareness of figurative use of language in poetry and songs, while understanding of poetic structure is demonstrated in *'it rhymes . . . but it cannot rhyme also'*, *'you can repeat lines'*. The children showed a clear understanding of the poetic form of writing. For six-year-old Nirmala, it was *'nice words'*; perhaps Nirmala was thinking about the nice words that create interesting images, beautiful feelings or humour in poetry.

Following this the children began writing their poems about the best experience they carried in their head. Parul wrote about how she played *Holi*, an Indian festival of spring. Her sense of fun and humour is appealing.

'I Played Holi' by Parul

From early morning
We filled our spray guns
And our buckets
With gulal*
And sprayed and splashed everyone around
Half of my face was red
And half of it was blue
I looked like a monster!
My dad was walking around
With green hair and yellow face.

One silly man
Wearing a new suit
Was walking by our house
Me and Guria threw a bucketful
Of gulal water from the balcony
He erupted like a volcano
Me and Guria laughed like a hyena.

* vegetable dye

Namita's poem was the outcome of her visit to India; she talked enthusiastically about her experiences. Amid all this I picked out her description of the sun: *'In the morning the sun is soft and pink'*, and suggested that she use this as her first line. I asked her to recall further images of the sun as it moved through the day. My only advice regarding structure was *'try and follow the rhythm of the first two lines'* and to use new lines for new thoughts. Enthused with this and feeling confident she made her second and final draft. Here is Namita's final poem:

'The Sun Shines in India' by Namita

In the morning the sun is soft and pink
It looks like a lotus growing in the sky
I saw
People bathing themselves by the tube wells
In the streets

In the afternoon the sun is a ball of fire
And people are hot and sweaty
I got sunburnt
I saw
People sleeping under the
Cool shades of trees

At dusk parts of the sun
Just float in the sky
I saw
People coming home from work
And the birds flying back to their nests
At night the sun fades away and
Shines in another part of the world

As can be seen, the outcome was a very personal impression of a young Asian poet. The images are very personal. *'At dusk parts of the sun / Just float in the sky'* resonates with a young dancer's impressions of sunset over fluffy clouds, and reminds us of her comment, *'you write it however you like'*. Obviously her play with rhymes and rhythm in Hindi film songs helped her to ease into this structure effortlessly. Nirmala's use of getting 'sunburnt' is interesting in that it is not an 'Indian' cultural expression: 'catching the sun' is the normal use. Transposing her 'English' expression in her poem about the sun shining in India will make an interesting read for her Indian readers in India.

Further evaluation of Namita's poem suggests her development of literacy skills is also rooted in her experience of listening to poems in Hindi. Namita's father writes poems in his leisure time, and sometimes he reads them at 'Kavi Sammelan' (Poets' Gathering). We see Namita using all her available resources – literacy knowledge and literary skills, as well as literacy content and style from home, and school visits – to compose her poem.

At age eleven, Namita, on her return from her summer holiday in India – where she was taught to write fluently in Hindi by her cousins – proudly wrote a letter to her grandfather in Hindi using the Sanskrit (Hindi) script (see opposite). Namita was also proud to be able to join her father in reciting the verses of the epic poem *Ramayana*, and offer her own interpretations of it. Her younger sister Nirmala joins in as well. Writing about people's mother tongue, Fishman (1991, p. 4) noted:

> It is a very mystic, moving and powerful link with the past and an energizer with respect to the present and the future . . . The destruction of a language is the destruction of a rooted identity . . . intimacy, family and community.

Transliteration of Namita's letter in English:

> Dear Baba,
> How are you all? Everything must be going well. We are alright here. When is Mithlesh *didi's* wedding? We haven't got any programme to come to India at the moment. Papa's health is fine. How's Durgesh *didi's* health? How is your health? We remember you all very much. Nirmala cries a lot. Manoj is settled now. Papa is thinking about coming to India soon. He'll let you know about his arrival. How are Kuku's lessons going? How do you like my Hindi?
> Your daughter
> Namita
> P.S. Sending some photos

Namita's letter is wrapped up in 'family intimacy' (ibid.) and demonstrates her knowledge about cultural markers used in the Hindi writing system. She uses the respectable addressee terms 'aap' (respectable you) to show respect to her grandfather, and adds the suffix *'didi'* to show respect to her older female cousin. Namita ends her letter with 'aapki beti' (your daughter), again a cultural usage signifying close family roots. Learning about how language is used in Hindi extended Namita's knowledge about the writing system beyond English and enabled her to understand how language and culture work together, consequently developing a heightened awareness of writing in English. Bilingual children's literacy and cognitive skills are transferable between languages (Cummins 1984, 1996, 2000; Bialystok 1991, 2001). Currently, aged seventeen, Namita is preparing for A Levels in English, Maths, Economics and General Studies after obtaining Grade A in English and other subjects in her GCSE exams.

Five-year-old Sanjay loved listening to stories from the epic poem, *Ramayana*, full of mythological creations and stories, that his grandfather told him. I was his scribe and I structured the poem as it was narrated to me and kept rereading his composition back to him. His poem contains many mythologies about gods, beasts, demons and animals (the monkey god Hanuman was his favourite, because he flew like wind). It would seem that his experience and interest in mythologies influenced his own creation of myth in his poem.

Ms. Namita Gupta,
Effingham Rd.
London N8 OAE

प्रिय बाबा,

आप सब कैसे हैं? सब कुछ ठीक ही
चल रहा होगा। हम सदाँ ठीक हैं। मिथलेय
दीदी की शादी कब हो रही है? हमारा
इन्डिया आने का प्रोग्राम अभी नहीं है।
पापा की तबीयत ठीक चल रही है। दुर्गेश
दीदी की अब तबीयत कैसी है? दादा. आप
अब कैसे हों? आप सब की बहुत याद
आती है। निर्मला खूब सोती है। मनोज अब
सैटल हो गया है। पापा   इन्डिया आने
का विचार कर रहे हैं। आने की सूचना देंगे।
कुकू की पढ़ाई कैसी चल रही है?
मेरी हिन्दी आप को कैसी लगी?
                आप की बेटी
                        सप्रेम नमिता
P.S. कुछ फोटो भेजे हैं।

He was happy with his completed poem and took it home. His parents told me he memorized the poem and now persistently asks them to write with him.

'The Sun' by Sanjay

The sun was shining in my garden
Then came the clouds
And cuddled the sun very tightly
And the rain came down
Then came the snow
But the wind came
And blowed the rain
The cloud and the snow
All away
And sun was left
Alone in the sky

Mythologies provide children with very powerful stories and with equally powerful sounds of words in every culture, and should be seen as a rich resource to develop minority-language children's use of literary language, as is discussed in my language story (see Chapter 1). Based on the above evidence, we as educators need to give thoughtful consideration to social approaches to literacy learning in multilingual classrooms.

This concern is voiced in the following extract from a student-teacher's account of literacy learning experiences of two Gujarati-speaking children with 'significant others'. Fabienne Mas (1999), a French-English bilingual, writes:

Nishant and Dipika are two eight-year-old English-Gujarati bilinguals. Nishant is learning to read and write in Gujarati from his grandmother. Gujarati is mostly spoken at home but most written texts are in English, except religious books (i.e. Ramayana and other religious stories) . . . Nishant goes to the local library every Saturday where he chooses story or information books for himself and a book in Gujarati for his grandmother. He listens to Gujarati and Hindi songs on the Sunrise Radio and watches Bollywood movies on Zee (Cable) TV. He recently watched 'Duplicate', it's a very popular love film. Nishant is reluctant to use Gujarati in the school playground . . . because he feels he doesn't have anything to say in Gujarati, as his cultural experiences are not activated in school learning. Dipika also speaks Gujarati fluently, but hasn't started learning to read and write yet . . . but she loves taking dual language books home and her mum reads the Gujarati text and Dipika reads the English text. She goes to the local temple with her parents and relatives. Dipika watches Hindi films on video. Her favourite at the moment is 'Kutch kutch hota hai' (Something is happening), and she loves singing the songs! She speaks in Gujarati to some friends in the school playground and does not mind the presence of non-Gujarati speakers. Throughout the discussion both children kept on referring to cultural and religious events which highlighted the importance of Hinduism in their life. It appears that their linguistic and literary learning is mostly embedded in cultural and religious experiences.

Religious premises – mosques, gurdawaras, temples, synagogues and churches – are often the hub of life and literacy for minority people. It is a common meeting ground for the young and the old, where moral tales are told and recited and sometimes translated into English. In some premises children are happy to play around, switching fluently between languages. Books are sold on some of the premises and elders either buy these for children or encourage children to buy them. Holy books with their richness of literary language in parables and allegories are read or recited in many homes. In addition, many children learn to read and write using a different writing system and are exposed to different ways of learning and different ways of meaning-making. Religion seems to be a fluid context for literacy experiences as well as maintenance of minority languages.

The above accounts show the fluidity with which children's cultural knowledge is co-constructed collaboratively in a variety of social contexts; siblings, cousins, grandparents, community language teachers are all part of this learning. Gregory et al. (2004) argue that the rich contribution of these 'invisible' mediators and 'unofficial' teachers remains unrecognized in mainstream educational settings. It is important for educators to be aware of different kinds of support in a multicultural society than the school's accepted norm of reading books to or with the child.

Fabienne Mas (ibid.) concludes:

> Multilingual classrooms have been common for many years in cities throughout England and many European countries. Although most schools acknowledge and seem to value such linguistic richness in various ways (i.e. scripts in different languages on display, dual text books, etc.), I have rarely seen in my school experience in the last three years children's linguistic and cultural experiences being used for teaching and learning. The children are almost embarrassed to admit that they have another language. This may highlight the fact that 'multiscripts' are recognized but 'multiliteracies' are neither encouraged nor developed in any form in school, where only the teaching and learning of English is pursued. Obviously we need to ask, 'Are bilingual pupils therefore being given the educational experiences they need to achieve their full potential in learning English?' As a bilingual myself I believe that my understanding and knowledge of French helped me to learn English effectively.

Intercultural literate community of learners

The accounts that follow demonstrate that bilingual children's curriculum literacy development acquires life when it is co-constructed from both their learning worlds. We have looked closely at the range of 'cultural capital' (Bourdieu et al. 1977) that bilingual children carry in their head. Cummins (1988, 1996, 2000) argues that educators with *intercultural orientation* 'enable' bilinguals to learn energetically using the meanings they carry in their head, as opposed to educators with 'Anglo-conformity orientation', who tend to 'disable' them through their pedagogies. Being able to choose and evaluate their best available resources (Kress, 1997) to develop deep literacy in English development is crucial for bilinguals. Withholding their 'cultural capital' from their school learning creates *surface level* learning only, blocking their ability to apply their knowledge to advance their learning potential. (See Chapters 5 and 6.)

Intercultural approaches to literacy learning in school need to be guided carefully.

Language awareness activities in multilingual classrooms are valuable not only in creating positive self-esteem for the minority-language child but also in making the learning environment intellectually stimulating and linguistically alive. These intercultural activities endorse every child's identity, language and culture, including that of the 'English only' child, and help create an intercultural classroom community. It provides a collaborative space for children to look, listen and learn from each other and develop confidence to participate.

> [A] multilingual approach to language development helps to deepen children's understanding of what language is, how it works and how it is used in different contexts, which in turn strengthens the teaching and learning objectives at text, word and sentence level. When children's language learning goes beyond English into other languages, it not only provides the stimulus to learn a new language but also allows them to think about language more deeply and flexibly'. (Datta and Pomphrey, 2004, p. 1)

Fanoula Xeneki, a student-teacher working with a class of seven- and eight-year-olds, made 'Our Languages Book' to create an intercultural learning environment. Below is a collaborative poem from the book:

'Greetings'

These are the ways we say hello,
And put smiles on the faces of those we know
Ola in Spanish, bonjour in French
In Bengali it's keeta aachen or swagatum,
In Arabic, salam-alay-kum

How many other ways can we greet,
And put smiles on the faces of those we meet?
How are you? In Tigran it's Te-me-le-ki?
If you say Ti kanete? You'll be speaking Greek.
But rather than find out from a book
We can tell you in 3B
If you're fine in Greek you say kala,
In Tigran, tobuk.

When we meet we say hi!
When we leave we say goodbye,

Adios, au revoir, zagee,
Is what you will hear from class 3B!

The first two lines of the poem were suggested by Fanoula, the rest of the poem were children's responses to the meaning and rhythm embedded in the lines. There are many examples of language awareness work throughout this book

Another example of locating children's home literacy in school literacy learning was initiated by a child. The example given below was spontaneously written in class by ten-year-old Faisal. He recalled from memory a Bengali poem his parents taught him at home. A free translation was offered by the child. For non-Bengali readers it demonstrates what might be the nature of his literary language experience in Bengali:

Kheila [Play]

শীতের ছুটিতে গিয়েছিলাম
বাদামতলির মেলা।
তিনটি ছোট পয়সা দিয়ে
কিনে নিলাম লাটপটি।
তারেই নিয়ে একা একা
কাটাই অখন বেলা।
সাত সকালেই উঠেই করি
চাই টাকের খেলা।
ভুলো দিয়ে আপন মনে
আপন খুসরে জানি,
সোনারদের ডাক যে তখন
হৃদয় ভরে শুনি।

I went to the Badamtalir fair
At the end of winter
With three pennies in hand
I bought a plough
And spend hours alone in its company
I get up early in the morning
And play with land
Growing my own crop
And listen to the call of the golden corn
To harvest with all my heart.

Memorizing significant poems is a cultural norm in the Asian culture as well as in some other cultures. The cultural practice enabled Faisal to encounter the use of literary language in Bengali with the support of his family. Excluding these experiences in literacy learning in English creates confusion and 'language anxiety' in bilingual children's schema: they feel pressurized to learn about English literary language as a new concept (see Chapter 7).

In an intercultural community of learners it is crucial that teachers play the role of active listeners to identify best topics in children's talk and ask open questions to raise their awareness of sense of self. It is a process that needs to be developed and 'managed' collaboratively through shared talk and a range of literacy activities (Datta and Pomphrey, 2004).

In one of my language sessions a group of ten-year-old children started talking about the Chinese New Year and comparing it to the Hindu celebration of Diwali, the Muslim celebration of Eid and the Christian celebration of Christmas. The environment was vibrant with children's 'voices' switching fluidly between 'expert–novice' roles (Rogoff, 1990) in sharing their knowledge of different religious festivals. Amid all of this Yew declared that he was a Buddhist, and shared his knowledge about Buddha's life with the others. With great awe he talked about Buddha's meditation, that 'Buddha meditated for six years . . . for peace'. This seemed to have a profound effect on Yew in the poetry-writing session that followed. The children were expected to write their own poems after reading and talking about some sea poems. Here is Yew's poem:

'My Emotions' by Yew
I like the sea
When the sun sets on it
I can see the beauty of the colours
On the waves and in the skies
Red and orange
Gold and yellow
Swirling and dancing on the waves
It makes me feel calm
And beautiful

In his first draft Yew had called his poem 'Sunset on the Sea' and the last line read 'It makes me happy as a lark'. After reading the poem to his peers he changed the title to 'My Emotions' and created two new lines, *It makes me feel calm / And beautiful.*

> *'Why did you make these changes?'* I asked.
> *'Because it's about my emotions, my feelings,'* he said thoughtfully.

Ten-year-old Yew's sharing of cultural knowledge, feelings and cultural ways of thinking with his peers awakened a creative energy that allowed him to take an enormous linguistic leap in shaping his poem, from the concrete image of 'Sunset on the Sea' to the profoundly abstract 'My Emotions'. Yew's poem inspired Mitesh to recall his experience in a village in Gujarat on his holiday in the same thoughtful mode:

'Run Away' by Mitesh

Run from the town
Run from the noisy dirty streets
Where people are pushing each other
Groaning and grumbling
Run away to a village
Far far away
To watch the cows mooing
To watch the cows grazing
Sitting under a tree
Listen to the music in your head
You hear it
You sing it

You feel the wind running away
Run with it
Still far far away.

In my talks with the children's teacher I was told Mitesh was a 'reluctant writer' and that Yew 'tries hard'. When I asked the children, Mitesh told me he found writing 'boring' and Yew said 'it was okay' (see other poems in Chapters 6 and 7). 'At our peril we forget the considerable variety of experience and the diversity of construction of meaning that is owned by bilinguals and multilinguals ... It is in the richest interests of child development that minority language literacy and biliteracy is supported by parents, teachers, communities and advocates (of whom academics are one important voice)' (Baker in his Foreword to this book).

Puppets, play-scripts and literary fluency

Literacy artifacts across cultures are important in bilingual learning. Here we see how the bilingual children, comparatively new to using English as their medium of learning, respond energetically to write a play for their puppet show. Given below is the account by a bilingual support advisor in the Local Education Authority (East, 2000) about the importance of puppets, or enacting language, in bilinguals' literacy learning:

> I regularly use puppets to provide a context to help both monolingual and bilingual children extend their language experience. Class teachers frequently notice that quiet children are often more articulate and expressive when using puppets, and comments such as 'he doesn't normally speak that much in the class' or 'I've never heard her talking so expressively before' are common. Puppets are exciting and motivating and when children 'play' with puppets they improvise and interact with one another fostering speaking and listening skills either in English or a community language, and writing skills are developed through play-script writing. Working towards a collaborative outcome such as a performance or play-script is a rich co-operative activity that fosters the following types of language development.
>
> * Imaginative language related to the developing role of a character, who may speak using words and structures that the child has heard at home.
> * Technical language associated with puppetry such as 'character', 'dialogue', 'play-script'.
> * Transactional language essential to negotiating, planning and decision making among a group of children.
>
> It is important to have a range of puppets available, including puppets whose appearance and dress show that they belong to a variety of cultures, especially those represented in the school.
>
> A group of children produced a multilingual puppet show. Dialogue in their first language (French and Urdu) was repeated in English so all those in the audience could understand. However the drama of a speech tended to be carried in their first language and the translation was delivered without expression. The children also gave English translations in their written text as presented below.
>
> Extract from Scene 1: 'At the Magician's House'
> **Junaid** [magician]: I find a potion in the spell book.
> **Evans** [Magician's brother]: Less moi voire, ces une bonne chose.
> Let me see, it's a good trick.
> **Junaid**: Let's cook it.
>
> Extract from Scene 2: [Abdul goes to open the door. The evil auntie bursts in]
> **Evil auntie**: aacha bacho ab mei boss houn iss gar ka (in Urdu). OK children, now I'm the boss in this house.
> [The children are terrified]
> **Children**: Who are you?
> **Evil auntie**: mei tumari evil auntie houn, ha! ha!!
>
> When evaluating the work the class teacher was impressed by the children's creative use of language in the dialogue. She noted how confident the children were in their use of specialist vocabulary. She was impressed by the children's confidence in writing a play bilingually and the way the scribes incorporated features such as 'setting' and 'stage directions' into the script. She recognized the value of the transactional language in the negotiations and saw how supportive the children were of each other. The play-scripts were edited, redrafted and published by the groups.

Friendship literacy and collaborative talk

Here we meet three boys from different linguistic and cultural backgrounds in an early childhood learning classroom. Mehmet, Daniel and Sam were three seven-year-old friends, sharing Turkish, English and Berber speaking Algerian as their native languages and were at different stages of reading. I first observed them listening to a story read by the class teacher, and sharing their quiet but animated expressions of delight and surprise amongst themselves. Later, I talked to the group and asked them, *'would you like to share your favourite books with each other?'* Their eyes lit up at the prospect and they had no problems choosing their best book from the class library. Mehmet chose a book about *Celebrations* (Kindersley and Kindersley, 1997).

'What would you like to talk about?' This open-ended question seemed to activate making personal choices and stimulating learning dialogues. The collaborative talk allowed the boys to share linguistic, cultural and personal knowledge with one another as they moved in and out of 'expert–novice' roles (Rogoff, 1990) to make meaning at a personal level. The following excerpt is from a conversation that the three boys had around Mehmet's choice (Datta, 2004):

> Mehmet: [Showing the book] *This is my best book. Celebrations is a book of all celebrations around the world ... I mostly look at Turkish ones because I'm Turkish.* [Effortlessly opens the book to a page with pictures of children in colourful costumes and begins his interpretations] *Children's Day is a big festival in Turkey. This is the first President of Turkey* [pointing to another picture in the book]. *It's Ataturk and his strategy in war was very good.* [Commenting on the next picture] *[When] children celebrate in Turkey, they kiss their family's hands and put them on their foreheads, they [the family] give them money.*
> Daniel: *Is that what you do in Turkey?* [emphasis on 'Turkey']
> Mehmet: *Well we do it in Turkey and England* [emphasis on 'and']
> Daniel: *Oh that's good.*

We see Mehmet, a boy of Turkish heritage, as the expert on his cultural heritage, and Daniel, of English heritage, as the novice. However, Daniel is not a passive listener. Throughout the session Daniel uses inquiring questions to seek meaning against his own cultural knowledge and experience. He uses his own 'cultural capital' to understand the Turkish culture of his friend by 'comparing, contrasting and mediating between the two' (QAA, 2002), identifying similarities and differences and developing an intercultural identity. This challenges Mehmet to clarify his taken-for-granted cultural understandings and evaluate his links between his 'two worlds'. The extract also demonstrates how children's sense of self and emotions are closely entwined in their literacy learning.

Mehmet: [Continues reading and commenting on the text] *At Cocuk Bayrami – At Celebrations* [translating Cocuk Bayrami for his friends] *– we sing songs. My favourite song is about Ataturk ... I watched the children's festival in Ankara on TV, I saw children from China dancing. I like seeing children from other countries ... it makes me want to visit those places.*
Daniel: Do they give presents?
Mehmet: Well some people give presents.
[Seeing Sam not asking any questions, I asked him quietly] *Do you want to ask anything Sam?*
I'm thinking.
Daniel: Do they give cards? Like with a piece of paper they fold and draw a card. Like Christmas cards with little reindeer and . . .
Mehmet: Well no, they don't make cards but there is always . . .
[Suddenly sees a picture of Simit, a twisted dough ring] *That's my bestest bread. It's called Simit.*
Sam: [Speaking for the first time] *Has it got chocolate on it?*
Mehmet: Well no. It has sesame seeds on it ... I love it!
Mehmet: [Turning his attention to a picture of a sports stadium] *There's lots of sports in Ankara stadium.*
Daniel: What kind of sports?
Mehmet: Like wrestling – even the children wrestle. Here's a Turkish man in wrestling uniform [pointing to a picture] *and running. On celebration day the Boy Scouts give flowers and an army man gives a round circle of flowers like this* [he points to a picture of a wreath] *and lays it on the place in Ankara where Ataturk died.*
Daniel: Do they put a stick up, with flowers on it? You have like in churches.
Mehmet: [Does not respond to Daniel's question, he continues] *Well [when] grandpa died . . . Do you know in mosques . . . when someone dies or when praying there's two places, one for ladies' prayer room upstairs, and downstairs men's prayer room. But children can sit anywhere! When I go to the mosque I just run up and down, up and down . . . and when grandpa died, in the mosque*
Sam: [Interrupting] *He died? How? Did they bury him?*
Mehmet: I didn't see the burial but I saw his coffin and he was high up on steps.
Daniel: Maybe that's the steps to heaven. Is it?
Mehmet: Maybe, I don't know.
Daniel: Oh, he might have rose up to heaven.
Mehmet: Yeah.
Daniel: In Eid do they dance around?
Mehmet: In Eid yeah, they give cards . . .
Daniel: Oh they give cards? [Daniel at last gets the confirmation that Turkish people also exchange cards]
Mehmet: It says on the card, 'Eid Mubarak', and sometimes there's one in Arabic and one in Turkish.
Daniel: Oh ... [lost in thoughts]

It is evident that Mehmet's energy for learning flows from his cultural knowledge of one of his worlds: 'I'm Turkish' he says proudly. His friends legitimize this by showing keen interest in what he has to say and by asking questions for further interpretations. Daniel's line of questioning at every level is as powerful as Mehmet's narrative, he makes use of his own cultural wealth to understand how the two worlds operate culturally to satisfy his *personal learning*. He learned that cultures converge as well as diverge. Minami (2002) argues that narratives are excellent 'to make sense of experience in culturally satisfying ways' (p. 48). Engaging in narrative dialogues enabled Daniel, Mehmet and Sam to fulfil their personal learning goals. Moreover, evidence shows that children learn more about 'language and language behaviour' from their peers (Krashen, 1982, p. 30). Children create their own pathways to extend their literacy learning and seem to create their own way with words. This is also evident in Kenner's (2004) work, which shows young bilingual children talking fluidly about different writing systems that they encounter in their first language.

In another setting we see how collaborative learning creates an interpersonal space in which learners feel inspired and confident to take risks with their creative thinking. Two competent writers in a class of six- to seven-year-olds chose to write a play about a personal interest. Their teacher supported them with class reading of their play and asking open questions. Looking and listening to the ongoing process of play-writing by their peers, Paramjeet and Sasha felt inspired and confident to write a play as well. When asked what the play was going to be about they had no hesitation in declaring that they wanted to write a play about Jack and the Beanstalk. As friends they had already decided on the theme. The choice was very intelligent in that they knew they could use the story as a 'prop' for their own play. Evidence shows the use of existing story frames as props helps bilinguals to take risks with their writing, language and style.

When asked further, *'Do you want to call it "Jack and the Beanstalk" or give it a different name?'* their eyes lit up at the possibility – they said, almost in unison, *'Can we Miss?'*

They responded by operating at two levels to affirm their identities. Jack became Rani, a female Indian child, as the brave protagonist. The Giant became a 'she-giant' with a Greek name, 'Andrianna', because Sasha was Greek. It was interesting to see how they negotiated the dialogues. They were seen acting their characters in role to write the dialogue: play allows children to push cognitive boundaries (Vygotsky, 1962, 1978, 1986). Following their peers they too wanted to present their play to the class, and had already decided on their choice of actors and music. The other children were very impressed by the play.

> *Paramjeet's original script*

coming home soon and he
mite eat You uP.

Rani | o what Am I going to
do?

cupboard

mG | hide in The KBRid
avick BeFoR mY hass
comes Bak.

[Act 3]

daddy
giant | fe fo fam I KAn

Smell TheBLod of alittle

Indian girl.

mG | No m r dear there

Aint ANy little
Indian girL here.

The rest of Paramjeet's writing is in Chapter 6.

Conclusion

Learning in the multilingual classroom is best supported in an environment of 'intercultural literate community of learners' where meaning is negotiated and renegotiated collaboratively between peers, and teachers. Teachers in this community actively listen to children's talk about the wealth of cultural and literacy experiences from both their language and cultural worlds, ask for further elaborations and guide them to extend and integrate these resources to curriculum literacy learning in a variety of literacy forms, genre or style. They are always on the 'growing edge' of children's learning development. Bilinguals in these environments fluently engage in evaluating and synthesizing meanings intelligently from personal available resources for high learning outcomes and personal satisfaction. An 'intercultural literate' environment enables bilinguals to use their 'cultural capital' on an equal footing with native English-speaking peers and activating lateral as well as multidirectional thinking. Teaching and learning in this community is strong, inspirational and rewarding for educators and multi-ability learners.

The overall evidence from my work in this book and elsewhere (Datta, 2004; Datta and Pomphrey, 2004) suggests that bilingual children's development of literacy learning in English is necessarily an 'intercultural' meaning-making process. Language learning, by definition, is an intercultural experience. It is essential that bilingual children are encouraged to 'behold the world not univocally but simultaneously' (Bruner, 1986, p. 26). Kenner (2004) argues strongly for recognition of bilingual children's 'simultaneous worlds'. She argues that the mainstream society constructs itself as 'monolingual and Anglocentric, and tries to keep children's linguistic and cultural worlds apart ... We need to make the most of children's abilities to produce alternative ideas and see a situation from different points of view' (p. 124). Further, Alred et al. (2003) argue strongly that it is not sufficient to add to the teaching of English a 'dimension, which is called literature from other cultures' (p. 6). The role of intercultural learning experiences in education, exchanging meanings from young learners' different cultural worlds, is central to broadening their thinking perspectives, and enhance learning opportunities and outcomes in intellectually and personally satisfying ways. To this effect teaching and learning approaches in multilingual classrooms need to be carefully thought through to create meaning-making 'dialogues' in learners' heads using the entire repertoire of learning resources. This forms the underlying theme of subsequent chapters.

Bilinguality and Learning in the Early Years

Maggie Ross

> To have knowledge of another culture does not mean to be able to repeat one or two words in a student's language, nor is it to celebrate an activity or sing a song related to that culture. To acknowledge and to respect is to be able to understand and apply this knowledge to everyday classroom activities. It is to be able to make changes or modifications in one's curriculum or pedagogy when the needs of the students have not been served. (Lizette Román, quoted in Nieto, 1999, p. 144)

A group of three parents stand talking together in the garden as they wait for the nursery to open. They speak Spanish together, their children playing a short distance away. Suddenly, one of the parents, Manuela, notices that a small boy has started to climb the fence on the far side of the garden. Manuela breaks off her conversation and calls across to the little boy in Turkish. I do not understand the words, but know from her tone and from the young child's reaction that she has told him it is not safe to climb there. His mother comes across to meet him, calling 'thank you' and a greeting to Manuela in Turkish.

Manuela returns briefly to her Spanish conversation and then moves towards the nursery as the door is opened, taking her own child by the hand and beginning a conversation with her in English. *'Come on, let's go in the warm. Here, put your gloves in your pocket safely.'* Her daughter says goodbye, hugs Manuela while jumping up and down excitedly and rushes into the nursery.

Moving between different languages, making quick judgements about conversation partners and contexts, switching languages within and between sentences: all this is everyday communication for those who, like Manuela, speak two or more languages. Her children speak two languages fluently, and rapidly gain fluency in two others when they have the opportunity to use them during extended visits to family members.

For children like Manuela's daughter it is vital that as educators we recognize both the linguistic knowledge brought by bilingual children and our own role as involved and enthusiastic partners in language development. Manuela worked closely with staff in the school, and was able to feel certain that her daughter would be supported when she used any of the linguistic knowledge available to her. Children, parents and carers hear how staff speak about language and see the ways in which nurseries and schools respond to the cultural and linguistic backgrounds of the families. Staff who involve families in close partnerships in which learning is genuinely an exchange take time to ensure that communication is always as good as it can be.

Our own responsibility to communicate must be a priority. If we are unable to deliver the whole curriculum successfully through a shared language we need to be active and creative in ways which match the creativity and effort of young learners. The confidence to take risks, which seems to be important for children who are successful in second-language learning (Wong-Filmore, 1991), has to be matched by the expectation on the part of adults that time, space and imagination will be given in support. Practice moves forward when we learn with and from the children, parents and colleagues with whom we work. In this chapter there are observations of practice where educators have made simple, but often important, moves to support young bilingual children as they become members of their nursery or classroom community. The emphasis in these snapshots is on strategies which support young children's access to membership of the group, and on the responsibility which staff have assumed to look at some of the basic structures in their settings in terms of helping young bilingual learners 'join in' rather than remaining on the fringes.

Bilingual children in the foundation years

Early childhood practitioners are used to approaching their work with the intention that careful observation of children will inform practice. Because we want to start from the child, and to allow for creativity and exploration, we may feel that we offer all children good access to learning. The way in which many staff work with bilingual children and their families has undoubtedly given many young learners a security and sense of value with which to begin their learning. The early childhood curriculum recognizes the importance of emotional well-being, and the different learning styles or dispositions of young children. Bilingual children need all this, but also a clear understanding of the ways in which first and second languages are developed, and of how linguistic and cognitive development are intertwined. Young children learning a new language deserve 'a rich language context . . . matching the learners' individual approaches and language needs. Mere participation in simple forms of interaction in early childhood settings is not sufficient to result in significant second language acquisition' (Clarke, 1999, p. 24).

There are many different family and community contexts in which young children grow up speaking more than one language. Some are fluent bilinguals by the age of three, others learn their different languages sequentially. Frequently, young children enter early childhood settings in the earliest stages of learning English. Educators need to build their own knowledge of the different language communities to which these children belong, working closely with families to do this. All children coming into a new nursery or classroom experience unfamiliar expectations and new forms of language. It is vital that educators understand and acknowledge the experiences and expectations of families from diverse linguistic and cultural backgrounds (Gregory, 1997).

Kenner (1997) has documented the language and literacy experiences of young bilingual children gained at home, through contact with extended family, in the community and at school. Once these experiences have been recognized and valued at school these young children are confidently able to draw on this wider knowledge and skill in school. If practitioners do not consider home literacy learning children are not able to progress as they should.

Arguments for the provision of bilingual education have been carefully explored in work which looks at issues of both identity and cognitive development (Corson, 1994; Skutnabb-Kangas, 1981). It is important for all young children to be able to draw on and learn through the languages which they are already able to use proficiently, extending conceptual understanding and language together. However, for most bilingual children in early childhood settings there is no bilingual curriculum. For many there is no adult present with whom to share their first language, and neither is it unusual for a child to have no peers with whom to share this language.

Case studies have shown how important it is that educators work in ways which support children drawing on their first language and literacy experiences (Kenner, 1997; 2004), and that they view bilingualism as 'an asset which will increase children's linguistic awareness, cultural sensitivity and cognitive functioning' (Whitehead, 1997, p. 98). But research has also shown that a young bilingual child may often have much more limited access to the early childhood curriculum than his or her peers who speak the majority language fluently on entry (Drury, 1997, 2000).

Planning to support bilingual children

Where practitioners are able to share the languages of the children with whom they work, their understanding of children's needs and their ability to make and implement plans which meet such needs are of a different quality. Children's learning can take place within the supportive environment that is provided by adults who are able to move between languages as they work with children, or in a 'one person, one language' model of practice where children have opportunities to work in their first language with one key adult and in their second language with another. Where we are not yet able to provide a bilingual curriculum we need to think about the essential elements which must be in place in order for children to have the fullest possible access to a shared curriculum. We need to be creative in our thinking, continually assessing the demands made on children and identifying all the possible approaches we could use to widen this access.

We need to consider:

- our partnerships with families and the local community, including local community schools;
- how we are able to involve adults who do share languages with the children;
- how we can plan for and provide an environment which is as receptive as possible to children's choices about language use;
- how to develop ways to support children learning together, supporting each other in their first languages;
- when it is appropriate to focus on some key language for specific experiences, and how to do this in ways which support new learning, and which do not negate children's own contributions;
- how to observe, assess and plan for progress in language;
- what we can do to make it possible for assessment to take place in home languages;
- how we can organize time so that young bilingual children do not get lost in the bigger group, but have sufficient opportunities to work closely with an adult;
- what we need to do in order to create an ethos in which linguistic variety is valued and developed;
- how we can maintain creative and rich approaches to both oracy and literacy which fully recognize linguistic diversity.

Planning for the beginning

Manuela, with whom this chapter opened, knew that her young daughter Ayse was able to gain access to the nursery through her increasing command of English. Ayse was able to use English very effectively, and when she did not understand a particular word or construction she was usually confident enough to ask. She was also able to use her knowledge of Turkish (her first and most fluent language) to enjoy playing with, and sometimes translating for, other children in the class. She would also use Arabic words for some things. Manuela knew that the school welcomed this linguistic knowledge and would support its growth.

Mohsen came into the school in a very different situation. At four-and-a-half he spoke Urdu fluently. He was not yet speaking English, although he had some understanding from hearing his brothers speaking English together and from the language used in the wider community. He was familiar to some extent with the 'outward' routines of the school day: standing still when the first bell rang; lining up at the classroom door at the second; knowing that his mother would come to the other door in the afternoon. His brothers had gone through these routines each day. But inside the classroom everything was new to him. He had attended a playgroup but had not had a place in this particular school before. For Mohsen, it was important that the staff who looked after him in his first classroom had thought about the ways in which school might be more difficult for children with whom they could not communicate in a shared language.

The routines were not rigid, but were consistent. Personal and social development was carefully planned for. Time was given for children to move through the routines with adults and with children already familiar with them. The other spaces in the school were explored in small groups. To make the rhythm of the day easier to understand, photographs of some of the key routines were displayed and these photographs could be taken round or held up as time for changes approached. There were pictures of children washing their hands, children lining up, children at dinner, children in the playground.

Photographs were used as much as possible in resource areas and in the trays of equipment. They were also used imaginatively at other times. At group times, when children talked about what they had done or what they would like to do next the photographs could be drawn on for support, and there was also a box of resources – blocks, a paintbrush, a doll and a teacup, scissors, glue, a book, a spade for the sand. The items in the box reflected the resources generally available and specific ones used in that session.

Key language was identified when new learning was introduced, and staff were careful to offer opportunities for all children to talk in small groups with an adult each day. Story sessions and singing were important times for developing language learning, drawing on the languages spoken by children in the class. At group times, including whole-class times, the children sat in a circle so that they were able to see each other, as well as the adults. In this way they were able to see the gestures and expressions of other children as they talked or sang. It also created a culture in which children could legitimately use these other forms of communication to share meanings.

Mohsen moved fairly rapidly through a stage in which he used mainly single words in English to express his needs, to simple phrases which conveyed a wide range of meaning and in which he used intonation and expressive tones and gestures to question, tell or exclaim with surprise. By the end of his first term he had become a confident member of the class. *'My mum say take this book home. Read this book.'* And talking about his painting, *'I make little like this [showing with his fingers together]. Mouse hiding.'* And taking the picture around at tidy-up time Mohsen could say, *'Jenny say tidy up now. Tidy up now [loudly]. You put doll there.'* It was important that staff observed what Mohsen enjoyed doing, who were the children with whom he worked confidently, when he spoke English confidently, and how he was able to use words and increasingly complex syntax to express his meaning. A very important support for Mohsen was the opportunity he had to work with a member of staff who could speak Urdu. In these sessions he had the opportunity to understand so much more, and to express much more fluently what he had done, seen and felt, what he wanted to find out or explore next, what might happen in a story. Only a picture which brought together the knowledge of Mohsen's mother and all the staff could begin to fully describe Mohsen's skills and knowledge. Mohsen did not go through a 'silent period' beyond the first few days during which he watched closely and followed other children. However, the support offered in his classroom provided a framework within which children who were 'silent' for longer could become members of the classroom community and share in the learning.

Observation and assessment

The creation of a supportive environment which recognizes linguistic diversity is a beginning. We also need to observe bilingual children across the curriculum and in different groups and situations, in order to evaluate their access to learning and their participation. The study of four-year-old Meera by Kenner et al. (1996) shows how important it is that our observations consider children in different contexts. Observation of Meera's use of English in different situations provided evidence of creativity and control of language. An assessment of Meera made from more limited observation would have described a far less fluent communicator. The observations and reflections of the class teacher, language-support teacher and researcher together provided a richer picture of a young child's language use in the nursery.

Paffard's (1999) broad yet detailed observation also provided significant information about Hana as a language user. At age four, Hana was not yet an interested writer but was a fluent and creative oral communicator, a 'teller of tales' who was able to use her increasing command of her second language to hold an audience. Forms of assessment which do not take into account the full linguistic profile of children risk giving a very limited and inaccurate view of what they are able to do, and therefore of what we need to do to support their progress. Any assessment must be based on a broad understanding of how language learning is taking place, and of the complexity and sophistication of bilingual children's skills. Much of the observation we do is during our interactions with children, and informs how we support children, even during that particular conversation or shared experience.

Seema shared a book with Anya and their class teacher. The girls were five years old, and in the middle of their reception year. The girls read a version of *The Little Red Hen* which was familiar to them from class story sessions and from the times they had pored over the book together in the reading corner. As they came each time to the refrain 'Who will help me . . .?' the two girls joined in with the teacher's reading. Anya was much more confident of the actual text, Seema quietly moved her lips. Afterwards, Seema was asked to read the story to the teacher. She skipped over the pages of the book until she found a familiar picture and began to read, '*Who will help me?*' Turning over the page, she read again, '*Who will help me?*' The adult pointed to the adjacent page with the text 'Not I said the cat'. Seema looked up at her, but said nothing. The adult read the text and this time Seema looked down at the page. As the story came to an end Seema skipped off the chair and went to find another activity in which to absorb herself.

The teacher's previous assessment of Seema was that she used only one or two words in English to stand for longer sentences – '*Me go*' '*Finish now*' – and usually chose to remain quiet in group or whole-class times. So for Seema this 'Who will help me?' said with expression was a leap forward. Closer observation and awareness of what was happening might have meant that Seema was supported so that she could enjoy a successful experience, in which she read the phrase each time it occurred. She might have been able to read the full question each time alongside the teacher, developing both her confidence as a reader and her use of the 'book language' she needs to become familiar with to be a successful reader.

Seema was confident and purposeful in a maths activity involving the children exploring boxes, and making their own simple nets for containers. On this occasion as she worked she was talkative. 'My mum,' she said, as she cut out a shape she had drawn in thick pen on sugar paper. The adult working with her in this session thought for a minute and, not sure what Seema referred to, responded in an interested voice, 'Your mum?' 'My mum do,' said Seema, pointing to her dress. The adult quickly realized that Seema referred to the sewing which her mother did, and suddenly thought about the pattern cutting. 'Did your mum make that dress?' she asked. 'My mum make,' said Seema. 'Make like this, and like this', demonstrating how her mother worked at the sewing machine. She then lifted up the hem to show the stitches. 'It's beautiful,' was the reply. 'I like sewing too.'

At the end of that session when the children shared their work Seema held up her box. She was asked how she had made it, but either she did not understand the question or did not feel confident enough to answer. The adult who had worked with her on the activity asked Seema again, but used carefully chosen language and an object to help her understand the question and support her reply. 'How did you make it?' she repeated. Then she expanded, 'Did you cut it out?' and reached for the scissors. 'Cut like this and like this.' Seema was able to respond. The adult could also add that Seema's mum made her dress, and to do that she had to cut out the pattern and the fabric. All the children could then share this link with Seema's experience and possibly with their own.

The adult's ability to listen, to analyse and to use language to extend children's learning through a shared context both gave Seema an opportunity to share her own experience in a way which made links with her school learning and offered her support for her developing use of English. In this way she could become confident in using her second language. Early years staff use this practice with all children. For bilingual children in the early stages of a new language the difference may be that an adult needs to be even more sensitive to the words and phrases which children can use to express their meaning, as well as to the communication intention. Patterns in a child's developing speech in his or her second language may then be supported through use of similar, but extended, examples from the adult (Siraj-Blatchford and Clarke, 2000). The adult had noted the significance of this experience for Seema, and was observant of the phrases and words which Seema had already used. She made sure that there was an opportunity for her to use and build on this language, and to practise it confidently during the sharing time with the class. Seema did not often have opportunities in school to work with other children or adults with whom she could speak Punjabi. It was important that she could be as fully involved as possible in the shared constructions of meaning, and supported as well as possible in opportunities to develop her fluency in English. At the same time the use of story tapes and songs in Punjabi supported Seema's identity as a fluent speaker of her home language and as a child able to take the lead in language experiences when she shared these tapes with other children and adults.

Language for learning

Young bilingual children need what all language learners need: many, many opportunities to hear and speak the new language in shared contexts. Although there are differences in cultural and linguistic practices within both communities and families, the practices by which young children become fluent language users almost certainly have much in common. Children develop an understanding of the social and linguistic contexts and learn the language attached to different people and situations. Within early years settings all children becoming familiar with new adults, wider groups of children and new routines, expectations and experiences will find support in the regularity of some of the frameworks and shared experience. For bilingual children less familiar with the language used by staff there needs to be careful thought about the creation of shared understanding.

Clarke (1999), through her research in a bilingual pre-school setting, has identified three phases through which young children progressed as they became more fluent in a second language. In the first of these phases English was 'mainly used to accompany interaction rather than to mediate interaction' (ibid., p. 23). In the second phase children were able to use some of this accompanying language in their interactions. In the third phase children could use their second language as the 'main carrier' of their interaction. The importance of the quality of the interactions with adults, which emerged from this work, is significant for all educators of young bilingual children.

Anwar made a model road for the toy cars. Observation of his play led adults to decide that they needed to create an opportunity for children to hear and practise language which would help them to share resources more comfortably. Anwar could use scissors, glue and paper effectively: looking carefully at the width of the track, he chose to widen it by adding a strip of card, which he fixed with tape. He was able to ask for more tape in English by telling the adult *'this finish'*, and showing her the finished roll. He was also able to share his work with another child. *'Car go fast, and then one go over here'*, he said, demonstrating this by making his cars go over the road and imitating the engine noise. He was creative as a communicator. However, when another child approached and wanted to share the new tape, Anwar was protective and snatched it quickly away. The other child suggested that Anwar could have the tape back afterwards – *'I only want a little bit, then you can have it back'* – but Anwar was unable to respond calmly and the adult, while helping him to share the tape, realized that he may not have been able to take part in a conversation about sharing and turn-taking as confidently as he was able to tell others about his model.

At circle time the children talked about what they had made. The models were placed in the middle of the carpet for each child to pick up as they described their work. Anwar enjoyed talking about his road and cars: *'I made one road, and cars go fast there, two cars go'*. He used a mixture of tenses, perhaps copying the model of 'I made' from the beginning of other children's descriptions. But a further and equally important intention for the staff in this session was to offer children models of language for turn-taking and sharing. Some of the toys were collected on the carpet and adults and children asked to be passed things, asked to share, pretended to argue. Role-play was used to offer simple models of some of the language useful for negotiation and turn-taking.

Another nursery team used a similar opportunity for bilingual and monolingual staff and students to model by asking each other how to ask for things in different languages. This was a short session which adults and children found fun as the adults tried to pronounce things correctly in each other's languages. It also showed the children how the adults needed to ask each other for help and support in order to share linguistic knowledge. It also created a situation in which children and adults were spontaneously using language to talk about language. Adults paused while they thought about how to explain how something could be best expressed, children offered examples and together something important about making meaning was explored. This experience was one in which the bilingual children and adults drew on knowledge which was special, but which could be shared with others.

Hanna, Abdullahi and Razia worked together in Arabic to make boats which they hoped would float in the water trough. Fluent talk in Arabic accompanied the activity and the children remained uninterrupted for twenty minutes. At the end of the day Abdullahi's mother, looking at the boats with the children, could tell the practitioner that they had made lots of boats which sank, and got very wet, and that the children thought they needed some more margarine tubs from home because they were plastic and would not get soggy.

The adult watching these reception class children at play was involved with another group of children during the session. Her brief observations of the water play had shown that the children had indeed made lots of boats which sank, and they had got extremely wet, and both enjoyed the experience and coped well with helping each other to dry the area and take off wet clothes. However, being unable to follow the Arabic conversation she overheard, she had not known about the conclusion reached as to the suitability of different materials or the plans to bring appropriate containers. The involvement of a parent in reflecting on the day had brought important new knowledge, which could be taken into account in planning for future experiences.

Abdullahi worked very successfully with a range of children in the class, and one of his favourite times was when engaged in small world play with an older boy, Andros, who enjoyed story-telling, using boxes and bricks to create sets for the characters. Andros was also bilingual and spoke fluently in both Greek and English. Together in this play the children were sometimes silent, but sometimes Abdullahi echoed his friend's English monologue as the characters were brought into action. Often there were no words, but wonderfully expressive sounds to show the rushing, bumping, falling and flying which were part of the story. An understanding that gesture and movement are important aspects of communication encourages this kind of shared meaning-making, and, Emblen suggests, may be particularly important in second-language learning (Emblen, 1990). Sometimes Abdullahi's mother was able to stay and tell the story in Arabic with him. Sometimes the props used by Abdullahi and Andros were brought into the circle for story-telling time. Adults also made time to share the play, and to create stories with individual children and in small groups, also trying whenever possible to revisit in these small groups the stories used in larger whole-class times when some children may easily become 'lost'.

Moving towards literacy

Sound and rhyme play, songs, word games, poems, are all important experiences, and children need opportunities to repeat and practise these time and time again, just as they need to practise the greetings and phrases of routine language. Visual support, and the sharing of meaning across different experiences, helped Anna as she read. She sat with the book she had chosen from the box. It was a short Christmas story with pictures of Father Christmas, trees, stars, presents and elves. The story was quite complicated and the pictures did not reflect the text very closely. Anna, however, went straight to the illustrations which drew her into the story. She was familiar with the book from group story time, and began reading to the visitor she had brought over to the book corner. *'Christmas now, and Christmas coming, and now Christmas. Then Christmas . . . and now Christmas.'* Turning the pages, she read with great expression. Coming to an illustration in which Father Christmas was shown with his hands upturned, wondering how he was going to get the presents ready in time, Anna looked at her audience and, turning her own palms upwards, sighed deeply and looked concerned. She repeated this two or three times before turning the page.

In this story Anna used the illustrations to hunt for things she knew about and wanted to share. The Christmas tree led her to take the visitor by the hand to the tree in the nursery. *'Come, come, we have tree.'* Together they began to look at the stars and the coloured balls on the tree, matching some of the colours to the decorations on the tree in the book. The adult said she loved the way the stars turned round and round, and Anna echoed, *'round and round'*. Then she moved to one of the balls and made it turn: *'round and round, round and round'*. The freedom to move into different spaces as she made sense of the story for herself and her audience helped Anna to work in an independent way.

'Come. Sit down.' Anna took the visitor by the hand and led her back to the book box on the carpet. This time she chose a story about a farm, where two children were looking at donkeys. It was the donkeys which held her attention. The adult had tried to begin reading the story from the beginning, but Anna showed that she was not interested. Turning confidently to the page with the donkeys Anna was immediately involved. This time Anna's language was not narrative, but there was a great deal of naming. *'Look horse, and horse, other horse. Legs, legs, horse, and horse. Look ears.'* Each time Anna followed the line of the legs or the ears with her finger. She allowed the adult to join in. *'This horse has long ears too. Yes, here's the horse, and look here, it has started to run.'* Anna's two fingers began to run across the page at this point, and she laughed. *'Table, table'*, pointing to the tails.

A little later Anna returned to the book area. She held in her hand a small cardboard figure of a horse that she had found. One of the nursery staff noticed this and helped her to find another book about horses: she had not been present earlier and did not know which book Anna had shared with the visitor. Each time Anna had made connections which interested her, there had been adults who noticed and responded. She needed the time and space she was given to think about what she wanted to say. Being supported as a communicator by adults who really listen is likely to lead to children developing confidence in their use of language.

The richer the experiences of sound, the greater the possibilities for developing young children's inventiveness and sharing enjoyment. Opportunities to use language in playful ways often arise out of very common, everyday experiences.

Children singing 'The Grand Old Duke of York' took the song into their play in the nursery garden. The children's play made something more interesting out of the song as the big blocks became steps and the refrain became *'Up, up, up, up, down, down, down, down!'* This was taken up by other children on the climbing frame, and then *'me up'* was heard, followed by *'I'm up too'*, *'I'm the king of the castle!'* and more. In this way children were responding, modelling, extending language for each other in playful ways. That play lasted through the afternoon, with a great deal more language used about position and movement, and several other songs were sung in the garden.

The following day the game began with the same use of the blocks as steps up and down, but the first child to march up and down on them counted *'one, two, three, four'* as he went. And that became the game, up and down the blocks, up the climbing frame, along the paving stones. One of the adults started counting in Bengali *'Ek, dui, teen'*, then added, *'un, deux, trois; bir iki uc'*: playful fun, but offering important linguistic experience. Young children also draw on their knowledge of more than one language as they make puns and funny word rhymes or make up nonsense from the different sounds they play with.

For all children within classes where a range of languages are spoken there are special opportunities to explore the differences and similarities between languages. If we want to help children develop phonological knowledge, listening to a range of languages can help them understand what phonemic structure really is. By looking across to other languages in order to compare, children can begin to understand something more interesting about sounds and their use and representation. When learning how to write her name in Bengali while Sonny's mother was working with a group in the nursery, Caroline asked with great concentration to be shown which character represented which sound in her name. Later that same day she chose a book with Bengali text, and looking closely at the print searched for characters which were like those she had used in her writing in the morning. Sonny's mother had both shown her how to form the characters, and had talked with her about the way in which they represented the sounds. When she wrote her own name, she had also talked with Caroline about the sounds which were different from those familiar to Caroline from her knowledge of English. This learning had taken place in a context created by adult and child out of a shared interest. A later experience for Caroline involved her writing the English caption for paintings of a favourite story while Sonny's mother worked on the caption in Bengali, both displayed together at the top of the board. Caroline also chose to listen to the Bengali story tapes, and enjoyed joining in the repeated refrains. All the children shared these tapes with adults, helping them to enjoy listening to, and joining in, different languages.

Caroline was an inventive language user, a confident early writer working in a nursery setting in which many children spoke different languages, but where all children had opportunities to be playful and creative. Parents gave generously of their time to work with the staff in many different ways. Shared stories and rhymes were told and read. Children made up their own texts for work they had done. Sometimes this text was an oral description to share, and at other times it was written down for children. In the same nursery, Jamie, fluent in Twi and becoming fluent in English, loved to play with language, and used every opportunity to try to use new words he had heard. When he was asked to tell an adult about the picture in which paint whirled around a figure, he described the woman as having *'dis, disa, disappointed, disappeared down the hole!'* Louis made his children *'trip trap, trip trap all the way'* to school. Edith's shell was *'like ear, like round and round'* and her moon *'curling'*. These three bilingual children used English to describe, retell and create meanings. They also needed spaces in which to share their home languages with other children in story, play and investigation.

The staff also had the support of bilingual parents and carers, older children and students who all contributed to the language curriculum. The involvement of staff was key to the success of this wider team. Adults who are interested enough to find out about the languages of the community within which they work, and involved enough to learn something of how those languages are both spoken and written, are better able to create an inclusive language curriculum.

Resources which support meaning-making

Literary language, which includes simile and metaphor, often develops successfully where children have opportunities to express meaning using different representational forms. Good communicators draw on everything they can to share meanings and adults need to plan for ways in which they can make meanings more accessible to all the children in a group. Visual support is very important, and puppets, storyboard figures and other props support young children's involvement in story. Music also adds to enjoyment and creativity in the telling. Edith 'danced' the sun, and later a dragon.

Children also need props for other experiences, so that they have support while they describe what they saw, what they did, and how they did it. Ways of creating displays which help children to revisit, think and talk about things which interest them can be developed using a wide range of representational forms. Early childhood settings can offer many examples of different ways of exploring and representing meaning. Children can draw on these as they remember and revisit learning, and bilingual children may be particularly supported by these opportunities. A chart made by the children about the insects found in the garden might be placed next to reference books and drawings. Musical instruments which children are free to play might be placed near photographs of a visiting group of drummers, accompanied by text recording some of the children's thoughts about the performance. Paintings inspired by a favourite story can be drawn on when the story is shared.

A collection of shells with the drawings and clay models they inspired, some string spirals and sewn 'shell' shapes all supported the talk which led to Edith's description of the shell as *'like ear, like round and round'*. Cooking utensils which were used to make gingerbread were displayed with a copy of the story and a recipe card. Talk centred on this display and in the role-play area children were cooking their gingerbread using similar utensils. Edith, whom staff supported as she moved with increasing confidence in role-play, cooked real gingerbread and then replayed this the next day. As she played she listed her ingredients, and then offered the pretend food to everyone as she walked around the nursery chanting, *'Run, run as fast as you can. I the gingerbread man'*.

Children need opportunities to choose different ways in which to remember, act out or retell. Where young bilingual children revisit ideas through these different resources they may choose to use English or to share a different first language. Adults can help them to remember by using resources alongside children and can offer models of associated language.

The ways in which a room is laid out can be instrumental in supporting children's development in language. Quiet corners and protected spaces enable children to work in privacy and offer places where it may be easier to listen and hear what is said, or to use language undisturbed by adults' or other children's questions.

Nicole and Baffour were creating roles for themselves in the role-play area. Both bilingual, their shared language was English in which Baffour was able to communicate with great fluency, while Nicole was just beginning to use some words and phrases to join in stories and conversations shared with adults. They were moving between the cooker and the table, where they had carried cups and plates, and some empty biscuit and tea cartons. Nicole was laughing loudly as Baffour sat down and began to drink from one of the cups. He said something to her, and she returned to the cooker and came back with a pot from which to spoon out some food. As an adult approached, Nicole looked up and laughed again. The adult had come over because she heard Nicole's enjoyment. Nicole had found it difficult to settle into the unit, and usually worked very quietly with other children, playing alongside them but not joining in their chatter or laughter, although she brought things to adults to show and share. Baffour and Nicole did not usually work together, but here they were clearly partners in the play. 'That looks delicious,' said the adult with great feeling. 'May I come in?' 'Come in,' said Baffour and drew up another chair. 'It's my birthday.' Nicole laughed, caught the word birthday and danced. 'This party, birthday cake party', and collected another cup and gave it to the adult.

For Nicole a significant step had been made in terms of her developing confidence in the nursery. Her involvement in both the actions of the play and the language accompanying it was linked in important ways. This kind of shared experience was something which the staff knew they wanted to develop for Nicole, and they planned to support her play in the role-play area because it seemed to offer her a space in which she felt able to share with another child in this way.

Mai also made clear choices about her use of language. The school situation did not provide a bilingual curriculum for her. Mai spoke Chinese happily to an older child and her sister in the same school at playtime, even when other children or adults were nearby, but she chose not to use Chinese in the classroom, although there was another child with whom she might have communicated in this shared language. When children were invited to offer songs, to count, to say hello in other languages at various times in the term, Mai listened. She was working with staff who respected her choices, and continued to build on opportunities to reflect the languages and dialects of all the children. One day Mai offered some Chinese writing. She chose to join a group of children who were using some Bengali primers, copying some of the characters and sharing what they knew. Some of the young writers were familiar with only English, some with Arabic and English, others with Bengali, Arabic and English. Mai drew some characters in Chinese and offered to show her friends how to do this, laughing at their efforts and helping them to try again. When an adult approached, and asked whether Mai could show him how to write the characters too, she did so. Adults' interest in learning to write an unfamiliar script is as important to children as our interest in learning spoken language. Mai's writing came from her home learning, and reflected the writing her sister was learning to do at her Saturday school.

Wider literacies

For all children, an awareness of different forms of writing and different scripts is an important part of the linguistic knowledge we would want them to acquire. Choices about how to use scripts need to be thought through carefully. Notices and labels in languages spoken, read and written by families in the local community need to be meaningful, with real purposes. Children need to have books in different monolingual texts as well as bilingual texts. Books may specifically reflect the literacy of home, and include stories, poetry and primers as well as newspapers and magazines with which children are familiar. Settings which acknowledge and reflect the wider literacies of all children provide greater support for children as they develop their knowledge and skills.

Hassan's written Turkish was first used in the classroom when children were making their own newspapers to share their news with older children in the school. Hassan created a simple script in which he repeated a few keywords he could attempt at six years old: the words for mother, father, house and his siblings' names. Set out like a real newspaper, this was accompanied by drawings of the events he wanted to talk about. Hassan had not been asked to write in Turkish, but, together with a friend who also spoke Turkish, he asked the teacher if he might do this. Writing in a variety of languages was a regular feature of the classroom, and children could therefore feel confident that their choices would be accepted.

For Bola and Sarah, shared writing came from the cartoons they watched together when videos were played during rainy lunchtimes. For Bola, the provision of comics, books and posters about these favourite cartoon stories was also important, as it offered her a way into shared conversations as she pointed out and named characters, and copied some of the actions with which she was familiar. In this way Bola was able to enjoy a shared world with other children. Experiences of writing in which she was closely supported by adults also helped her to extend her knowledge of English as she and Sarah made their own small books. Videos of stories or other children's programmes in home languages would have given further opportunities for children to share experiences through this medium.

Visits outside the classroom setting also quite often lead to significant changes in confidence and involvement for some children. The excitement of a visit to the park allowed Rosa to communicate with other children and adults in both Portuguese and English. She started by imitating the noise made by the ducks as she raced up and down the path by the pond. This became excited chatter about the ducks, a dog and what other children were doing. In Portuguese she talked both to children who understood Portuguese and to adults and children who did not, but her communication was powerful. Back at the nursery she was able to tell other staff that she had seen the ducks, making the noises and using phrases in both languages in her excitement to share. Photographs of a park were found, and a story about a duck, also toy ducks to accompany a song and, later in the week, a counting game. Perhaps most importantly staff took Rosa back to the park for another visit. This time they took the nursery camera. Talk was an important part of the experience, and adults listened, responded and extended language. One of the staff commented that she had not only been unaware of how much Rosa could communicate to others in English, but also been surprised that she could understand so much of her Portuguese, even though she herself had no knowledge of the language. Shared contexts suddenly made sense to her in a different way, and this knowledge helped her to observe more closely, and to develop new strategies for supporting Rosa's language development. Greater attention to what she was able to say in English as well as to what she wanted to communicate, but struggled with, led to more effective support from the staff. Planning for the park visit had been minimal. Visits were frequent and this was not seen as a major or exceptional outing; the park was local, and familiar to the children.

Reflections with Rosa after the second visit led to discussions about ways in which the photographs could now be used before each visit to ensure that all the children knew where they were setting off for, and to support work on some key language about going out together and the park itself. Photographs of the local area and of places familiar to children from both their home and school lives can be drawn on to support bilingual children in many ways: to help them understand where they are going to go during a trip out; to talk about where other adults or groups of children have gone; to revisit experiences shared in the group; to focus on when talking about experiences with family and so on.

Video-recording an outing also enabled Stephen to share what he had done when he returned to the nursery. Stephen spoke Spanish, and had only just begun to use English words. Watching the video, he could name some of the things he had seen and all the children in the group. He could turn to others watching, and, even without talking, share the memories with them. He could understand much better what other children were talking about because it was based on shared visual support. Again, the staff involved used what they had learned from this observation about the effectiveness of the video-recorder. It became a more valued tool to extend opportunities for bilingual children on further visits and on ordinary nursery days.

The stories drawn on in this chapter are brief extracts from sessions in early childhood settings. Surrounding these episodes are many experiences in which sensitive adults worked in ways which supported the development of shared meanings. Staff were observant about children's linguistic development, and creative in their use of strategies to support children as they developed both their understanding and use of a new language. They expected to understand what children wanted to say, and to make their own meaning as clear as possible.

Early childhood has a long and rich tradition of observation-based practice. We need to ensure that our understanding of good practice genuinely reflects the needs of all the young bilingual children in our settings.

> Children need well-educated educators with knowledge at their fingertips, adults working with them who: see what is happening, understand what they see and act on what they understand. Just seeing, just understanding, is not enough. The next essential stage is to take children further along their own learning pathways. This is a marker of quality in any early education provision. (Nutbrown, 1996, p. 45)

Adults who do not share the first language of the children whom they care for and teach need to be active and committed in their search for other ways in which to make it possible for all children to become full members of the early childhood setting. This means looking at the small details of everyday practice within the wider discussion of a curriculum which recognizes linguistic diversity.

Rhythmic Language, Creativity and Fluency

4

Manjula Datta

Young children learn a language interactively by listening, looking and actively participating in a variety of cooperative, sociocultural contexts, through countless songs, rhymes, poems and stories and meaningful interactions with peers or adults. Through these linguistic and cultural tools young children encounter the rhythm of a particular language; they enjoy repeating, reciting and rehearsing these in their playful activities, in their monologues. In these playful moments children demonstrate their skills of being 'creative' with their language use or expressions. All educators are familiar with children's love for nonsense words or rhymes in any language.

The aim of this chapter is to look at ways of developing bilingual children's creativity and fluency in English in early childhood settings, as this would affect their proficiency in reading and writing in English later. Central to language learning is Chomsky's (1957) argument that every new-born child is equipped with some type of *innate* predisposition towards language learning, however this 'latent potentiality' needs to be activated and supported in social contexts and peer-learning. In most cultures the learning of the mother tongue or the first language occurs in a variety of social encounters – language is culturally transmitted.

At the centre of any language study is *phonetics* or human speech sounds. Every language has distinct 'sound patterns' or *phonology*. The native speakers of any language acquire the sound patterns by operating within the sounds of that language, in many ways, modes and forms. *Syntax* denotes the possible arrangement of words defined by the rules of a particular language. It shows the acceptable grammatical relationships between words, or *semantics*. 'Language can therefore be regarded as an intricate network of interlinked elements in which every item [word] is held in its place' (Aitchison, 1992, my insertion), and derives its meaning by its interrelationship in the sentence. Another aspect of language, which is an essential knowledge for curricular literacy learning, is known as *pragmatics*. It deals with how language is used in different contexts and for different purposes, but how to use language cannot be 'predicted from linguistic [grammatical] knowledge alone' (ibid., 1992), therefore thoughtful consideration is necessary for language planning for young children, especially in multilingual classrooms.

The stated aim of this chapter could be encapsulated in Clark's (1976, p. 29) observation of young fluent readers: 'auditory memory for sounds in sequence, and tasks involving completion in a language context are the areas in which the group as a whole appears to be particularly successful'. The notion of 'auditory memory for sounds in sequence' would suggest fluent semantic and syntactic knowledge of English. Clark considers this crucial to develop fluency in reading (and writing). Her subsequent observation of 'tasks involving completion in a language context' would suggest that the young readers are able to use their fluent semantic and syntactic knowledge to predict text, and develop the ability to read (and write) fluently. To be able to predict or anticipate text at word, sentence and text level ahead of decoding is a high level reading skill and is crucial for developing fluency in reading. This is further discussed in Chapter 5.

For emerging bilinguals the ability to predict in English fluently would require internalization of 'sounds in sequence', semantic as well as syntactic. To this effect we will look specifically at ways of developing auditory memory of 'sounds in sequence'. Writing about verbal or auditory memory Neisser (in Barrs and Thomas, 1986) observed that some kind of 'rhythmic grouping' of words facilitates verbal recall from memory. In this chapter we will look at how this tool could be used for developing fluency in English in multilingual classrooms.

However, developing fluency in speech, and consequently reading and writing, should be an *additional* experience for bilingual children in that the songs, rhymes, stories and poems they have encountered in their first language should form a part of their school learning as well. This ensures transferability of cognitive and literacy skills between learning and language development. A collaborative partnership with minority-language parents, teachers or other adults in school with monolingual English-only teachers facilitates this well (Datta and Pomphrey, 2004). Many teachers and student-teachers use these resources effectively as discussed below.

A class of three- to four-year-old nursery children was seen singing and enacting robustly a song in Yoruba taught by a student-teacher. I also observed a class of five- to six-year-old children listening intently to a story in Bengali. The rhythm of the story and the use of magnetic story props and the student's story-telling skills using tone, intonation, and rising and falling voices created a profound effect on the listeners. The non-Bengali pupils made some intelligent linguistic inferences and exchanges around story words, for example, *gaajor* or carrot, *paani* or water, *gadha* or donkey. An 'English only' child commented that he enjoyed the repetitive rhythmic expression of *choltey-choltey, choltey-choltey.* He learned the Bengali expression in one story session – rhythm supports retentive memory. When he was told it meant 'walking-walking, walking-walking' he seemed very pleased at learning another way of saying 'he walked and he walked'. Stylistically these repetitive expressions or sound patterns are used to emphasize any significant action or meaning in Bengali and other Indian languages. Jenny remarked, 'I like stories in voices', perhaps implying she enjoyed the 'sound-patterning' in Bengali. Such activities in multilingual classrooms create metalinguistic and multidimensional thinking for every child.

In the next section we will look at how caring adults in all cultures use rhythmic utterances with babies and toddlers to engage their minds.

Children's monologues and fluency

New-born infants in all cultures hear language as a medley of sounds. Gradually they become aware of different tunes and tones of a particular language and the growing infant recognizes language as 'patterned sounds'. Caring adults support the process by using ritualized speech and a range of physical gestures – facial expressions, eye contact, laughter, playful movements – and constant repetition in many contexts, in many voices. Gradually the infant shows signs of awareness of language as a 'shared activity' by responding with energetic body movements and an array of happy noises and chuckles. Bruner (1975) believes this early 'mutuality' of an interpersonal intention and responsiveness between the adult and child is an essential starting point of language learning. This is strengthened by a range of cooperative games, hiding and seeking, sharing cultural artifacts including books, and the child begins to associate language with 'shared doings' or play. We can say language learning begins as '*social speech*', listening and interacting emotionally, socially and physically.

With active participation in a range of repetitive and stimulating contexts a child's 'social speech' develops into '*speech for oneself*' or monologues (Vygotsky, 1962/1986). The child begins to use speech or 'sounds in the head' to assist and organize solitary exploratory activities or play, and thus actively engages in planning speech in different activity contexts. The child's monologues reflect and resonate with patterned grammatical utterances acquired in repeated social encounters and other forms of ritualized linguistic rhythm and shape. It is not an organized speech comprehensible to or meant for others. For example, when the child makes a 'running commentary' on an ongoing activity, some of the action may itself form the connecting link in the child's monologues or represent words for the child (Britton, 1972). Such 'enactive' speech is crucial for the child to make sense of play, internalize speech and develop the ability to think in words or use language to think. 'Enactive representation is based . . . upon a learning of responses and forms of habituation' (Bruner, 1966, p. 11), this is very relevant to bilinguals' learning of the second language. It enables beginner bilinguals to engage in monologues in their second language and, for most, this is likely to begin when they start school.

All bilinguals seem to engage in linguistic pattern-making in these enactive monologues using both their languages. For example, four-year-old Hakan practised the pattern of counting in twos – his latest discovery – alternating between English and Turkish while running up and down the stairs. He displayed the characteristic bilingual repetition by switching languages in his play. 'Bilinguals like to repeat in both languages' (Gumperz, 1982) any learning of outstanding significance. We encountered Nitya in Chapter 2 engaged in an imaginative monologue while travelling in the car. She seemed to be matching the names of animals in Hindi and English, which she had recently acquired: '*Tota maney [means] parrot, bandar maney monkey,* ...', thus creating a 'personal lexicon' for her bilingual mind. Listening to the sounds in both her languages and making word pairs was a linguistic pattern practice monologue for Nitya. Linguistically, bilinguals' monologues give us insights into their language-learning processes. They are also the most important aspect of their solo play to engage in '*sustained and fluent*' speech.

Such is the *tour de force* of this linguistic pattern playing, it is observed that when young minority-language children first start school their popular play at home is often 'patterned tone and intonation' of their new language, especially that of the teacher's voice in different classroom rituals. The absence of conventional words in English is filled in with nonsense words and play with sounds continues unhampered.

Developmentally, monologues are gradually directed inwards and internalized into *inner speech* (Vygotsky, 1962/1986). At this stage the child's use of language does not wholly depend on the 'immediate present'. The child is able to verbally recall experience or events from memory. This is considered the beginning of the child's new faculty to 'think words' (ibid.), or to engage in 'verbal thoughts'. This is a significant development for young language learners in that they learn that meaning can be derived entirely from word or meaning structures and this is crucial to their academic achievement. For bilingual learners trying to achieve academic excellence in the second language, it is vital that they are given opportunities to listen to repeated use of grammatical and meaning structures in different contexts to develop deep 'inner speech', to engage strongly in verbal thoughts or to learn how to use words in communicating meaning or thought.

Recalling past events or experience requires *selecting and ordering* of significant experience to represent meaning. Thus language reduces flux to order. All first-language learners acquire these skills well in repeated social encounters with significant others and siblings and are able to play with these sounds in their playful monologues or storying as discussed above. In the bilingual context the lack of repeated sounds and playful explorations in their second language results in 'gaps' in their schema of 'inner speech', and I believe this affects their sustained meaning structures, which manifests in bilinguals' insecurity and anxiety with the second language. It is very important that they build up a fluent repertoire of 'auditory memory in sounds'. The ways of building up a fluent repertoire are considered below.

Bruner (1968) argued that any learning could be represented in three models. The first is *enactive* or learning through action. We will look at how enacting or 'doing language and literacy' (Datta and Pomphrey, 2004) help young bilinguals to learn and develop fluency in a new language and subsequently draw on these resources to engage in personal learning. The second is *iconic* or visual organization or representation of knowledge; emerging bilinguals use this tool flexibly to represent personal experiences and ideas, especially before developing fluency in the new language. We will see how five-year-old Zubair uses this tool as a narrative maker in his 'ghost story'. The third is *symbolic* or representation in words or language. We will look at how role-play and the use of rhythm in language encourage bilingual children to make creative responses in English in early childhood settings.

Rhythmic grouping of sounds

In all cultures children respond energetically to 'rhythmic grouping' of sounds and meaning in rhyme and poetry, and children are known to show a particular facility for repeating and playing with these oral and aural sounds. What this signifies to a young child is echoed in the words of Dylan Thomas (in Roberts, 1986):

> The first poems I knew were nursery rhymes, and before I could read them for myself I had come to love just the words of them, the words alone . . . and these words to me [were] the notes of bells, the sounds of musical instruments, noises of wind, sea and rain . . . I cared for the shapes of sounds . . . and the words describing action remained in my ears.

For bilingual children memorization and recitation of poems, rhymes, songs and stories provide an essential foundation for learning the conventional meaning structures in the second language. Repeated and creative play with these sounds encourages fluid memory recall, and this is a significant aspect of literacy and developing fluency. In most cultures this forms a part of school or family life, and it is not considered to be mindless rote learning.

My personal experience of teaching and learning, as well as evidence from children's work throughout this book, suggest that creative memorization of significant linguistic experiences is for bilinguals an empowering tool and an active force to scaffold and generate new meaning structures. *Creative memorization* scaffolds 'solo discourse' (Moffet, quoted in Britton, 1972) that all readers or writers engage in. Encouraging bilinguals to engage in repetitive retelling of stories enables them to rehearse and become creative with narrative discourse. In many cultures poetry recitation forms a part of the curriculum: 'I know what I remember' seems to be the underlying theory. Creative memorization of texts for bilinguals works at two levels: *first*, they learn to read in 'chunks' using tone and intonation; *second*, they become familiar with narrative rhetoric. This obviously requires teacher knowledge of a good collection of texts with language in a flow, with 'speech vocabulary' (Britton, 1972), reinforced by collaborative reading activities.

> Sound structures of a text are essential ingredients for memorizing patterns of words and help prediction as well . . . good readers do not commit to memory individual words but the phrase structures of a story. The individual words flow from the structures. (Bussis et al., 1985)

On a wider map of learning English as a first, second or third language around the world in different cultural contexts, singing popular nursery rhymes or playground chants and poems gives new learners the opportunity to play with the phonology of English and its rules. Chanting 'Ring-a-ring-a-roses' holding hands and dancing in circles and enacting a dramatic 'fall down', or running up the hill, real or pretend, singing 'Jack and Jill went up the hill' and then come 'tumbling after', not only act as physical stimuli but also provide active language-learning experience. The children receive language emotionally, aurally, linguistically and physically. Other sources of such fluid use of language are playground rhymes and chants in all cultures. The sounds and tones travel from country to country taking on different cultural colour and connotations, but the enactment and pleasure accrued from such rhythmic pattern practice is universal. In the multilingual context they are chanted in many languages. In Calcutta I watched my eight-year-old niece, Shaonli, fluidly performing playground chants in English, Hindi and Bengali. Words synchronizing with brisk action seemed to roll off her tongue and reminded me that for children language is a 'performance' across all cultures. She performed the following chant in English, with each word accompanied by a different hand gesture, and as the chant picked up pace so did the action sequence. The chant is repeated at ever increasing speed until players can no longer sustain verbal or physical synchronization and the 'winner' concludes with a triumphant YAM!

Ham cheese hamburger
Sauce potato chip chip chip
Sauce potato chip chip chip
Cream roll – mutton roll – chicken roll – egg roll – YAM

The action song in Hindi narrated the full life cycle from birth to death!

Physical pleasure in making sounds, oral as well as aural, is bound up with language learning and language use. All cultures have an array of action songs, rhymes or clapping games that have an enchanting as well as a soothing effect on children. However, educators must enable bilinguals to practise and enjoy sound patterns and meanings in their first language to make learning a very personal experience. Many children have been known to become 'moody and withdrawn' in 'English only' classrooms, and many fail to realize their full potential in English (Bullock et al., 1975, Chapter 20). We must encourage bilinguals to talk, recite and sing in their first language as a multilingual classroom ritual. Songs, rhymes and poems in English should be an added experience rather than a 'subtracting' experience (see Chapter 2). Nadia's fluency in Bengali enabled her to visualize potential fluency in English. In some excellent early years practice teachers and other adults include songs and rhymes in many voices in classroom rituals and children are eager to recite them for sheer oral and aural fun.

Some schools have adopted a policy of keeping bilingual children's languages active in their learning process. For example, Yasmin Ali, of

Whetley Primary School, says that the school has developed a policy of using nursery rhymes and stories from children's languages and cultures (Cunningham, 2000). Sometimes children are exposed to important mathematical concepts. Here is one in Urdu, with English transliteration:

> *Naana jee ki topi goal*
> *Naana jee ki topi goal*
> *Naanee jee ki choor-ee goal*
> *Suraj goal, chanda goal*
> *Mummy kehtee thalee goal*
> *Teacher kehtee aloo goal*
> *[Grandad's hat is round*
> *Grandad's hat is round*
> *Grandma's bangle is round*
> *The sun is round, the moon is round*
> *Mummy says the plate is round*
> *Teacher says the potato is round]*

'We can now sing "Heads, Knees and Toes" in Urdu ... and English ... When we sing "The Wheels on the Bus" one verse will be in English, the next in Punjabi and the children don't bat an eyelid.' (ibid., 2000)

I have seen Bengali children singing and enjoying a very popular numerical rhyme in an East London school, 'Dosh-ti Chhana' (Ten lambs), keeping the rhythmic beat with swaying their heads and tapping their laps. The gist is how the lambs get eaten up one by one by predators. The setting of the poem must be a village where these occurrences are common. The rhyme resonates with the numerical concept in the song 'Ten Green Bottles' in English.

Another example is that of the teacher singing a traditional rhyme in Jamaican English and how this affected one particular Jamaican child emotionally. Marcia did not have a long concentration span, but when suddenly surrounded by some familiar sounds her eyes lit up and awakened her desire to belong to the learning classroom.

> **Brown girl in the ring**
> *There's a brown girl in the ring,*
> *tra la la la la,*
> *There's a brown girl in the ring,*
> *tra la la la la,*
> *There's a brown girl in the ring,*
> *tra la la la la,*
> *For she like sugar and I like plum.*
>
> *Then you skip across the ocean,*
> *tra la la la la,*
> *Then you skip across the ocean,*
> *tra la la la la,*
> *Then you skip across the ocean,*

tra la la la la,
For she like sugar and I like plum.

In playgrounds children's fluidity with play and imagination around the rhyme inspires them to create new action and words inside a ring.

Phonological awareness of a language is the crucial *first step* to learning to read (Goswami and Bryant, 1990), as well as learning the language. Bilingual children's knowledge of these rhymes spans two languages, thus enabling them to develop a metalinguistic awareness of common linguistic features of rhyme and rhythm operating between two languages. Evidence shows that when rhymes from other languages and cultures form a part of learning in the classroom, 'English only' children develop cognitive and metalinguistic understanding of how rhymes work across cultures. In 'inclusive' classrooms children have fun singing in another language with rhythm and beat. It is interesting to analyse the cultural themes and journeys of some of these rhymes. Here is one in Turkish that is popular with children:

Kücük kurbag-a

Kücük kurbag-a
Ellerin nerede?
Ellerim yok
Ellerim yok
Yüzerim derede

Kücük kurbag-a
Kücük kurbag-a
Kuyruğun nerede?
Kuyruğum yok
Kuyruğum yok
Yezerim derede

[Little frog / little frog / where are your hands? / I don't have hands / I don't have hands / I swim in the pond

Little frog / little frog / Where is your tail? / I don't have a tail / I don't have a tail / I swim in the pond]

In London schools and nursery settings I have also seen children making meaning by dancing fluently to popular Iranian, Turkish, Indian, Ghanaian, English and other music or songs as part of their 'sharing time'. Teachers as well as children look visibly pleased with these social and enactive learning sessions. I have been told that the children never forget to bring tapes or other artifacts to these 'show, tell and do' sessions. Such sharing of experience energizes every child to develop a voice in culturally diverse classrooms, and motivation to learn is high.

Rhythm, creativity and fluency

The evidence from my research shows how the rhythm in the human voice triggers the imaginative force in children's thinking. Four-year-old Chanel was sitting beside an adult in the nursery in the graphics corner. They were watching a sudden downpour of rain through the window. The adult initiated a game of word play with rhythm and tone.

> *Adult*: Oh look it's raining, it's splashing everywhere
> *Chanel*: It's splattering everywhere
> *Adult*: It's thundering
> *Chanel*: It's splundering.
> All this time Chanel was feverishly colouring her paper with 'rain' using blue, purple and black. Then she started cutting slits all around the paper.
> *Adult*: What's that?
> *Chanel*: It's raining, it's raining everywhere

The use of rhythm and images in the adult description of rain seems to have triggered rhythmic thinking in Chanel's responses. She joins in the linguistic pattern-making energetically and uses an imaginative or nonsense rhyming word, 'splundering', to carry on with the game. It also helped her to move fluidly from a two-dimension to creating a three-dimensional effect; this gives us an insight into children's minds – play pushes cognitive boundaries.

In early years settings there are many contexts where children use patterned language in their cognitive development in recurrent indoor and outdoor activities. In story reading some pattern practice occurs in children joining in with repetitive refrains in stories or while playing some creative literacy games. However, for bilinguals to develop strongly in narrative speech we need to look at specific literacy strategies directed at developing fluency, at more ways of creating memorable sound patterns in many shapes and in many tones in school learning. Repetitive playing with these sounds will help internalize or 'store speech' as well as generating more. This section offers some 'tried and tested' ways of extending bilinguals' development of narrative language in early years and beyond, which are based on the principles discussed above, and in Chapter 2.

The strategies encourage memorization of words in sequence and involve acting or dancing to develop fluency in speech and meaning in the second language. Adults and children collaboratively create the verses around everyday experience in the nursery setting or universal themes that any child can relate to. The adult takes the leading role in this process (see discussion of Vygotsky in Chapter 2), either initiating ideas or building on children's ideas. These rhythmic patterns of words, with lots of repetition in lots of enjoyable contexts, engage bilinguals in a fun way to support fluency in English.

Learning is a cumulative process. The narrative tunes in bilinguals' heads create the awareness to listen to and accommodate new tunes and extend learning. This encourages generating more narrative language. All children have an 'innate propensity' (Chomsky, 1972) to create language. For example:

- Activities on rhymes may include extending or writing *alternative nursery rhymes* drawing on children's experiences. Bilinguals feel secure to take risks within the given structure.

Rain rain go away
Come again another day

Not on Monday because I go swimming
Not on Tuesday because I play out
Not on Wednesday because I go to my nan's
Not on Thursday because . . .

The rhyme continues to include the seven days of the week. Sometimes children produce nonsense reasons out of sheer fun!

- In the early years setting we have many contexts where children engage in repetitive activities, for example, playing with dough. We can use ritualized enactive language to help bilinguals build a repertoire of 'narrative sounds in the head'. They can use these in their creative monologues or generate more at home or school.

Squeeze squeeze squeeze the dough
Squash squash squash the dough

Pat pat pat the dough

Pinch pinch pinch the dough
Roll roll roll the dough
Roll it harder harder harder
Look I have made a . . .

Children can add the name of whatever shape they visualize. Similarly, play with water and sand as well as outdoor play activities offer opportunities to experiment with repetitive meaning structures.

- Dramatic situations with tone and body language set the mood of the world that children are about to enter with words. These images help bilingual children to remain focused on context and generate meanings from past experiences. Sounds of words and patterns of language resonate with images they have in their heads. In the example below the teacher's choice of a dramatic first line produces equally dramatic responses from five year olds. It is important that the starting lines should contain the potential and possibilities of a range of responses from a culturally diverse class of children:

Adult

Telephone telephone
Ring ring ring [spoken with urgent tone]

Children's responses

Dial 999
Fire fire fire
Burning burning burning
Everything everything everything
Call the fire engine
Call the fire engine
Quick quick quick
Water water water
Quench the thirst thirst thirst

The flow of repetitive pattern enabled even beginner bilinguals to compose responses fluently. A range of poems was written on the same theme and different beginnings gave different responses, most of which were personal.

- Seasonal themes are explored for a range of cognitive development in early years settings. The poem 'Blow Wind Blow' was enacted in the playground one spring afternoon with four and five year olds. The objective was to use narrative language to describe experience and feelings. Here the student-teacher took the initiative to set the mood of the poem: she engaged in a kind of monologue reflecting on her own sensations and then started the first two lines of the poem. It was quite a ritualistic performance, with the teacher and children holding hands and feeling the wind and making up the poem as they gently ran against the wind. At the beginning the most articulate took the initiative to respond, but within a repetitive pattern and rhythmic grouping everyone eventually joined in and felt confident to offer personal responses.

Adult

Blow wind blow
Blow on my face
Blow on my . . .

Children's responses

Blow on my hair
Blow on my arms making them tingly
Blow on my belly making it tickle

Adult

Blow over the tree tops

Children

Blow over the roof tops
Blow over house tops
Blow over chimney tops

Adult

Blow in the sky

Child

Make the birds fly

It is interesting to note how the children responded to the teacher's change of direction in thinking and image-making. She encouraged them to develop wider views of life and experience. The children were thrilled with the experience and made several poems on wind, rain and storms following the same format. Similarly, on a hot summer afternoon the following poem took shape with the teacher's 'wonderings' in the outdoor play area in the nursery setting with a very linguistically mixed group of children.

Teacher

Oh I am so hot!
What shall I do?
Shall I sit under that tree?
Shall I . . .

Children

Shall I go swimming?
Shall I go to the park?
Shall I have an ice cream?

Teacher

Shall I fly with the clouds?

Child

Shall I fly with the birds?
Shall I fly with the leaves?
Shall I fly with the flies? [the child giggled loudly]

In this poem the adult included imaginative or 'I pretend' experiences. The children were equally adept at responding to it and wanted more.

- Autumn occupies young children with a range of activities and observations. Sometimes these could be shaped as poems for children to enact and memorize. In the poem below a student-teacher led a dance-like movement pretending to be a 'falling leaf', and started the pattern of rhyming words. The children responded with ideas of a 'falling leaf', dancing behind him, and internalizing language and meaning. This strategy of learning relates to a well-known method in second-language learning known as the Total Physical Response (Krashen, in Duley et al., 1982, p. 25), where the main focus is on enactment of language.

I am an autumn leaf
   Falling from a tree
    Twisting
      Twirling
        Circling
          Dancing
            Floating
          Dropping
        Dropping

> *Dropping*
> *On the ground.*

We discern a few underlying factors that develop bilingual children's ability to engage energetically with creative responses: *first*, in all the above examples we saw how children's responses were mediated by rhythmic grouping of words (sound patterns), role-play and teachers' use of language and images; *second*, the use of rhythm in language seems to trigger rhythmic thinking and awaken associated images in children's minds; *third*, the familiarity of the themes in children's lives and thoughts enabled them to actively participate in their creativity; *fourth*, the collaborative nature of learning, looking, listening and learning from each other energized multi-ability children to take risks; *fifth*, the ability of knowledgeable adults with shared awareness of bilingual children's linguistic resources and their ability to learn English through rhythm, rhyme, songs and role-play helped in creating a range of proximal development zones to develop fluent use of English narrative language and literacy (Vygotsky, 1962, 1978, 1986). (See discussion in Chapter 2.)

Books, rhythm and creativity

Books written by children's authors offer memorable 'sounds in sequence' for bilinguals to tune into and engage in deep-level meaning-making. We will see how Nadia's growing knowledge and memory for narrative conventions was supported through repeated rereading and retelling of stories (see Chapter 5). Listening to and reading books with ritualized use of language, affects younger bilinguals' development of fluency in grammatical structures and creativity, as well as providing a great source of fun.

Rod Campbell's book *Dear Zoo* is like a treasure chest for young bilinguals. The story line provides rhythmic grouping of words that are easy to hold in memory in sequence, and the interactive flaps offer specific vocabulary and a context for a range of talk; for example, geography, language and rhyme. The poetic style of the text generates further images that children can play with. Talking about the camel, for example, a group of under-fives made up a chant-like poem with their teacher, keeping close to the language used in the book:

> *He was too grumpy*
> *He was too lumpy*
> *He was too humpy*
> *He was too bumpy*
> *He was a grump-along, lump-along, hump-along, bump-along camel!*

Bilinguals also seem to have a lot of fun in other uses of patterns, for example, Michael Rosen's poems 'What if . . .', 'After Dark', and others in *Under the Bed*, while Wes Magee's book *Madtails Miniwhale* provides fun with shapes and words.

Responses to text and meaning structures

Children's books with rhythmic groupings of words or stylized use of language are very helpful in allowing bilinguals to listen to and play with narrative sounds of the English language. Children should be given appropriate contexts to make personal responses using these structures wherever appropriate. A group of six-year-old bilinguals chose to read *The Tiger Who Came to Tea* by Judith Kerr. This book offers a variety of narrative patterns, inviting the possibility of involving children in playing language games. Following a '*ring at the door*' the story takes on a rhythmic pattern, '*I wonder who that can be*', and goes on,

> It can't be the milkman
> because he came this morning.
> And it can't be . . .
> Because . . .

Children can create their own possible visitors with 'because . . .' or they can change the language pattern into a series of questions:

> 'Can it be the postman?'
> 'Can it be . . . ?'

Bilinguals should be encouraged to play with idiomatic and proverbial language to develop fluency in English.

Further along in the text the repetitive pattern of language describing the tiger's consumption of anything edible or drinkable in Sophie's house can help bilinguals to use the structure and add their own ideas and substitute synonyms for eating or swallowing. As discussed above, rhythmic grouping of words and further image-forming helps fluent recall and memory of words. Playing with these structures provides stress-free and valuable experience in narrative language, and writing their own responses helps children internalize language.

Talking books and fluency

Bilingual children's fluency can also be mediated through 'talking books'. If sensitively chosen, these books offer moving pictures to create images of text and good understanding. Children can work in pairs, reading, talking and rereading text; specific texts could be set to direct identified contexts for talk. I have seen children having enormous fun in interacting with *New Kids on the Block* poems by Jack Prelutsky (1993). Equally popular is *Harry and the Haunted House* by Mark Schlichting (1994). However, these must be supported by further talk and play to be effective.

CD-ROMs containing animations and spoken text provide an interactive, multimedia presentation of stories and poems, which have become known as 'talking books'. Wood (1999) writes:

> The majority of Talking Books imitate real books by having 'pages' which turn in the direction you would expect pages in a book to turn. There is often a 'cover page' with the title, author and illustrator and, where there is a collection of stories or poems, a content page allows the children to choose which one they would like to read. The mouse is used to activate hotspots on each page, which usually consist of animations or sound. Words, sentences and paragraphs can be read and re-read by the computer if the child chooses to click on the appropriate area of the screen. In this way, the child is in control of their own learning and able to listen over and over again to all or part of a story or poem. In turn, this allows them to become more familiar with the sound, purpose and meaning of words and the way in which sentences work. In the same way in which pictures provide visual cues, graphics also offer further information about the text on each page. In the context of Talking Books however, the graphics may become animated and so provide a richness of information which is not possible in the static pages of a conventional storybook.

As an educational resource, it appears that there is great potential in the use of talking books to encourage and assist in the process of learning to read. The Talking Books Project (1995–6) showed that there had been significant gains in both accuracy and understanding. In addition, it was reported that some children's attitudes towards reading improved and confidence increased. This was particularly evident with the boys who, in general, appeared to show the most significant gains in word accuracy. My observations suggest that these multimedia forms of text could be an active resource for meaning-making for bilinguals in that abstract words are made more accessible through images, both lexically and semantically. We have already discussed the important role of images in bilinguals' development of fluency in literacy. If used appropriately, multimedia texts provide context for peer-talk as well as practice in reading, considered crucial for bilinguals' literacy development. Kress (1997, p. 154) affirms the use of multimodal forms of text and meaning-making if children are to 'successfully enter their own paths to literacy'.

Play with words

Chukovsky (1963, p. 98) believed that the child plays not only with toys but also with '*ideas*'; the latter constitute most of the popular language games that children play. Having fun with words is common to all cultures. I can remember how as children we used 'word reversals' as part of our playground-speak and being fascinated by the upside-down world of Tagore's *Ultadanga*. 'Nonsense and sense are part of the same pattern, as are fact and fiction' (Meek, 1985, p. 48). Play with words and language helps children challenge language to confirm boundary norms. The fun involved provides a secure context to play with linguistic risk. Having fun using nonsense words or *anti-language* (ibid.), making rhymes, telling jokes, are all rich contexts for language development that have the potential to look at language as an object and help reduce language anxiety for bilinguals. Here are some riddles, step poems and similes from Gray's unpublished (1999) work with eight-year-old children:

'What am I?'

Stripes as black as the night
On a sunny yellowy orange background
Claws sharp like broken glass
Teeth pointed like giant thorns
What am I?

What am I?

Bumpy, lumpy, humpy, greeny skin
A long mouth that opens like a car-park barrier
Please come and see my hurting tongue – I bit it by accident
Do you want to play snap?
What am I?

(By Suhel and Ahmed)

Coca Cola

Cola bottle
　　Bottle bank
　　　Bank robber
　　　　Robber's car
　　　　　Carwash
　　　　　　Washroom
　　　　　　　Room service

(By Suhel, Luke and Ahmed)

Hot Colour

As red as
Thundery lava erupting from an angry volcano
The burning sun in the clear blue sky
Fire flickering with dancing flames
A hot chilli waiting to burn your mouth . . .

(By Ahmed, Shukri, Asma and Daniel)

Playing with rhythm, images and words supports bilingual children's literacy learning and helps them develop different meaning and grammatical structures playfully and emotionally. This helps them to take a controlling interest in their English language development in a stress-free and collaborative learning environment.

Visual texts and creativity

Young children begin by using available tools for writing to make marks on paper, slate or whatever else is available. Developmentally, a child's undifferentiated mark-making goes through gradual changes to represent meanings symbolically, when 'meaning and form are indistinguishable wholes' (Kress, 1997, p. 9). 'They make signs which are founded on a motivated relation between meaning and form, signified and signifier' (ibid., p. 73). Children's significant experiences and the people around them occupy a very special place in a variety of forms. In the examples below many facets of this evidence in young bilinguals' writing can be seen: 'the human voice is an elementary part of writing' (Graves, 1983, p. 163).

It was a hot summer afternoon and May Wei was sitting in the graphics corner by the window. Bright sunlight flooded the room.

'What is this?'
'Lots of suns', May Wei replied.

In the sample below, Anwar represents a tragic boat accident in his parents' home district of Sylhet in which 25 people were killed. The tragedy had a profound effect on his family and community in London. To be able to express his feelings iconically allowed him to come to terms with the tragedy; it would seem to be an experience of *catharsis* for the young writer.

In another sample, five-year-old Raki thoughtfully documented her knowledge about writing from various contexts of learning: home, school and the mosque. The vibrant picture with a very carefully drawn bird flying towards the house might have a significant tale to tell. Raki is also playing with the concept of how to form words by using consonants and vowels in Bengali. The sample is very interesting developmentally in that both forms of representation are juxtaposed energetically and intelligently. Both tell us about Raki as a bilingual writer and her breadth of understanding of the written language.

It is very important for bilingual children to talk about their 'iconic representations' (Bruner, 1966, p. 11), as in so doing they learn how to

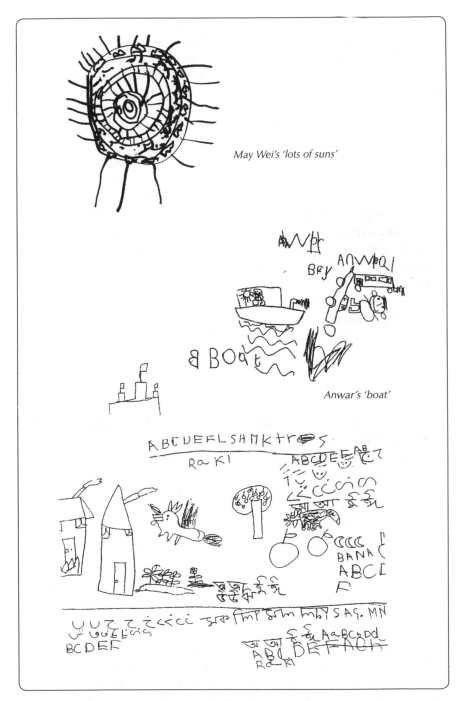

May Wei's 'lots of suns'

Anwar's 'boat'

Raki's complex combination of words and pictures.
(Reproduced by permission of QCA.)

make verbal representation of meanings in their second language. I believe that young bilinguals should be positively encouraged to make meaning iconically, as images have no language barriers. They can convey the whole text of meaning in their head from both their learning worlds rather than producing 'incoherent expressions or ellipses'. Storyboards should be used more comprehensively in multilingual classrooms. Children do not see the world only in words; rather they behold it simultaneously in images and words, in fact images precede words.

Making the transformation from drawing to 'disembodied signs and symbols' or writing is mediated through self-knowledge or topics that are most important to the child. Some bilingual parents believe that their children's writing should be 'accurate' (Gregory, 1996, p. 31) from the early years. However, this must be seen as 'passing the knowledge on' to the next generation in one's mother tongue, and cannot be replicated as a model of learning to write in the second language. This understanding should be shared with parents if they express anxiety over their children's written language. Evidence shows 'children's early experience of the writing process is . . . significantly influenced by the sense they make of the writing instruction and advice they receive from teachers and parents' (Gundlach, 1981, p. 147).

Cultural literacy, creativity and fluency

Five-year-old Zubair, a Bengali-English bilingual child wanted to *write* a story. He especially wanted to write a ghost story, '*aami ekta bhooteir golpo likhba* [I want to write a ghost story]' he said, sitting in the graphics corner in the classroom with his other Bengali peers. Zubair's choice of a ghost story was interesting in that the culture of telling ghost stories is a popular literary activity in most Bengali homes. Grandparents and countless visiting aunts and uncles are often requested to tell ghost stories. Zubair 'drew' his story deftly in six complete pictures, with excellent details indicating his potential as a writer. Children do not think in words only: 'Make-believe play, drawing, and writing can be viewed as different moments in an essentially unified process of development of written language' (Vygotsky, 1978, p. 116).

It is crucial that drawing as a form of representation is promoted strongly in the multilingual classroom to enable children to use their cognitive and cultural resources creatively and help them to develop confidence in communication in English. It is also a very useful strategy for early writers to use. Visualizing the story – characters, settings and episodes or events – helps emerging writers to think about what they are going to write, and how. Drawing children's attention to details helps them to think about details in their written texts.

ভূতের গল্প

In one place there used to be eight ghosts and one rabbit living together

১) এক জায়গায় আটটি ভূত তার একটি rabbit একসঙ্গে বাস করিত।

One day the big ghost wanted to eat up the rabbit.

২) একদিন বড় ভূতটি rabbit টিকে খাইতে চাইল।

The little ghosts picked up the rabbit and ran out to the police car and hid in it. When the big ghost went out the little ghosts went and hid under the big ghost's bed with the rabbit. The big ghost came back and broke his bed.

৩) ছোট ভূতেরা rabbit টিকে নিয়ে পালিয়ে গিয়ে police কারের ভিতরে লুকাইয়া রহিল। বড় ভূতটি বাহির হইয়া গেলে ছোটো ভূতেরা rabbit টিকে নিয়ে বড় ভূতের বিছানার নিচে লুকাইয়া রহিল। বড় ভূতটি ঘরে প্রবেশ করিয়া বিছানা ভাঙ্গিয়া ফেলিল।

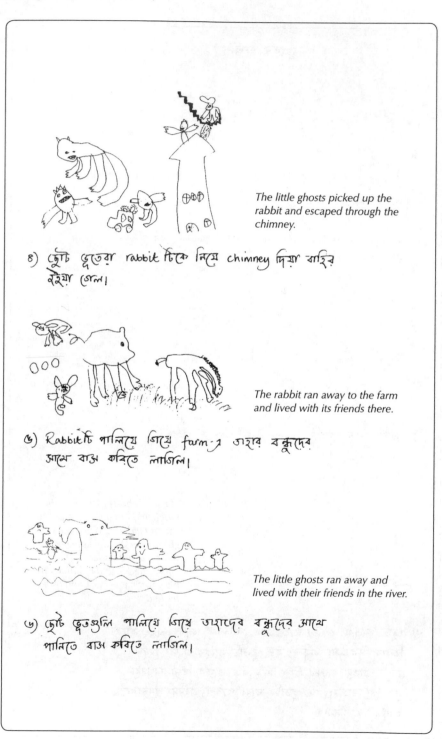

The little ghosts picked up the rabbit and escaped through the chimney.

৪) ছোট ভূতেরা rabbit টিকে নিয়ে chimney দিয়া বাহির হইয়া গেল।

The rabbit ran away to the farm and lived with its friends there.

৫) Rabbitটি পালিয়ে গিয়ে farm-এ তাহার বন্ধুদের সাথে বাস করিতে লাগিল।

The little ghosts ran away and lived with their friends in the river.

৬) ছোট ভূতগুলি পালিয়ে গিয়ে তাহাদের বন্ধুদের সাথে পানিতে বাস করিতে লাগিল।

'When only the rational aspects of learning and development are stressed we deprive ourselves of the full range of the human ability to think' (Duffy, 1998, p. 6). The classroom culture of encouraging children to draw their experience and thoughts enabled Zubair to represent fluently what he knew about stories and thus avoided bilingual language anxiety to set in. Conversely, his teacher could make a true assessment of his cognition of narrative making. A full analysis of Zubair as a narrative maker is presented in Chapter 6.

Conclusion

We may conclude that 'doing' language and literacy (Datta and Pomphrey, 2004) in many modes and many forms in stress-free environments with teachers as collaborative partners supports bilingual children's development of a cognitive, linguistic, emotional and motivated relationship with English. The use of images and rhythm in spoken language or written texts triggers some kind of rhythmic and visual thinking which help develop creativity and fluency in their new language and literacy, in words and images: 'Only increasing fluency and understanding, independence and response are signs of progress' (Meek, 1982, p. 132). Having collaborative fun and freedom to express thoughts, feelings and ideas on familiar themes and personal experiences, with appropriate support and cooperation from knowledgeable adults, act as powerful mediators of literacy learning in early childhood. Moreover, keeping both their languages and cultures together for learning helps make learning a cumulative experience and helps invest in their bilingual identity as learners.

The following activities help extend this development:

- some of these patterned verses can be written down in large print and displayed with children's drawings;
- use of textured paper for writing helps children to feel the letter shapes and the flow of movement that is needed in reading and writing;
- some of the verses can be memorized collaboratively and used as a regular classroom ritual to repeat, recall and generate more;
- some words can be used to raise awareness of letter shapes and combinations to form words;
- making small individual books with word-processed poems with children's own illustrations helps make learning to read and write very personal and affects motivation deeply.

The role of the teacher is one of an expert partner, linguistically aware of the possibilities of learning using rhythmic language in many forms and a deep understanding of teaching and language learning as a joint enterprise.

Bilingual Readers and Personal Learning

Manjula Datta

All the higher functions originate as actual relationships between individuals.

(Vygotsky, 1978, p. 57)

We saw in previous chapters how the underlying factor of sharing knowledge creates adult–child and child–child learning relationships which are crucial for the development of language and literacy of the bilingual child.

In this chapter we will look closely at some significant case studies of bilingual readers learning to read in the second language and examine the complex interplay of linguistic, social, cultural and psychological factors as well as the part played by 'significant others' in this development in both their learning worlds. We conclude by highlighting the need to construct a framework of knowledge-based understanding and pedagogy that encompasses the complexity of reading and making meaning in the second language.

Central to this development is our knowledge and understanding of the intimate relationship between language, culture and cognition discussed in Chapter 2. Monolingual speakers of English use this knowledge, albeit implicitly, with ease in their thinking, reading and writing. Bilingual children need to feel secure with taking meanings from both their language and cultural worlds for literacy learning in English. The case studies in this chapter testify to this. In Chapter 4 we saw five-year-old Zubair blending cultural artifacts from both his worlds to create his very unique 'Ghost Story'. The bilingual mind makes meaning interculturally, in that the learner interacts with both their learning worlds to arrive at a best possible meaning.

> Excluding one or the other world from their schema results in surface level meaning or making feverish attempts to elicit deeper meanings. Intercultural approaches to language and literacy learning in multilingual classrooms allow children to think 'beyond English' at word, sentence and text levels, which enriches every child's literacy learning, as 11-year-old Tom remarked *knowing another language makes you more sensitive to use language.* (Datta and Pomphrey, 2004)

Further, language educators in multilingual classrooms need to develop a shared knowledge and understanding of the individual needs and strengths of readers and 'guide' them into their proximal zones for further development; learners move from personal to proximal zones with guidance from adults or more competent peers (Rogoff, 1990; Vygotsky, 1962, 1978).

The case studies in this chapter exemplify many images of teachers: peer-teachers, student-teachers, class teachers, support teachers, researching teachers – all rooted in sociocultural or collaborative approaches to learning (see Chapter 2). These teachers have one common denominator, in that they understand the significance of incorporating children's wealth of cultural experiences to support development of deeper level skills in reading. We sample how sociocultural approaches allow children to create a personal relationship with curricular reading in an additional language, in what could be construed as a short period of time in each study.

The reading process and the bilingual child

Traditionally, in all societies being literate meant having 'technical mastery' of reading and writing and the teaching of these skills has been prioritized in literacy learning. However, in recent decades research evidence based on close observations of children engaged in reading and writing suggests that they actively engage in meaning-making processes in reading and writing.

A crucial development of children learning to read is cognitive awareness that 'speech sounds' can be written down or encoded in print, that print carries meaning. Bilingual children may have this awareness in two or more languages. In Chapter 4 we see how five-year-old Zubair 'draws' his 'Ghost Story' in Bengali. We also see five-year-old Raki demonstrating her knowledge of writing (and reading) in three languages: Bengali, English and Arabic, playing with the concept of how words are formed in Bengali by adding vowels to consonants. Having an opportunity to transfer such essential knowledge and skills from one language to another is crucial in bilinguals' literacy development.

Children learning to read draw on different kinds of information about language – graphic, semantic, syntactic and bibliographic – to make sense of written text. Graphic information is visual, and children need to develop 'visual analysis skills' or grapho-phonic skills to decode it.

However, reading is not just an act of decoding print word by word, rather an interactive processing of meaning in print. Children learning to read in their native language are competent language users. They bring to reading a wealth of fluent oral language and implicit control of syntactic and semantic knowledge including a cultural understanding of language in context. The grapho-phonic skills are more effectively used for accuracy and fluency when they are supported by 'high-level strategies' (Clay, 1979, p. 2) of prediction using syntactic (grammatical structures) and semantic (content-meaning) cues. Fluent readers integrate these sources of linguistic information or cues to read, intelligently scanning to confirm, reject or correct their hypotheses. Correction may involve going over what was read previously, rechecking cues, especially grapho-phonic cues, to verify meaning, that 'at any point in time . . . the reader has available to him the sum total of his experience and his language and thought development' (Goodman, 1982, p. 40). Goodman emphasizes that the ability to *predict* is central to fluency in reading development. A preoccupation with phonics is not a panacea for bilinguals' underachievement in reading as the case studies show. One of the central issues in bilinguals' reading development in the second language is how to develop their ability to predict. A second important issue is how to help develop their fluency in reading, the ability to 'chunk meanings together'; this would imply fluency in language use.

Bilinguality, talk and reading

Teachers in multilingual classrooms are aware of bilinguals' over-reliance on the phonemic decoding of words when reading. Operating between two languages makes it easier to learn abstract rules but in concentrating too hard on phonemic decoding they fail to interact fluently between the local and global meaning of text. They fail to engage with connected discourse in text, especially literature. Interactive talk is central to bilinguals' development as readers, and I believe it is the only way to ensure bilinguals' deep engagement with literature. A five-year project in five Nordic countries on how bilingual children learn to read concluded that bilinguals learn to read through speaking: 'Learning to read and language learning are primarily based on oral work . . . or *Reading through Speaking*' (Andersson, 1997, p. 23). Reading, speaking, listening and making connections with text and life experiences in both their worlds encourages bilinguals to take risks with thinking, meaning and reading.

Books play a crucial role in bilinguals' additional language development. For example, reciting and enacting *Rosie's Walk* or *We're going on a bear hunt* or *The Leopard's Drum* and many such books written by children's authors with a rhythmic pattern of language and narrative style offer many playful opportunities to bilinguals to learn about grammatical structures in English, for example, use of prepositions, sequencing of meaning, story phrases, etc. All these are crucial knowledge for children's development of literacy in all its forms. Locating onset and rhyme or activities on phonic skills in interesting texts allow bilingual children to develop these skills meaningfully and holistically. Creating opportunities for bilinguals to use popular story structures as personal 'story props' are useful strategies to develop their writing. We see six-year-old Paramjeet using this strategy to write her play 'Rani and the Beanstalk' very successfully in Chapter 6.

The strategy of 'co-creating text' (Meek, 1988) helps bilinguals to connect text meaning to life and life meanings to text, using their linguistic and cultural experiences. It is only by being involved actively and creatively in the construction of meaning that bilinguals learn to situate themselves as readers, and enables them to develop deeper literacy skills. They feel confident to 'ask questions' (Britton, 1972, pp. 81–2) and to take risks with their own ideas and interpretations. The very nature of this talk is purposive. Collaborative talk gives them the opportunity and space to listen to and participate in literacy and literary talk, and to learn to coordinate different perspectives, from both their worlds 'simultaneously' (Bruner, 1986, p. 26; Kenner, 2004). This is also exemplified in children's writings in this book. A comprehensive study of empirical research demonstrated that bilinguals learn English deeply from their reading experience (Krashen, 1993). This would suggest an effective reading policy must be informed by knowledge and understanding of how the bilingual mind works.

Multimodal literacy

The concept of literacy is also challenged by the current multimedia world. These new forms or modes of representation and communication must have a recognized place in the school language and literacy curriculum (Kress, 2003). In their everyday life children come across and use 'visual' texts as natural literacy resources in many ways and many forms; they learn from experience how these texts work to make meaning. Most bilinguals are known to watch avidly their favourite programmes on satellite transmissions from their root countries, in their own language and culture; when given the opportunity they talk fluently about their experiences, often comparing these with their television viewings in English, and having a lot of fun. It would seem 'being bilingual' eases them into such evaluations. Most importantly children enjoy these programmes in the company of their family and friends; rich communication of ideas, comments and analysis form an integral part of this intercultural talk. Moving images on the big screen played a significant part in my personal development, opening up my mind to seeing how language works in different contexts and for different purposes (see Chapter 1). We saw Zubair using these resources creatively as a story maker in Chapter 4. Most classrooms in Britain are fitted with ICT facilities today and young learners are using them as a natural resource for learning development in all curriculum areas.

For bilinguals audio-visual texts have many advantages. They make learning a social activity in that working with a friend or a peer encourages collaborative problem-solving talk, thus developing literacy-based speaking, listening and meaning-making skills; they also encourage bilinguals to integrate thinking and images from both their worlds to produce a 'cohesive' text. The demands of a literal text are dependent on the child's ability to read and understand words and complex meaning structures in English; appropriate use of visual text helps them develop these skills. I have often seen bilingual children in early years settings immersed in audio-visual texts, or 'talking books'. Visual images in talking books help provide support to hold events or episodes 'in memory' and with repeated listening this helps strengthen their access to the written word.

I also believe that production of these books in different community languages would not only validate children's own languages in school but would help strengthen their linguistic and literacy development. However, teachers must recognize that talking books offer a good and interesting practice in reading that helps bilinguals to tune into the mode of narrative language, but they do not replace books, peer-talk or teacher-talk in developing literacy. To conclude, we can say that the concept of literacy has been redefined to reflect technological advances in society, and all children must be enabled to learn and use ICT skills to their advantage for personal and social development at local, national and international level.

Case studies

Nadia and personal learning goals

Nadia was a rising six-year-old Sylheti-speaking Bangladeshi girl who went to an inner-city school in London. The school population consisted of almost 95 per cent Sylheti speakers with roots in Bangladesh. Sylheti is a dialect of Bengali, henceforth it will be referred to as Bengali. The sheer number of speakers in school meant that Bengali was used freely. Nadia had a close network of friends with whom she spoke in fluent Bengali. When I met her she spoke very little English and, according to her teacher, she was approximating Level 2 of Hester's (1990) 'Stages of English' development in that she was 'becoming familiar with English and was able to hold simple conversations in English . . . was more interested in communicating meaning than correctness'. Her teacher also told me that she was 'happiest' when she worked with the Bengali mother-tongue teacher in small groups using mostly Bengali. She was beginning to 'emerge' as a reader but 'still needed a lot of support'. The teacher's comment drew my attention to Nadia and led me to look closely at what kind of 'support' Nadia needed as a bilingual reader.

In this case study of Nadia we look specifically at the crucial role played by 'significant others' and a 'competent peer' (Vygotsky, 1962, 1978), her friend Samia, who shares Nadia's home language and culture. The study clearly shows Samia's perception of Nadia's immediate reading needs, which she provides cooperatively in all the reading sessions. Adults in the classroom and community playing different parts in this development, all rooted in sociocultural approaches to literacy development.

The whole process of Nadia's development into a fluent reader took eight months in all and included two school holidays. Her story of becoming a reader can be broadly divided into three stages. In Stage One we get to know Nadia as a learner and a reader and look at what cognitive and literacy skills she had acquired from both her languages and cultures at this point of development. Stage Two looks closely at strategies to support her development of *fluency* in reading, and Stage Three looks at Nadia as an independent reader. Children's learning development may include recursive curves as well. Each stage of Nadia's development has been subtitled and is supported by a significant quote from Nadia.

Stage One: Getting to know Nadia

Making choices: 'I want to read these …'

Children's learning is best observed in social settings where mutual relations between peers and adults impact learning outcomes (see Chapter 2). I invited Nadia to bring two of her friends to our reading session to encourage collaborative talk. It was interesting to see Nadia's choice of friends, Samia and Tasnim. Samia was obviously a peer model for Nadia. Samia was a very confident, fluent and highly motivated reader, and according to her teacher she was a 'little adult', very helpful towards others. Samia spoke fluent Bengali and English, while Tasnim was a close friend and an emerging reader like Nadia. Tasnim spoke Bengali fluently and could converse in simple English. Nadia and her friends were born in Britain and came from a similar socio-economic background. The parents were immigrants from Bangladesh. The children's fathers were all skilled workers and none of the mothers worked as they had young children to look after. They were all literate in Bengali but their spoken English was limited. Bengali was mostly spoken at home although the children switched between languages with their siblings.

Nadia brought a pile of books to our first reading session. These were:

Brown Bear by B. Martin
The Great Big Enormous Turnip: A Traditional Tale
Wilberforce Goes on a Picnic by Margaret Gordon
Dogger by Shirley Hughes
Rupa Naamey Haathiti (The Elephant named Rupa) by Aditya Sen

On being asked about her choice of books, Nadia said, *'I want to read them, I like them, they're funny.'* Looking through the collection it became clear that Nadia liked humorous and mostly animal stories. They all had a repetitive grammatical pattern and varied from simple prose to poetic use of language. Nadia had heard these stories in class; otherwise the choice seemed quite personal. *Rupa Naamey Haathiti* was an interesting choice. The story was written in Bengali with a handwritten translation of the text by Nadia's mother-tongue (MT) teacher pasted on each page. Nadia told me that she liked the story and that she had heard the story in Bengali and English. Perhaps the book held an added interest as her teacher had translated it for her.

Nadia's love for stories: 'Shall I tell in Bengali?'

Nadia loved stories; the source of this love spanned two worlds: Bengali and English. She had a good knowledge of 'story grammar' – how stories begin, build up to a climax in the middle and how they are resolved in the end – and this came from both home and school. Her experience of listening to an array of rich sounds encompassing both her languages and cultures immersed her in the story world. This proved to be essential knowledge for her reading. Nadia was quite a story-teller herself.

I invited Nadia to tell a story and her response was prompt: *'Shall I tell in Bengali?'* (she knew that her audience shared her language). She chose the story of *Topiwallah* (The Hat-seller), a traditional Indian tale. This seemed to be a popular choice and her peers responded in excited anticipation. She used her eyes, face, voice, along with pitch and gestures, to carry the meaning beyond words. Part telling, part mimicking she made the characters come alive. Her audience was gripped, eagerly nodding their heads and saying *'Yes, yes that's right'*, reassuring me of Nadia's accuracy in sequencing the story. I detected a familiar 'pattern' of children's story-telling in the tale: *'taaley nanhi . . . taaley nanhi'*, 'and then . . . and then'.

Given below is the transliteration of Nadia's story in Sylheti (a dialect of standard Bengali). I have put in some full stops in the written text to help comprehension. I have also added some narrative 'hooks' in Bengali that Nadia uses in her story, to highlight the universal grammar of stories across languages and cultures. Nadia begins:

Ek din ekta topiwala asil nani ... One day *ekta* (a) topiwallah came [to a village] and he went to sleep. and the monkeys saw that he went to sleep and um ... [when] he was sleeping. and all the monkeys came and took everything [the hats] and, left just one hat [on the topiwallah's head]. *Ar khotobil badeh nanhi* ... then and after sometime when he [topiwallah] got up and saw that he had nothing and he looked up, and they [the monkeys] were laughing, [because] they saw there was only one hat [for the man], and they made monkey noises. and the man looked up and um ... what ever the man said, the man did *oi shokol monkey* ... all the monkeys, did. what ever the man did *'thara ali copy khoreh'* they kept on copying. *'ar khotobil badeh thara ekta figure khorse'* and after a while they [he] figured out something. *'beta tho nani falay di-se, falay di-soin na?'* the man threw [his hat], threw it, isn't it? (seeking approval from her audience who were seen nodding their heads saying 'yes, yes, that's right' looking at me), *'thoki shokol monkey-o falay di-soin'* so all the monkeys threw [the hats]. and so *'o shokol tha thulya gese-gi.'* he picked up everything and went. *'shesh'*. Finished.

Transliterated by Aysha Sultana (2006) from a video clip. Aysha, a fluent Bengali-English bilingual is a trainee-teacher on the PGCE Community Languages course at London Metropolitan University.

Nadia was a lively narrative-teller. She embellished her story with ingredients that would appeal to her audience as well as maintaining a dialogue with them to keep them engaged. Being able to tell her story fluently in Bengali when her English was at an early stage of development not only allowed Nadia to use her narrative skills purposefully but also made her feel emotionally secure. This was important for Nadia as it helped her develop a positive self-concept and a sense of pride in herself. It was especially important as I suspect Nadia knew that she did not have an adequate grasp of English to tell stories the way she could do in Bengali. We also note some word 'borrowings' from English. This is a characteristic language behaviour of a bilingual child with a bilingual audience. This became clear when I asked Nadia if she could repeat her story in English. I wanted to assess her narrative skills in English. She began with equal enthusiasm, voice and pitch. Here is a transcript from a video clip.

> One day there was a Topiwallah and the man was sleeping and all the monkey take the caps and one monkey put the cap on the Topiwallah head and . . . and they all laugh and when the Topiwallah got up and he sees there's no cap . . . and . . . [long pause] . . . and . . . [long pause] . . . and . . . [long pause] . . . then when he do the thingy . . . and . . . some of them do this [waves her arm] and when he sees something and throws the cap and he get everything to him . . . and he puts his head in the thingy and he takes it. Finished.

In the process of telling the story I saw Nadia's face gradually losing its original expressions, her voice losing its original vitality, her body withdrawing gradually. She did not have adequate meaning structures in her repertoire to share the 'narrative twist' in English. However, she continues by interspersing her narrative with non-linguistic gestures and her limited English vocabulary and grammar. Finally she said in a small voice, 'finished'. Her audience remained quietly seated.

However, within this we see that Nadia's story knowledge is clear. She begins her story well, introducing all the characters as well as the element of conflict: 'all the monkey[s] take the caps [away]'. But her inadequate grasp of grammatical structures or 'how to mean', and vocabulary, were major handicaps in her story of Topiwallah in English. In the process of telling the story she mixes up tenses which she does not normally do in her conversational English. In the story she uses some vocabulary replacement utterances – 'thingy', 'something' – and uses physical gestures in an effort to continue to tell her story, for example, 'some of them do this' (waves her arm). Compared with her vibrant story-telling in Bengali, Nadia found telling the story in English very stressful. We have looked at how to develop fluency in meaning structures in English in Chapter 4; bilingual children will gain enormously by doing the activities suggested in that chapter.

Personal goals and models: 'I can't read – only Samia can read'

As well as her love for stories Nadia was inspired by her reading models who also provided her with a vision of fluent reading. When invited to read a book of her choice she declared, *'I can't read – only Samia can read.'* Tasnim nodded her head and repeated *'I can't read also [either]'*. This was surprising as both were on different levels of class reading scheme books. On being reminded of that Nadia responded with facial gestures: *'No, no I want to read these'* (pointing to her pile of books). Tasnim was more skilful and said, *'That's for Wednesday morning, we want to read* Brown Bear *now'*. This was followed by a duet rendering of *Brown Bear*, which may be interpreted as somewhere between 'fluent' reading and the chanting of Quaida (Arabic alphabet) in their mosque schools, with rhythmic body movements, and rising and falling tones. Both Nadia and Tasnim tried to identify words in the text as they read.

Nadia's comment that *'only Samia can read'* was insightful for a young reader. What was Nadia's perception of a reader? Samia chose books freely to read. She read fluently and independently using many voices and faces. She also loved talking about what she read; she was happy with happy characters and sad with sad characters. Reading was always fun to her. Nadia couldn't do any of those things, she could only look at some interesting books she would have liked to read. In short, Nadia wanted to be a free, fluent and fun-loving reader like Samia. This was Nadia's image of a 'reader' and her understanding of reading, at a metacognitive level. She was determined to pursue it.

Nadia's relationship with her teachers: 'I have to watch Miss Burns ...'

'How do you think you will learn to read?' I asked Nadia. She responded with some consideration: *'I have to watch Miss Burns very carefully [when she reads]'*. As well as a peer model Nadia's long-term 'image' of a reader was her class teacher. I saw the children sitting on the carpet as the teacher's story-telling skills unfolded – voice, pitch, tone and facial expressions – her whole body moving with the rhythm of the story. The class teacher's love for language and literature in these 'literacy events' was visible to the children, and when language is expressive at both verbal and non-verbal levels, bilingual children are moved by the new language. Nadia sat completely spellbound, while Tasnim seemed lost in the story whirls.

Nadia liked her teacher. On an individual level she gave Nadia a 'sense' of her second language. Nadia saw an image of a teacher whose use of language was fluid and went beyond 'instructional language'. It touched her on many levels: personal, linguistic, intellectual and imaginative. She used English to express her feelings, her thoughts and ideas, her likes and dislikes. She shared with the children her anecdotes of funny moments and crises on holidays. In turn the children were inspired to share their experiences of festivals and holidays, mostly in Bangladesh. The teacher modelled Nadia's 'internal dialogue' that she wished to make her 'own' (Bruner, 1966, p. 124). Nadia's teacher understood the needs of bilinguals to develop an *image of English* that is a 'tie and a tool' (see Chapter 2). She developed an image of English which energized Nadia to cross linguistic and cultural boundaries in search of a voice in English, her second language. Many bilinguals distance themselves from learning English because their experience of it is limited to its functional use as a tool for instruction, or for assessing comprehension by asking short and 'closed' questions that require 'accurate' answers or to express teacher dissatisfaction with the level of bilinguals' work. To learn English well it is imperative for bilinguals also to relate emotionally to English.

Nadia's classroom was alive with children's voices, asking questions, describing, explaining, hypothesizing, gossiping, and telling stories. It demonstrated an active partnership between teachers, children and parents. There was fluid use of language at every level. Two support teachers, a Bengali-speaking EAL (English as an additional language) teacher and an MT teacher worked alongside the class teacher for three mornings a week. Once a week all the teachers engaged in tutoring children in phonic skills in different targeted groups as well as using reading scheme books for practice. Some parents joined in as well. These 'team-teaching' sessions were planned carefully with shared knowledge of learners, and the children seemed secure in their groups and with the guidance they received. A collaborative ethos permeated the whole learning environment. The MT teacher was observed switching between languages; for example, he showed them phonics in Bengali rhymes to support children's understanding of phonics in English. The EAL teacher taught mostly in English, but repeated in Bengali whenever she wanted the children to remember something of significance. A bilingual likes to repeat a statement of significance in both languages. This is known as 'bilingual repetition' (Gumperz, 1982), and it helps bilinguals to internalize learning or remember facts. A range of word games was used to allow children to have fun with the sounds of words and to strengthen their knowledge of phonics – rhymes, alliteration, onomatopoeia. The adults also heard all the children read, monitoring their progress and making notes of their needs. This knowledge was systematically shared in planning meetings as well as with parents. Having adult minority-language resources in the classroom for talking to parents proved to be crucial in children's learning achievement. Most parents came to school regularly to talk with the teachers about their children's learning.

Relevant to the classroom environment outlined above is Cummins' (1988, p. 137) model of 'Empowerment of minority students: a framework of intervention'. He posited that at the heart of this model is the notion of a teacher with 'informed intercultural orientation', that minority students are 'empowered or disabled as a direct result of their interactions with educators in schools' (ibid., p. 138). We have argued in Chapter 2 that bilingual children learn best when they are able to interact with both their languages and cultures to make deep *personal meanings*.

Switching languages for learning: 'That doesn't make sense'

There were frequent switches between languages in the classroom as well as in my reading sessions. When Nadia, Tasnim and other children sought help from each other with 'difficult words' the help came bilingually in that the children predicted the word spoken in Bengali while the word was given in English. Sometimes the children were heard to disagree, making comments such as *'that doesn't make sense'* or laughing at the nonsense word they thought they came up with. The children used both their *linguistic referents*, Bengali and English, to make sense of text. Cognitive and linguistic skills are transferable. Nadia used her wealth of literacy and cultural knowledge in Bengali, as we encountered in Chapter 2 to develop her reading skills in English. Her love for stories of all kinds, singing in all her languages, and dancing, were all part of her literacy repertoire.

Bengali was mostly spoken at home the children switched between Bengali and English. It was not a monolingual home. We can see that Nadia's sources of meanings spanned two cultures, and two or more languages. Her literacies, including oral skills, encompassed English and Bengali as well as use of metalanguage in translations and language switches (see Chapter 2), while Arabic was mostly memorized to recite the Qur'ān. The advanced linguistic skills, and perceptions of different ways of saying and doing things that bilingual children bring to school learning should be cherished and advanced through school education.

Assessing Nadia's reading: 'I like the part …'

Nadia chose to read *Wilberforce Goes on a Picnic* by Margaret Gordon. It shows her strengths and highlights her needs. It was a familiar text for Nadia. *'Do you like the story?'* Here is a transcript from a videoclip:

Nadia scans the pictures and says,

'I like the part when he put the roller in the man's lorry . . . and the part . . . [she looks through the book] . . . in this page when Wiberforce [for Wilberforce] is greedy and is naughty and he kicks something and his granny tells him off.'

The extract says many things about Nadia as a reader: that she loves talking, and can scan text to find her favourite parts, and that at this stage she was a keen 'reader' of pictures. We can also see that her first observation is incoherently represented in language. The episode refers to the picture of Wilberforce holding a roll of toilet paper out of the car window with the paper stream unfurling and flying over to a lorry behind. She spotted this in a very 'busy' illustration showing a traffic jam. But the text (page 8) reads, *'Off they went through the town . . .'.* She scans more pages until she comes to her next 'fun' episode, and once again she reads the picture rather than the text, *'Grandmother unpacked the picnic'*. In both instances she created her own text and did not make any connection with the written text. This behaviour can be interpreted differently, but based on evidence from her reading skills I feel Nadia found the written text uninspiring, or perhaps she was confused as the text did not relate to the illustrations.

When she had finished talking, Nadia returned to the text and started reading. Here we first encounter Samia taking on the role of a 'more experienced peer' (Vygotsky, 1962, 1978) to guide Nadia:

1. *'One day Wilberforce went on a picnic.*
2. *He wo . . . woke [hesitates] woke up Gr . . . Grand mother [hesitates and repeats] Grandmother and Grandfather [repeats whole sentence fluently again].*
3. *And had an e . . . eno . . . ['enormous' says Samia] enormous breakfast.'*

The text on page 4 reads,

4. *'Then he cleaned his teeth and brushed his ears.'*
Nadia ignores the text and 'reads the illustration' which shows Wilberforce squirting toothpaste on the mirror. She says,

'And then he put toothpaste on the thing then . . . '

Samia interjects, *'Not thing . . . on the mirror, anyway you have to read this.'* Samia points her finger at the text and reads, *'Then he cleaned his teeth and brushed his ears.'* Nadia continues reading.

5. *'Grandmother pa . . . cked [hesitates; Samia says 'packed'] packed the picnic [and repeats the whole sentence fluently].*
6. *Grandfather star . . . ted the car.'*

In her anxiety to make sense of the text Nadia read word for word. Concentrating on individual words she often lost track of meaning and repeated some words or sentences fluently to hear the sounds of the words as she knew them or to make sense of the text. She found the process frustrating and tiring. Nadia made only two predictions at word level using sentence-meaning contexts; for example, 'grandfather' in line 2 and 'breakfast' in line 3.

Nadia's limited range of vocabulary or grammatical structures did not help her to 'anticipate words' (Clay, 1976, p. 2). We note from the above extract that Nadia was happy with conversational everyday English using simple syntax, for example, *'when Wilberforce is greedy and is naughty and he kicks something and his granny tells him off'*. But when she had to *describe* an event encountering a whole text of narrative language, she was constrained by her inadequate knowledge of 'how to mean'. Nadia needed 'a lot of support' (her teacher said). We also note from the above extract that Nadia seemed to keep the worlds of print and illustration apart (line 4). She did not show any connectivity in her reading approach, which Samia demonstrated well in her reading and talking.

An episode from Samia's deep and fluent involvement with reading from a video clip illustrates this point. Samia is reading *Horace and Maurice* by Dick King-Smith. Samia reads the first page accurately and with expression. The illustration shows the mother feeding Horace with a *string* of sausages. After finishing reading the page Samia comments:

> *'But they can't eat sausages like that . . . they need [to] cut [them] in half. He don't like anything to drink so he cries all the time . . .'*
>
> Samia flicks through the book showing illustrations of the crying baby.
>
> *'. . . look . . . he's so skinny!'*
>
> Samia turns the page and reads all the text before saying:
>
> *'He's very naughty, he doesn't like anything. Sometimes and one day . . . you can see this picture and he's [pointing to the cat] eating Horace's dinner, and he's eating the cat's dinner, it's funny.' (Samia laughs)*
>
> Samia reads all of the next page fluently with tone and intonation. She follows the text with her finger, sometimes pointing to each word but mostly sweeping across a whole sentence or phrase, eager to know what happens next.
>
> She turns the page and announces:
>
> *'That's why he's crying so loud – he wants to eat the cat's dinner. That's why . . . Look, Mrs Primrose is putting her fingers in her ears. She doesn't like the baby.'*

Throughout the exercise Samia was reading and talking about what was happening and making comments, flicking pages back and forth to make connections with what had happened before and to have a view of what might happen next simultaneously. She used the pictures to extend the meaning of the text, to read beyond the literal. She read in whole phrases using her reading strategies in 'an integrated way' (Clay, 1976, p. 2). Nadia needed to use more strategies and integrate them to read well and fluently through repetition and rehearsals.

Nadia's specific needs

We can say that Nadia had *three major needs* in her development of fluency.

First, it was essential for Nadia to develop fluency in English quickly. 'The best reading teachers are those who help children to become independent readers quickly' (Meek, 1982, p. 27). It was a dangerous situation for Nadia, who had set her own goal and was trying hard to read fluently (for example, rereading sentences for fluency, see above) but she was not able to predict and was becoming frustrated with her efforts. Sometimes at such crossroads of literacy some bilinguals fall by the wayside, some like Nadia keep on pushing, and yet others end up with a high level of 'phonic skills' of reading only without making sense of the text and get trapped in what is known as the bilingual 'switching-off syndrome' (Datta, 1998) and accept their 'assigned levels' of inadequacy. Nadia wanted to become a *fluent reader* as quickly as possible, so that she could have fun reading all the books that Samia and her teacher read.

Second, it was crucial for any teaching strategies to keep Nadia closely connected with her love of literature in both her languages. It was through her love of stories that I came to know her as a learner or reader. Her narrative fluency in Bengali gave me insights into her potential development in English and enabled me to consider the nature of strategies to meet her needs effectively as well as to keep her strongly motivated. In one sense Nadia's needs were not far from her strengths, and it was essential to locate her strengths and weaknesses on a continuum of learning, rather than respond to them in isolation of the whole image of Nadia as a reader.

Third, as a non-native speaker of English, Nadia's major need was to develop grammatical structures to 'affect fluency in expectancy as to what types of word are likely to appear, and in what order' (Vernon, 1971, p. 62). This would enable her to use high level strategies of prediction and self-correction rather than relying on phonics as the main strategy. Nadia's anxiety to read word by word was due to her insecurity with grammatical or narrative structure and inadequate vocabulary. We must recognize that native speakers of English and bilingual children have different starting points in reading in English. The former scaffold their spoken language to reading in school, and thus learning remains a continuous process (see Chapter 2). Scaffolding for bilinguals to continue learning happens at a different level. We saw Nadia had a range of skills in Bengali, including her fluency in Bengali narrative speech. Evidence shows that these skills are transferable (see Chapter 2); therefore scaffolding for Nadia must keep her wholly engaged with narrative speech in both languages. This would allow learning to take place at a more *personal level*. Also, as a bilingual, the whole notion of interrelationships between texts in English and Bengali would be a very important part of her literacy development.

Based on the above discussion a number of strategies were used creatively for Nadia's development.

Stage Two: How was Nadia supported?

Texts and group dynamics played a major role in developing Nadia's syntactic and semantic structures in narrative language. A developing pattern of cooperation and leadership within the group (Vygotsky, 1962, 1978; Rogoff 1990), including support for individual initiatives, proved to be crucial to Nadia's development of fluency in reading at this stage. A range of texts with repetitive and patterned use of language was selected to help her build up a repertoire of 'narrative tunes in her head in English' as well as keep her strongly motivated to read fluently. The following books were collectively chosen to support her development:

> *Burglar Bill* by Janet and Allan Ahlberg
> *The Shopping Basket* by John Burningham
> *Handa's Surprise* by Eileen Browne
> *Dear Zoo* by Rod Campbell
> *Don't Forget the Bacon* by Pat Hutchins
> *Goodnight Owl* by Pat Hutchins
> *The Tiger Who Came to Tea* by Judith Kerr
> *Not Now, Bernard* by David McKee
> *Quick, Let's Get Out of Here* by Michael Rosen

Exploring texts: 'I wonder' and 'what if' questions

The objectives of these sessions were twofold. *One,* to raise the awareness of how semantic and syntactic choices are made to create meaning in text; for example, how writers create good, bad, sad, funny, angry characters, or interesting, funny or sad episodes or events; in short to experience the magical power of words, and words in sequence. The children were encouraged to role-play characters and situations to develop a 'feel' for language. *Two,* they were encouraged to read beyond the literal by using a series of open-ended and interrelated questions to enable them to build up a sequence of images in their head. They were invited 'to go inside the text', by exploring 'possible worlds' embedded in episodes or texts. The questions were repetitive in pattern to enable the young readers to understand and internalize how texts mean. For example, *'I wonder what's going to happen next?'* or looking at alternatives, *'I wonder what would have happened if . . . ?'* or *'I wonder if this can happen somewhere in the countryside or in another country?'*, or looking at feelings, for example, empathizing with sadness, anger or happiness, '*I wonder what she was thinking when she said that?*' or '*I wonder how he felt about . . . ?*' or '*I wonder why the writer has used such expression or description . . . here?*' or '*I wonder if it reminds you of something that you've read before . . .*'.

'I wonder' questions rather than 'tell me' communicates a sense of 'invitation to further thought' (Bruner, 1986, p. 126); 'tell me' invites recall only. The technique of questioning by teachers to create dialogues in readers' minds is crucial for bilinguals' cognitive and linguistic risk-taking. Developing perspectives is an essential aspect of literacy learning; it encourages development of an independent mind – a pathway to becoming an independent reader.

Examples of role-playing situations to develop perspectives and encouraging the use of narrative structures, for example 'telling the tale of the Fox' in Pat Hutchins' *Rosie's Walk*, or telling 'the tale of the animals' as they land in a strange place in Rod Campbell's *Dear Zoo*, or what the animals in John Burningham's *Mr Gumpy's Outing* felt, or what their expectations were as they went into Mr Gumpy's boat one by one, or telling the tale of the monsters when they saw Max in Maurice Sendak's *Where the Wild Things Are* or 'what if' the children were one of these characters adds strongly to developing thinking and creative perspectives; it also affects creating their own characters in their writing. There is no right or wrong answer in such learning. Nadia did not feel anxious about her language or her ideas (see 'Affective variables' in Chapter 2). For her it was an enjoyable experience of learning to talk as well as talking to learn, experimenting with self-expression in many ways and internalizing learning and having fun.

Reciting texts to develop literacy skills

Reciting or retelling stories is one of the most ancient art-forms in all cultures. Many ancient myths predating reading and writing have been passed from generation to generation and have survived to the present day. Tellers of these tales were helped to recall the story line by the *rhythmic pattern* of language and *story images*. In their retelling some stories merged with others, and others were created to suit a different audience, to carry different social meanings, over the centuries. Similarly, choice of texts with rhythmic language and meaningful images allows bilinguals to hold the narrative in memory. Responding to Nadia's need to develop fluency in narrative and grammatical structures, the group was encouraged to read, reread and recite selected texts to one another regularly. The intended objective was not an exact imitation of the text but rather an experience of a 'transformative and creative' process (Kress, 1997, p. 73). The children were encouraged to add their own creative expressions when retelling within the structure of the overall story. Bilinguals need the sounds of grammatical or narrative structures in their heads to take risks with their own narrative-making. The young readers were encouraged to repeat stories in Bengali to keep in touch with fluency; a bilingual always 'repeats' significant experiences in both languages (Gumperz, 1982).

In Samia, they had a model of an accomplished narrator in English. She was Nadia's 'internal dialogue' (Bruner, 1986, p. 26), who was also strongly motivated to broaden her own literary horizons.

Through such repeated meaningful activities, Nadia went through a 'steep learning curve' for nearly a term. An episode of Nadia's reading in this stage suggests that she had begun to read in 'phrase units', attempting to memorize chunks of grammatical structures from text. She had also developed her own reading routines – *'I liked reading about "Holiday", I take it home and read it every day'* – and thus Nadia brought home and school closer. Rereading texts had given her a lot of confidence in reading and she enjoyed using the ritual at home as well. In the extract below we see Nadia talking about *My Holiday* (by Sukimo), choosing to talk about what she liked in the text.

> *'I have been enjoying [reading] about My Holiday. I take it home and read it. It's about a little girl who goes to [the] seaside. Her little brother is called Ned. She has got a lot of nice clothes and she has books, her brother has got a fishing net and then she plays all the time. Some of the time they play in the sea and they throw ball and catch it, they go up the mountain and her mum and dad . . . and they play games. Then they go inside when it's pouring with rain.'*

We can see from the above extract that Nadia has been able to convey the flavour of the story in sustained narrative speech using simple narrative structures. She has developed a sense of connected and interrelated narrative speech. There is a flow in her narrative and her use of language shows a marked clarity in textual coherence, which was one of her primary needs.

With her developing fluency in English, Nadia was beginning to predict and self-correct and use her phonic skills intelligently, without losing the sense of meaning. With growing maturity she will read, connect, anticipate and reflect on events and relate to past memories of texts, almost simultaneously. Fluent readers enact the whole relationship between reader and text. Nadia chose to read *Mog in the Dark* by Judith Kerr, a text she had not read before, but she had heard the story. Although repetitive in tone it has a variety of grammatical structures, and exploring the text would be a valuable learning experience for bilinguals. Here is an extract of miscue analysis of her reading; all her miscues are noted in parentheses in the text:

> Can I read Mog? I want to read Mog in the Dark. Nadia quickly located the start of the story and began reading with confidence:
> [Page 5, the story begins:]
>
> 'Mog sat in the dark.
> Mog thought in the dark.
> Mog sat in the dark
> And thought dark thoughts.
> Mog thought, I am here.
> I am here in the dark,
> But where are they?'

She read the text fluently and her familiarity with the story enabled her to attempt intonation and enjoy the text.

> [Pages 6–7]
> Nadia scans the page and quickly locates the text:
>
> 'They are in the house.
> My [people – Samia gives her the word] are in the house.
> My [basket – Samia gives her the word] is in the house,
> And my supper is in the house.
> But I am not in the house.
> I am here.'

> [Pages 8–9]
> 'And who [else – teacher gives her the word] is here in the dark?'
>
> [Page 10]
> 'Dog . . . Mog [self-corrects], who is that?
> Who is that in the dark?
> Is it a b . . . [bird – Samia gives her the word] bird?
> Birds are not bads [self-corrects] bad.' (While reading this sentence Nadia was no longer looking at the text on this page but had already focused on the text on page 11.)
> 'But it migh [may – self-corrects] be a big bird.'
> Nadia points her finger at the text and follows each word as she reads:
> 'It may be a big bird with [teeth – word given by Samia].
> A big bird with teeth can be bad.'

Throughout the text her reading voice was tentatively showing expressions in her reading. She was beginning to read in chunks, predicting and self-correcting but still needing collaborative help.

Stage Three: Nadia becoming an independent reader: 'Shall I sing it?'

What can be termed as Nadia's third phase of reading development was marked by her self-confidence. With her developing fluency in English, her 'reading voice' was confident and she read with ease. She was carrying a fresh pile of books.

I Know an Old Lady Who Swallowed a Fly by Nadine Bernard-Westcott
The Elephant and the Bad Baby by Elfrida Vipont and Raymond Briggs
Peace at Last by Jill Murphy
Under the Bed by Michael Rosen and Quentin Blake
Writings by Olivia Bennett
Horace and Maurice by Dick King-Smith

At this stage Nadia's choice of books included selections that would tell her about things she wanted to know, something new to add to her repertoire of reading. Picking up *Writings*, I asked her why she had chosen this book: '*I like looking at the pictures and read about them*'. The text had samples of many scripts including Arabic but it was quite advanced; it would seem she liked the idea of a book with different scripts and perhaps related it to her own experience. I also noticed she had chosen *Under the Bed*, again because she liked the poems.

The following is an extract of her reading from a video clip:

Nadia picks up *I Know an Old Lady Who Swallowed a Fly* from her pile and reads the title on the front cover. She opens the book and scans a few pages and says, '*Shall I sing it?*' She turns to the back of the book where the lyric is written above the notes. Nadia starts singing, following the words in the text with her finger. Samia and Tasnim huddle up to Nadia to 'read' with her. Samia follows the text carefully and whenever Nadia falters she immediately points to the words and enables Nadia to pick up the song again without stopping for long. Nadia sings in tune throughout.

We will recall that Nadia loved singing in both her languages. Throughout these sessions Samia played a significant role in supporting Nadia collaboratively and unobtrusively. Nadia observed and listened to Samia reading intently; she took a keen interest in what she read. 'Children learn more language behaviour from members of their own peer group' (Krashen, 1982, p. 31). Nadia seemed to have constructed her own theory of fluency.

As the group dynamics strengthened it was interesting to note that the children seemed to be 'learning in chain'. For example, Nadia added most of Samia's books to her pile when she had finished reading them. This challenged and encouraged Samia to look for new experiences, including poetry and non-fiction books. In turn, Tasnim quite unconsciously followed Nadia's reading interests and started adding some of Nadia's books to her pile for future reading. When a collaborative group works well it seems to adopt a collective behavioural pattern and is driven by a collective force, and encourages individuals to cross learning boundaries and to develop an individual voice. Physically, too, they were poised to 'learn in chain'. Nadia seemed to be the connecting link and sat between Samia and Tasnim. At times one could see the image of 'three heads together' poring over a book.

Reading in chain: 'Can I read more?'

The following is an account of Samia, Nadia and Tasnim reading in chain in an episode from a video clip. The session took place in the library. Samia entered the library and started to browse through the books. She picked up a few books and an atlas. Nadia had a collection of books from the class library and so had Tasnim.

> *Samia 'reading' an atlas, with Nadia and Tasnim looking on*
>
> Samia is looking at a map of the British Isles:
> *'This is Scotland and this is ... [she searches for the word] ... England ... Edinburgh, this is where Miss Burns' mummy and daddy lives ... there's Liverpool ... Wales ... Birmingham ... Birmingham's got a football team and racing [track] ... Northern Ireland ...'*
>
> Samia turns the page to a map of Eastern Europe and points to the key:
> *'These are all the pictures ... there they are [pointing to pictures on the map]. My friend's got that, she's got a map like that, but it's a big map. [It's] a children's atlas but her mummy likes to read, which, where she ... about Chile, because her dad went to Chile.'*
>
> When Samia turns to the page showing the Indian subcontinent she says:
> *'Oh that's nice ... I know the country because my dad knows someone living in Mumbai and ... [Samia finds Bangladesh on the map] ... when I was in Bangladesh I went to stay in Dhaka ... I used to play with my cousin brothers and sisters ... we used to feed a cat ... it lived in the street not like London ... (where people have pets).'*
>
> Nadia listened to Samia intently throughout, nodding and smiling.

Nadia had brought a fresh pile of books to the session. She wanted to read *Peace at Last* by Jill Murphy. On being asked whether she had read the book she replied, '*No, Miss Burns has ... I was looking at it in the morning*'. '*What do you like about the story?*' I asked.

Here's an extract from the video. Nadia begins telling the story and scanning the text for the best bits.

> *Nadia skimming, scanning and part-telling the story of* Peace at Last
>
> *'What I like about it .... He, the bear can't sleep because, you know the mother bear she keeps on snoring. Then he goes to the Baby Bear's room, then Baby Bear pretends he's an aeroplane and he goes NYAAOW [Nadia makes aeroplane sounds and laughs. The other children join in the fun and laugh with her.] And then he goes to the kitchen and the tap goes drip drop [self-corrects] drip drip drip', continues Nadia. Samia then says, 'and the refrigerator ...', but Nadia does not allow her to finish her sentence and continues to read, 'and the refrigerator goes ... hmmm [Nadia makes refrigerator sounds and points to the hmmmmmmm in the text and they all laugh] and then he goes and Mr Bear says ... [Nadia points to the text, reading] "I can't stand this", [and adds] to himself [Nadia smiles and turns the page] and then he goes into the garden and you see the owl [she points to the picture] 'the owl goes too-whit-too-whoo, too-whit-too-whoo [Nadia enjoys making owl sounds, Samia joins in with the fun] and the cat goes snuffle, snuffle.'*

Nadia 'enacted' the above performance with poise and a glint in her eye that matched the energy of her story-telling feat of *Topiwallah* in Bengali at the beginning of this study. With her developing grasp of English, Nadia used higher-order skills of 'skimming and scanning' to 'part read and part tell' the story fluently, modulating her voice and pitch to match the 'tune on the page' (Meek, 1982, p. 22). Nadia was an animated reader. As well as enjoying the story she 'acted out' parts of the story, changing her facial expressions, making eye contact with her audience, creating dramatic effects and having fun. Her audience was gripped. When Nadia finished *Peace at Last*, I asked Tasnim if she wanted to read. Nadia interrupted and said, *'Can I read more?'*, looking at her pile of books.

Tasnim was beginning to show interest in talking about reading and demonstrated reading with some fluency.

Tasnim reading The Great Big Enormous Turnip

'Once upon a time an [hesitates, Nadia says 'old man'] old man . . . pl . . . [Nadia gives 'planted'] planted a little turnip and said "grow, grow, grow little turnip, grow sweet . . . [Nadia prompts Tasnim at the beginning of almost every line] . . . grow, grow, grow little turnip, grow little turnip, grow, grow, grow"'

Later in the story:

'Still ag . . . [Nadia corrects 'again'] again but still they couldn't pull it up.'

Nadia telling the story of The Crocodile and the Monkey in Bengali

At the end of the session I invited Nadia to tell a story in Bengali. She instantly began *The Crocodile and the Monkey*: *'ek din ekta coco . . . cocodrile aar ekta monkey, maaney ekta bandor chhilo . . ..'* Unmistakably it was Nadia telling a story – it had all the hallmarks of Nadia: the voice, the face, the body and expressive eyes. The audience prepared themselves for fun. But this time the story had bilingual features, English words located within the 'matrix' language or the major language (Myers-Scotton, 1993) or Bengali in this context. In this story we see that the linguistic sounds in Nadia's head are Bengali and English. The English sounds in a Bengali story are used unconsciously as a bilingual in the flow of the story with the implicit knowledge that her audience share the sounds as well. We note that her first story *Topiwallah* was entirely in Bengali.

This study demonstrates a case of *additive bilinguality* (Lambert, 1974) in that Nadia added another language to her first language. The factors that made it possible are clear throughout the study – school policy and resources, team teaching and the attitude of the teachers supporting children's bilinguality collaboratively with well defined working structures, including parents. All this contributed to Nadia's zest for learning, using the languages she had to serve the purpose. She was guided by an adult, who understood that her bilinguality was an asset in her literacy development in English, and who, along with other adults around her, believed in intercultural and sociocultural approaches to learning for a bilingual child, Bengali and English in this case. The result was to provide deep and holistic literacy development for a bilingual child. The process enabled her to transform and negotiate meanings interculturally from both her learning worlds. This was further strengthened by reading, rereading texts and narrating and talking to develop her use of meaning or grammatical structures in English, at semantic and syntactic level – this was her crucial need at the beginning of the study. The nature of support at all levels enabled Nadia to become a fluent reader, skimming and scanning texts to identify talking points or use them in her narrative recalls. Nadia was able to do this within a seven-month period, which included a summer holiday. It was essential that Nadia maintained a lively interest in Bengali as it was a major driving force and support in her literacy development and a part of her identity.

Zaida and teacher–pupil collaboration

There are many similarities between Zaida and Nadia and there are also many differences, as we shall see. They both come from Bangladeshi families with similar socio-economic backgrounds. Zaida is the youngest of three children and speaks fluent English and Bengali. Zaida's parents talk to her mostly in Bengali but she uses English with her siblings. At home Zaida has Bengali books. Zaida is learning Arabic through her religion Islam and speaks some Arabic phrases, which she describes as Bengali. However Zaida did not confess to her knowledge of Bengali at school until after a long time when she 'felt safe' to reveal the nature of her bilinguality. Evidence shows that young children are 'sensitive to status issues of languages, quickly perceiving where power and prestige are located' (Baker, 1996).

We can say that for Nadia her Bengali was a strength for learning and contributed to her positive self-concept, while for Zaida it would seem it was a cause for concern. The story of Zaida, a fluent Cockney speaker (a London dialect of English), becoming a reader is very different from Nadia's. Here we see how the learning environment can affect a child's identity, self-esteem and potential to learn. We also see how Karen, a student-teacher, applies her knowledge of bilingualism, and sees the importance of supporting Zaida's identity in class by providing an environment of 'an intercultural community of learners', where everyone feels emotionally secure and benefits from peer learning. Unfortunately, there are many 'silent voices' like Zaida, from minority ethnic communities who feel 'excluded' inside the classroom. The study shows teachers can affect children's learning strongly.

Need to become a member of the class community

The study draws on Karen Gray's (1999) study of Zaida as a bilingual reader. Karen's study was part of a PGCE course at the University of North London (now London Metropolitan University). Karen writes:

> Zaida went to an inner London school where children's home languages included English, Arabic, Bengali, Fanti, Greek, Gujarati, Turkish, Polish, Spanish and Yoruba. Although there were some shared languages, including Bengali, the children were never heard using them in the classroom or playground. Zaida was often a solitary figure in the playground and seemed withdrawn and isolated in class. In her teacher's opinion she was a 'moody and withdrawn child'. Zaida had a low self-image in school whereas at home she was described as a very 'bubbly child'.

We looked at the role of 'affective variables', or the relationship between cognition and affect in bilinguals' learning development, in Chapter 2. This relationship is true of all children, but for bilinguals it can carry an extra sense of rejection by peers because of their linguistic or cultural differences. Evidence shows that in the bilingual context children's learning achievements are as much an outcome of their personal strengths and skills as of a social and cooperative environment in the classroom. It was essential for Zaida to become a 'social member' of the class community quickly, as Zaida's 'alone ness' seemed to be a major block in her learning and self-confidence. Considering the presence of many languages in the classroom it was thought best to involve the whole class in collaborative and cooperative language awareness (see Chapter 2) activities that would raise an awareness of children's languages in the classroom, and the topic itself will be interesting for all children.

Language awareness work

We looked at books in different languages and saw that some were similar to English, for example, Polish and Turkish, while Indian and Arabic scripts were different. We talked about the shape of scripts, that every language has an alphabet but the letters or symbols have different sounds. At this stage I avoided singling out any particular language – knowing the sensitivity of the situation in the class. I wanted children's attitudes towards different languages and people to change through the process of doing a variety of activities. It was essential to have a globe to hand as well as a map of the world on the wall. A map seemed to act as a catalyst, children were seen to be gravitating towards it with naturally occurring talk about places and languages. We then did some work around scripts that we looked at.

We traced the journeys of these scripts from countries of origin to Britain and the journeys of the languages in the class to countries of origin. We also traced the journey of English to some major parts of the world. As well as talking about places where the children had heard other languages – playground, neighbourhood, television, holidays – the children started collecting some common phrases in all the languages spoken by children in the class. There was a flurry of activity going on with children following journeys of different languages on the map or the globe – literacy skills in map reading developed very fast as a result of everybody working collaboratively – and the class was alive with linguistic discourse!

The language awareness work strongly motivated children and much of the work seemed to be child-driven after initial attempts by Karen. Zaida began to regain her self-worth as she opened up gradually and was able to share her bilinguality with the rest of the class.

It is hard to ascertain exactly how her bilingualism was formed but from my reading (in particular Romaine, 1995) I would say that Zaida's experience was 'simultaneous' bilingual acquisition. In support of this is Zaida's fluency in an English London dialect featuring strong influences from Cockney, such as consistent use of double negatives and idioms. However, a limiting factor in putting together her language history was lack of opportunity to talk with her mother, whose tangible discomfort in school resulted in fleeting visits of necessity.

Assessment of Zaida as a reader

Here are some further episodes from Karen's profile of Zaida as a reader.

> When I first met Zaida she was reluctant to read aloud in small groups; her peers pronounced that she was 'unable' to read well. I also observed that at story time she liked sitting quite alone, near the teacher observing her every move, her every expression. I found her often in the 'reading corner' actively choosing and poring over books. Her favourite books were *The Jigaree*, which she read again and again, *Sam and the Frogs*, and Spot flap books. In reading time she preferred to read with one other class member, Charmaine, who was a good reader, or myself.
>
> Zaida reading *Sam and the Frogs*, a familiar text
> Zaida substituted spoken language for written language on several occasions. For example, on page 4 the text read, '*The digger was going to fill in the pond*', which Zaida read as, '*The digger was going to fill the pond up*'. Similarly, on page 10 the text read, '*At home, Sam had a tank*', which Zaida read as, '*At home, Sam got a tank*'. Further on, on page 16 the text read, '*But there were no frogs*', which Zaida read as, '*But there wasn't no frogs*'. Sometimes Zaida would self-correct these linguistic miscues, but

mostly she continued to read at a pace she liked, especially as her miscues did not alter the meaning of the text.

Zaida reading *Clever Clara* by Jill Hamilton, an unfamiliar text

Zaida was very keen to read the text fast, and on page 2 she read *'smashed'* for *'washed'*, two rhyming words with a different onset. She paused to self-correct if she recognized she had made a miscue. We see her substituting spoken language again. On page 7 *'Why can't you be like your brother'* was read as *'Why can't you be like normal people'*, but as the meaning of the text was not affected she did not attempt to self-correct. However, from page 12 she read the text with strong rhyming elements grapho-phonically and accurately. By the end of the text she was able to read previously unfamiliar words without hesitation.

As we can see, Zaida is showing the beginnings of a fluent reader, predicting, checking meaning and self-correcting. She had formed a good relationship with Karen and enjoyed talking about books 'in a very lively fashion'. This was encouraging, and without this many bilinguals seem to 'switch off'. From the above episodes we learn that Nadia and Zaida's 'starting points' as readers were different. Zaida was a fluent speaker of English albeit in a London dialect, her peer language, and Nadia liked talking in Bengali at the beginning of the study. Both loved stories, enjoyed reading and were lively readers once they had developed confidence. Like Nadia, Zaida's primary need was to develop fluency in written English to enable her to engage with text more 'accurately', and this would also develop her writing skills.

Given below are some examples from Karen's work on words and narrative structures.

Supporting Zaida's language and literacy development: 'I've seen snakes in Bangladesh!'

We began by reading 'The Jumblies'. The children loved the poem and asked me to read it again and again. We talked unceasingly about the wanderings, about the preposterous nature of the Jumblies' travels. The children had great fun. We talked about sounds and shapes of words – rhymes, alliteration and onomatopoeia. The next session began with talk about and chanting of some playground rhymes. The children were surprised to know that they are a part of authentic rhyming poetry! Making up some of our own rhymes followed.

I started them off: 'I dropped a pound'. The children brainstormed words containing 'ou' sounds. Zaida suggested 'sound'. Other words included 'ground', 'pound', 'down'. We all noticed the irregularity in grapheme–phoneme relationship, which highlighted an important aspect of the English written language. The poem read:

I dropped a pound
On the ground
It made a sound
When it fell down

I stopped here for children's responses. Zaida was lost in thought and then said excitedly: 'The drain!' It was the children's idea to perform the poem orally together with claps to emphasize the rhythm.

The children's high level of interest in making up poems encouraged me to look at alliteration. This would also extend their vocabulary using meaningful contexts as well as help them with spellings. We wrote a collaborative poem on snakes. This was a small group activity and everyone had a voice. The work began with children reading their favourite poems on the carpet. I began by sharing my experience of seeing an adder in Dorset and how it made me feel all 'tingly'. This was the start of stories around 'snakes'. The children were vociferous about their experiences, in Bangladesh, Nigeria, Turkey, Scotland, Iran . . . Tobias talked about 'suddenly coming upon a snake on holiday in Wales', while Yasmin said she was frightened of snakes. Zaida was excited and talked about snakes she had seen in Bangladesh, in the zoo, with relish. Following their stories, which were necessary to engage their minds, I asked the children to think about 's-words' that conjured up images of snakes and within minutes the whole class was 'hissing with s-words!' Zaida offered 'slithery and smooth'. Other words were 'hissing', 'silent', 'shiny', 'shimmering'. We talked about where snakes lived; 'in the ground', 'under leaves' were two ideas. I wrote down the words as they were suggested, encouraging the children to spell the words. I scribed the first line on the easel and the following lines were composed by the children. The title was thoughtfully worked out in the end.

The Slithery Snake
The snake slithered
Under the grass
Shiny, slithery
Zig-zaggy, smooth

The snake slithered
And hissed
And slinked [this was my contribution]
Under the ground

One child said it was a 'very snaky' poem. Others commented that it looked 'good and was easy to read'. A new descriptive word 'zig-zaggy' was invented in the process. The children's enthusiasm and concentration was very high: they worked hard to get their spellings right using all the skills they had learnt. A poetry craze took off. Zaida chose poetry books now, including the ones I had read with the class, for example, 'The Owl and the Pussycat' and 'The Jumblies'. She drew and modelled her impression of the Jumblies.

Towards the end of my three-month study Zaida was seen choosing a much harder book, *The Old Boot*. Zaida and Charmaine read together more and more. They collaborated to read *The Old Boot*. Zaida took risks decoding new words and they continuously chatted about the pictures in relation to what they read. Zaida also urged Charmaine to read chunks of text to her.

The Old Boot featured mini-beast life in an abandoned boot.

'Why did you choose this book?' I asked.

'I need this [book] now because the others, the other books are too easy.'

A new Zaida had emerged who read confidently, took interest in Bengali at school, made friends and became a humorous and much appreciated class member.

Bilinguality is a multidimensional phenomenon. Different contexts and different needs demand different strategies. However, in all contexts small group mixed-ability peer learning is crucial. In all contexts 'affective variables' play a major role in bilinguals' learning development, and the children's relationship with their teachers is a highly motivating factor. In the bilingual context the driving force for reading seems to be the 'construction of meaning' approach. It is interesting that Karen saw this as a web of many factors, language, culture, socio-psychological, i.e. Zaida's self-esteem. She created an energizing intercultural collaborating literate community for children's learning, which endowed Zaida with a 'much appreciated and respectful membership' of the class.

Kasi and cultural literacy

In this study we encounter Kasi, a ten-year-old African-Caribbean boy who speaks both English and Patois, along with the profiles of Nadia and Zaida as readers. It shows that literacy development in the multilingual context is a complex process. Teacher knowledge and understanding of children's bilinguality and cultural identity and the resources that children bring to school learning is an essential factor in minority children's reading development.

We share student-teacher Ian Taylor's (1998) report on Kasi as a reader whose attitude and motivation to reading depended on his cultural and personal interests, and self-concept. He writes:

Kasi is a very sociable and talkative boy who talks with his entire 'self' – words, face, body and voice – but struggles with his academic work and is often in trouble with his teacher. He experiences difficulties when 'confronted' with reading. He seems to 'confront' texts rather than read them and this conveys his attitude to reading. During reading time he prefers talking to other children, telling tall stories rather than reading. This may have been exacerbated by the fact that because of his low achievement in reading, he was expected to select simple reading scheme texts from the Special Educational Needs Coordinator's room while his classmates selected books from the class library. This implicit 'exclusion' was a source of great embarrassment to him and when asked to read to me he became quite anxious and employed a number of avoidance strategies. When he settled down to read with me he was tense and agitated, concentrating intently as if he were taking an exam. The tone, intonation, pitch and flow, along with his expressive body language in his talk simply wasn't there when he was reading. Kasi read word by word without making much sense of the text. He relied heavily on phonic cues and made frequent errors, substituting words closely resembling in graphemes, such as 'looked' for 'look', 'was' for 'went', and 'you' for 'your', which he left uncorrected. It seemed that for Kasi the acquisition of skills including ability to read was devalued because 'what he had learned to read added nothing of importance to his life' (Bettelheim, 1976, p. 4).

Responding to Kasi's needs: 'My gran told me Anancy stories'

Kasi did not have any problem with words; he was articulate, fluent and loved talking. His friends enjoyed his talk and he had a lot of friends. He needed a strategy that would boost his self-worth, respond to his interests and encourage transfer of his 'talking voice' to his 'reading voice', in other words to develop his interest in the written word. It was necessary to consider how to help him to make the best use of his oral skills and to establish a sense of ownership of reading and books.

Encountering and playing with written words encouraged his enjoyment of words for learning and literacy development. Resources were displayed that reflected his culture so as to foster favourable attitudes towards reading and to motivate him to read. Reorganization of the class library to include simple yet imaginative texts helped Kasi to relate to reading. Also, positive reinforcement through 'circle' and 'golden time' to enhance his sense of self, and the model of an Afro-Caribbean adult reader (Ian) to talk about text, helped in changing Kasi's behaviour towards reading. But most significant of all was his response to the Anancy story used in a reading aloud session. He seemed excited to be able to tell Ian, the student-teacher who himself was an African-Caribbean, and his peers, that he remembered being told Anancy stories by his grandmother in the Caribbean.

Ian, his teacher, concludes:

This seemed a significant development point for Kasi. The reading of the text was followed by a number of reading and writing activities around Anancy stories. Kasi developed the Anancy theme to make his own book, writing the script collaboratively with me. Slowly and over a period of time he became more relaxed reading with me and started to enjoy sharing and talking about books. I also noted how he was able to use his 'animated talk' to tell Anancy stories to his friends and how they too became interested in the tales, and wanted to read the text.

We can say that the Anancy stories proved to be of significance to Kasi's reading development. The stories helped Kasi, a sociable minority-language boy, bridge the gap between his ability and reading achievement in school. It would seem denying Kasi his personal interests in reading created the gap. From then on Kasi chose books from the class as well as the school library. Kasi learnt to use advanced strategies – predicting, self-correcting, checking grapho-phonics if what he read didn't make sense – with more and more confidence. I shared my interest in reading with him and also told him what I used to read when I was his age to further encourage his emotional engagement with books and to extend his reading horizons.

We may conclude that teachers' shared knowledge and pupil–child relationship are crucial in bilingual children's language literacy development in English. In contrast, a lack of shared knowledge leads to 'excluding' learners in the classroom as well as 'disabling' their future learning potential (Cummins, 1996). Ian's intercultural collaborative approaches to literacy learning were crucial for Kasi's development and his newfound learner-identity.

Salina's dialogues with her teachers: *'an appalling book – don't read it'*

In this study we have an excellent example of one of the ways of 'guiding' a young learner to become a critical and an independent reader, within the constraints of demanding teaching schedules. It demonstrates a learning relationship that is rewarding for co-participants in children's learning, teachers, the child and parents.

Many schools encourage pupils to keep 'reading journals', but what interested me about ten-year-old Salina's journal was the 'silent dialogue' that developed between Salina and her teachers, Ms Perry and Ms Keats. Rogoff (1990) terms such teaching and learning as 'guided participation' (p. 191), in this case writing comments in Salina's reading journal, demonstrating a shared understanding of her *proximal* conceptual development in the higher *zone* of thinking and reading. One of the most important underlying factors of children's learning development – teacher–pupil relationship – is very visible here. It is trusting, collaborative and inspiring. I have selected a few reviews that provide glimpses of this relationship, showing Salina's obvious delight in books and how her teacher matches that delight in her comments.

Salina is an avid reader who consistently reviews between two and four books a week, giving each book a star rating ranging from * for *'an appalling* *book – don't read it'* to ***** for *'brilliant and excellent – read this'*. She particularly enjoys horror and comedy stories but also reads an impressive range of books including information books on a variety of topics – from history, to astronomy, to sport. Salina obviously takes great pleasure in her reading and throughout her journal one can see her developing a voice and interactive style.

We can see that she interacts with her reading at a variety of levels. She interweaves the 'blurb' from the back cover of the book with personal narrative to make it her own. In this process she is developing familiarity with book language and an ability to relate it to real-life situations. In her journal entry for 6 November she writes *'Now I am determined to track a thief down. Any thief, any time'*.

Salina also shows a capacity to reflect on her reading to make sense of her experiences and growing awareness of the wider world. This also serves to illustrate how identity can impact on reading and reading on identity. For example, in her review of *The Caribbean* by Cas Walker she reflects that: *'some people in St Lucia are Muslims which is amazing!! to hear'*, and in *Earth Stories* by Ruskin Bond questions the information given with respect to her own understanding:

> *'some things I didn't understand and didn't make sense. Though some things I could understand. It was about how the Earth began. A strange process and I think it's not true. But I'm a Muslim so I believe in something else.'*

A further aspect is her ability to empathize with characters in the books she reads. For example, in a review of a book about Ann Frank she writes,

> *'I did not actually read her diary but this is a book about her and her family. I felt upset when I read this book because I know if I was in the same situation I would suffer and feel the same way she did. There were several sad bits but I think the saddest was when they all died in the concentration camp.'*

Salina's style of writing her journal is intimate, enthusiastic and honest, as we can see in the entries below with phrases such as *'so hello again'*. Her teacher's responses demonstrate her enthusiasm for reading, a deep knowledge of children's books and her emotional relationship with Salina, which affected her reading development so much (see 'Affective variables' in Chapter 2).

5 November

Dawn and the Halloween Mystery *by Anne M. Martin* *****

'Dawn has become a key witness of a robbery. The thief is still at large but Dawn is determined to track him or her down. Who is the mystery thief?

I knew the story would be scary like 99 Fear Street. *Again shivers run down my back and along my body.'*

6 November

'Continued today . . . So, hello again. I've just finished the book. Now I am determined to track a thief down. Any thief, any time. But as you know there haven't been any robberies lately on the news. Last year I remember reading a Baby-sitter Book [book in the same series] which was also scary. In the end it was a happy ending. I almost wanted to cry (why is it that happy endings want to make you cry?).'

20 November

Give My Liver Back *by Elizabeth Kiev. Illustrated by Katy Ferite* ****

'Johnny goes out to get some chicken liver. But he has a sweet tooth and spends all his money on sweets. Why did he have to go and dig up a person's liver? . . . "JOHNNY, I'M COMING TO CATCH YOU. GIVE MY LIVER BACK" repeats something or someone mysterious. Next day his father found him dead in the closet. Who killed him, a ghost?

(PS I know who did!)'

At the end of this journal entry Salina writes *'Comments,'* inviting her teacher to respond.

Teacher response: 'Do you think the title of the story is suitable? I have my doubts.'

21 November

A Woman and Dead Dog *by Anita Shear* ****

'A fantastically scary book which leaves YOU in deep suspense. Why? What?, and how? You've got to read it to believe it.'

Teacher response: 'How does the author make you feel scared? You could learn some "tricks" for your own story writing.'

25 November

Disasters *by Terry Deary* *****

'This book informs you about the disasters that happened which are perfectly true. One of the disasters was very upsetting. It was a disease called plague . . . a person could catch it within one minute and die the next. There was no cure or solution to the rats' fleas . . .

This is a brilliant book which taught me information especially about the plague.'

Teacher response: 'Did you feel moved by what you read? It always makes me terribly sad, Salina.'

1 December

Bill's New Frock *by Anne Fine* *****

'When Bill Simpson woke up on Monday morning he found himself a GIRL!! . . . This stylishly written book is a prize winner, it said so itself. Winner of the Nottinghamshire Book Award. It should be awarded book of the MONTH!! It's funny and very understandable because I know if I woke up and found myself a boy, I would scream. What I really liked or you could say LOVED about this book is how Bill shares his feelings. It's like the reader (in this case me) is inside the book involving the reader (me) along with the fantastic story. It makes you want to jump up with EXCITEMENT!! Reading on to find out what

happens next. It's incredibly funny!

PS Miss Perry or Miss Keats read this book, if you can!!'

Teacher response: 'Can you think of any advantages to being a boy? Or are you convinced that being a girl is best?'

3 December

The Wrestling Princess and Other Stories by Judy Corbalis *****

'If you thought that princesses were all soppy and always wait for husbands, well this book has proven you wrong!! The princesses in this book ride forklift trucks, pilot aeroplanes and kill dragons in clever ways . . .

Miss Perry or Miss Keats read this absolutely fabulous book!!'

Teacher response: 'This story really proves girls are as good as boys – and can do the same things as them.'

5 December

Glasses Who Needs 'Em by Lane Smith ****

'It's ideal for people who hate!! Glasses. This book might persuade people to wear them. I know a girl called Kimberley, this is just the type of book she needs at the moment . . .'

Teacher response: 'It's a good idea to make a story to convince people that wearing glasses is normal!'

15 December

Hunting of Jessica Baven by Irene Ballein *

'at first I thought it was going to be scary but I was wrong. There wasn't much conversation and it wasn't scary at all. There isn't much to say because I didn't enjoy it. This is my strong opinion . . .'

Teacher response: 'Is it suitable for an older reader? You can always re-visit books and change your opinion when you are older! I DID!'

31 January

Teacher comment: 'Well done Salina, again you have really kept me entertained with your fantastical reviews! This is the standard of a Level 5 writer – confident, sharing opinions, a wide choice of vocabulary and punctuation used to EXCELLENT effect!!! Please try and check your spellings – it will matter in marks between high Level 4 and Level 5. Go back through and correct spellings underneath.'

Salina's response: 'Thank you Miss Perry.'

Underneath, Salina's father wrote: '*I have noted your wonderfully encouraging comments about Salina's work. I am touched about her progress – I wish her to keep it up! Regards.*'

Salina's father recognizes the 'silent dialogue' that developed between Salina and her teacher as having a positive effect on his daughter's progress. As well as providing academic and emotional security, her teacher strongly encourages Salina's independence in learning. She doesn't direct Salina to specific tasks but rather raises pertinent points to guide and extend her development. In later reviews Salina's remarks such as *'This book is like a dream . . . I've learnt something from this. Firstly if you are writing about someone that had a dream, jumble up your ideas so that it makes sense but it doesn't . . .'*, and *'Maybe I might revisit this book when I'm older, and change my opinion. Like you say Miss Perry'*, echo her teacher's suggestions.

It clearly shows that this intimate interactive journal had a profound effect on Salina's self-perception as a reader. The opportunity to be in dialogue with a knowledgeable adult who shared her interest and enthusiasm for reading will be a lasting experience for Salina's academic life and beyond.

Conclusion

Literacy learning in a multilingual and multicultural setting is a multidimensional phenomenon, and, as we saw, different contexts need different responses. However, a few things are clear. Bilingual children's reading skills are best developed in collaborative intercultural literate settings, where cultural knowledge is generated freely by children and exchanged with peers and teachers in 'co-creating' text. Learning is negotiated at a *personal level*. Central to bilingual children's literacy development are their cultural meanings that they carry in their head; using these resources in their meaning-making process is crucial in developing deeper meaning and cognition required for high level literacy attainments in English.

It would seem that the best approach to reading for bilinguals is 'talking to read and reading to talk'. Keeping children's languages and cultures together as well as the integrative role of talk and open questions activates bilinguals' past literacy knowledge and meanings in school learning and literacy development. 'Without explicit attention to the social realities of diversity, many whole language classrooms . . . [remain] monocultural' (Maria de la Luz Reyes, cited in Cummins, 1996, p. 156). Bilinguals' crucial need in their reading development is learning how to use narrative or representational language, to read fluently and talk about text clearly, appropriately and coherently, using meaning from both their learning worlds. Absence of holistic talk can lead to control of phonic rules without an understanding of text or the underlying meaning structures. Inappropriate strategies cause deep language anxiety; we must understand that the bilingual mind actively seeks to make sense of learning and literacy meanings in their new language. This raises serious assessment issues in that if the pedagogy of teaching does not match with bilinguals' needs and strengths it leads to underachievement and consequent under-assessment of their potential, and subsequent teacher under-expectation, and underperformance by children. Bilinguals learn best in multi-ability collaborative settings with knowledgeable adult guidance. Evidence shows that peers and friends make very powerful models and *partners in learning*, where emerging bilingual readers situate themselves as readers and pursue personal pathways to literacy.

The teacher–learner relationship is crucial in this development, and teacher awareness of children's bilingual attributes and how the bilingual mind thinks, including home literacies as well as transferable skills and high expectations, are all important aspects of this relationship. 'All the higher functions originate as actual relationships between individuals' (Vygotsky, 1978, p. 57). We can conclude that bilinguals need an 'intercultural, collaborative and literate environment' to make meanings strongly in their new language. We see intelligent minds at work in such settings.

Bilingual Writers:
aami ekta bhooiter golpo likhba (I want to write a ghost story)

Manjula Datta

Our classroom was full of human knowledge, all of us knew something different and we were confident enough to share it with each other. We had a teacher who believed in us and gave us the opportunity we truly needed to reclaim our voices. (Frederickson, 1995, p. 255)

Five-year-old Zubair wanted to write a ghost story. We saw how adults around him enabled and supported his writing (Chapter 4). This chapter, along with Chapter 7, attempt to look closely at what makes it possible for bilingual children to develop high level skills to write strongly and purposefully. These chapters address concerns raised by Ofsted reports in March 2003 and July 2005.

The 2003 report stated that bilingual children *'need extra support long after they become fluent speakers [of English and that they] … struggle with writing.'* The 2005 report asks *'Could they do even better?'*, which would suggest that bilingual children's learning potential is not fully stretched by their writing. When we juxtapose these with what the TTA (Teacher Training Agency) survey showed, *'[that] … only 32% of NQTs (newly qualified teachers) considered that their training prepared them adequately to teach pupils from minority ethnic backgrounds'* (TTA, 2004), the immediate cause of the problem becomes clear. The content of the reports are corroborated by observations made by many in the profession as well as my own observations.

Meaning, purpose and audience are central to any message. Addressing these aspects in written constructs in an additional language is a complex phenomenon: there is constant interplay of linguistic, cultural and cognitive demands in the act of writing. The complexity of the process is expressed fluently by some children: '*I don't think I put in all the story things*'; '*I did the letter, I know how it's supposed to be written . . . and all that*'; '*You write a good story and they say "Oh this is rubbish!"*'. The comments encapsulate that cognitive development by itself is inadequate for developing their writing in English.

'The best writing is vigorous, committed, honest and interesting' (Cox, 1989, 17.31). It would follow that to address these attributes writers must have something of significance to say, and commit themselves to what they want to say, and how they want to say it, and in what form. Young bilingual writers can write 'vigorously' if they are encouraged to choose 'best topics' (Graves, 1983) from both their cultural worlds; '*children show most significant growth in both information and skills at the point of best topic*' (Graves, 1983, p. 21; emphasis added), or relate writing to personal experiences. This would suggest teacher knowledge of the possible range of literacy meanings and resources bilinguals carry in their head, and how these resources could be used to develop bilingual children's *communicational* (focused on the audience) and *representational* (focused on the maker) aspects of writing (Kress, 1997), which are 'central to any understanding of the form and meaning of messages, written, drawn or otherwise . . . children learn to write by skillfully drawing on their *resources*' [my emphasis] (p. 15). The freedom to 'draw on their resources' from both their learning worlds is crucial for bilinguals' development of writing. In Chapter 4 we saw five-year-old Zubair as a narrative-maker skilfully using all his available resources – a fund of stories in Bengali, his favourite media characters, images, enactment of story line and iconic as well as verbal symbols – to communicate his intended meaning to his audience. He used his rich conceptual understanding of story grammar from both his worlds to 'make' his Ghost story. How he negotiates this is discussed below.

The underlying theme of this chapter is to look closely at how bilingual children's range of literacy resources from both their language and cultural worlds could be drawn upon to write in many modes, forms and styles. The evidence shows that this provides a strong foundation for their writing development in English, as well as meeting the demands of the English curriculum. The process underlines essential teacher knowledge of 'how the bilingual mind works' and the importance of teacher–child and peer talk. Peer learning in this development is fluid, switching between writer–audience roles and creating a classroom environment of 'joint culture creating' (Bruner, 1986) (see also Chapter 2). It would seem that such joint partnership in teaching and learning triggers multidirectional thinking and imagination, as well as personal ways of responding to a best topic.

It is a matter of concern in the bilingual community that fluent bilingual speakers are still 'struggling' with writing (Ofsted, 2003) this despite most parents' deep commitment to supporting their children's learning development. Talking to young bilingual adults about their writing experiences in school it became clear that they found writing in school 'boring', except writing across the curriculum subjects, especially science, design and technology or geography, which they understood well. Most had difficulties with literary language; in my recent discussion with two GCSE students they claimed they 'know what to do (structure or procedure) ... but it's very difficult ... it's hard to put it together ...'.

'Children do not learn to write by being taught explicitly only, it is learned cooperatively and collaboratively in the company of significant others, peers or teachers. Adults in these environments have two special roles: they are fellow practitioners, and they are providers of possible content, and experiences' (Emig, 1981).

Bilingual children and the writing process

We will look at the writing process, making references to how Zubair negotiated the process in his 'Ghost story'.

Writing is a *thinking process*. In his 'Ghost story' Zubair shows his understanding that writing requires thinking. Much of his thinking was devoted to planning or composing a visual text. Children do not think in words only – children's gestures, play-acting and drawing enrich, inform and strengthen their writing development (Vygotsky, 1978).

Writing also involves weaving *previous knowledge* into the fabric of current meaning. For bilingual children this would include the wealth of cultural literacies, choosing best topics and ways of making meaning that they carry in their head. As a narrative-maker, five-year-old Zubair uses his love of ghost stories in Bengali – a popular genre in children's oral literature – as his best topic to compose a complex story demonstrating his knowledge of story grammar.

Looking closely at Zubair's story we see he has a good grasp of morphology. Propp (1968, p. 92) analysed story morphology or structure in terms of *'moves'*. He found that in most folk-tales in all cultures the first move – 'villainy' (wickedness, jealousy or unkindness) – is introduced at the beginning of a story. The proceeding number of moves depends on the complexity of the tale, but one move develops out of another logically and artistically. In Zubair's composition we see four logical moves that are compatible with some of Propp's 'moves'. The elements he weaves into his 'moves' are of great significance to young minds and demonstrate Zubair as a narrative-maker.

Zubair's tale begins with an 'initial situation' (ibid., p. 25), an appropriate setting in which the characters, including the future villain, are introduced. His *first* move, villainy – '*The big ghost wanted to eat up the rabbit*' – creates tension, 'disturbing the peace of a happy family' (ibid., p. 27). His *second* move can be described as a 'journey to defeat villainy' and arises out of the first move: '*The little ghosts picked up the rabbit and ran out to the police car and hid in it. When the big ghost went out the little ghosts went and hid under the big ghost's bed.*' In his *third* move the conflict reaches a climax and a sense of 'apparent failure to defeat villainy' prevails: '*The big ghost came back and broke his bed.*' In the *fourth* and final move we see 'villainy defeated', and a final denouement (ibid., p. 53): '*The little ghosts picked up the rabbit and escaped through the chimney. The rabbit ran away to the farm and lived with its friends there. The little ghosts ran away and lived with their friends in the river.*'

In many folk-tales we see the perpetrator of villainy suffer retribution, often violent in the resolving move, but such retribution is not explicit in Zubair's tale. However, if one interprets his story as an 'allegory of friendship' we see that the rabbit and all the little ghosts desert the 'unfriendly' big ghost and live happily with friends, while the big ghost loses all his friends and is left to suffer in loneliness.

In Zubair's ghost story we get a glimpse of how the bilingual writer's mind works. As a bilingual writer Zubair seems to be uniting his cultural and linguistic artifacts and experiences to construct his ghost story. The setting of his story could be Bangladesh, his country of origin which Zubair visits regularly, where traditionally ghost stories (*bhooteir golpo*) are a popular genre with children. In extended family situations such tales are told by grandmothers and aunts as well as visitors to the family. There is no specific place or time for stories. They are told sitting in courtyards, on verandas or on beds, whenever or wherever children can seek out their story-tellers. The story conclusion, '*The little ghosts ran away and lived with their friends in the river*', may relate to Zubair's holiday experiences in Bangladesh, where rivers and ponds are never far from people's homes and lives.

On the other hand, the setting could be in Britain as indicated by his use of *chimney*, a culturally significant artifact in Britain. He uses it skilfully to plan the escape route of his good characters. The image of Father Christmas coming down the chimney could not have been far from his imagination or thinking. Chimneys are not architectural features of houses in Bangladesh. At yet another level Zubair's story structure seems to bear nuances of media images of *Tom and Jerry*'s invincible flexibility which he so enjoys watching, particularly in the fluidity of the daring escape *'through the chimney'*. Zubair loved cartoons: was he creating a cartoon version of his intended meaning? Learning for children is now a multimodal experience and must be used in the classroom to develop children's literacy. Here we see Zubair's ability to weave stories from different sources, from the story worlds around him, which also demonstrate his intertextual skills.

His linguistic borrowings of English nouns – 'farm' and 'rabbit' – are probably influenced by a recent school visit to a city farm, and characteristically as a bilingual he retains the English words in a Bengali text, with the knowledge that his audience were his Bengali-English-speaking peers. Thus we see in Zubair's setting for his ghost story both his languages and cultures have merged or *integrated* to represent his bilingual voice. I have always been amazed at how closely the two worlds exist in bilinguals' schema. We can say that for Zubair, learning to write is strongly intertwined with his bilingual identity, and this must constitute *essential teacher knowledge* for his further development.

Writing is a *communicative process*. From his experience Zubair knew 'that's what writing does', that writing communicates messages, or stories to audience (readers). Zubair was well aware of his audience's taste for ghost stories. His choice of 'villainy' as a motive for his story was designed to have the desired effect. As a narrative-maker he develops the pace of his story with some swift 'moves', climaxing in the big ghost 'breaking' the bed under which the little ghosts and their rabbit friend were hiding. This violent act, with anticipation of more violence if the rabbit was caught, had his young audience on tenterhooks – gasps and cries! *'Is he or is he not?'* NO! The little ghosts and the rabbit make a dramatic escape through the chimney – sighs of relief at villainy defeated. 'Prior knowledge represents one central aspect of what students bring to the learning situation that makes input more context-embedded and comprehensible' (Cummins, 1996, p. 7). Zubair's narrative clearly shows a bilingual mind at work *evaluating and manipulating* cultural symbols from both his worlds to create the desired effect. He felt secure with the process as well as accruing personal satisfaction.

A child's language and identity are intimately bound up with each other (see Chapter 2). At a family level, the child sees many faces of language in everyday familial rituals and routines – religious and family mythologies, sad, angry or funny anecdotes, favourite television programmes in the home language as well as English, listening to journeys of all kinds, celebrating cultural, religious or family events – all wrapped up in narratives of all kinds interspersed with proverbial and metaphorical language. The child's literacy skills arise and develop out of these activities and the child begins to develop a sense of self.

It would seem that this image of self, language and voice undergoes a sea change for most bilinguals when they enter school. Here bilinguals face a language that is mostly didactic – right and wrong is clearly spelt out linguistically and culturally. Language teaching and learning follows a *formulaic pattern*. Talking about text mostly entails short responses to comprehension questions. Clear instructions are given on how a piece of learning is to be understood or constructed. In many cases there is a mismatch between teacher intention in the message and child reception or understanding of that message.

Such didactic teaching approaches present two major problems for bilingual children's literacy learning. *One*, they learn that school literacy is just an 'academic exercise', in that they need to answer teachers' questions correctly to be good at it. This causes deep confusion and anxiety among children with different literacy practices, where 'lived' experiences of children's literacy learning is considered important (see Chapter 2). *Second*, the implicit or explicit message given to children from minority language backgrounds is that what they know about language and literacy in their cultural settings is not valid in their literacy learning in English, which causes further confusion and anxiety. Olsen and Torrance (1981, p. 235) make this point succinctly, that 'school contexts function to gradually establish written text as *disconnected* [my emphasis] from the immediate context of students' lives'.

Over the years I have been struck by a 'sense of anxiety' in many language-minority children's writing in school, yet almost always I have been able to identify a phrase, an expression or a line which tells me about the voice that is struggling to come through.

Emerging voice of a new bilingual

It would appear that bilinguals' personal narratives are strong and often show 'unique blends' (Grosjean, 1982), even when the meaning structures in English are not well formed. In the sample below, eight-year-old Sri Lankan child Munsif, who had been in England for only two years, writes:

I would like to go to Sri Lanka by ship because they give you good food and it takes long. You get to swim in the sea and I like water because I like blue because it's my best colour. I like going by ship because it goes gently and goes slowly and the people are laughing and talking and the waves are talking to the people. Sometimes the sea blows the ship down and the wind helps the ship come up again. But I don't like flying because they give you ugly food in every aeroplane. I don't like flying because you can't relax and sometimes the wind blows the aeroplane to the sea and suddenly appears a tornado and broke the aeroplane. I don't like flying because you crash when the fogs come.

We can see a very powerful voice striving to come through. I also believe the best way of drawing Munsif's attention to his use of grammar, especially his use of tense, would be to enact the significance of passage of time in relation to his writing. Munsif does not mix up tenses in his conversational speech, additionally teachers should use his first language resources around use of tense to support his grammar in English. We can see that his grammatical weakness is not consistent in his writing. Any teaching of grammar for Munsif must be carried out in relation to the whole text rather than teaching 'bits' of grammar. Bilingual children, operating between two languages, understand grammar better if it relates to the whole meaning of a text.

As educators we need to engage in rethinking literacy teaching and learning approaches in multilingual classrooms to equalize opportunities for high learning outcomes.

Short precise answers . . . do not encourage students to draw upon personal experience, nor do they encourage students to explore their thinking as they write. (Carrasquillo and Rodriguez, 1995, p. 88)

Listening to teachers during my research it became clear that bilinguals are often insecure about 'what to say' and make poor representation of 'how to say' this confirms the above statement. Not being able to make personal connections with the topic of writing or to make meaning using their entire repertoire of experience inclusive of first language and culture, bilinguals become unsure about content (what to say), and this subsequently leads to insecure grammatical structures and style of writing (how to say). Thus bilinguals are left to make tentative guesses at meaning, purpose and audience levels in their written communication. Recent evidence, including my own work with children, strongly indicates that teaching methodologies that take account of personal, linguistic and cultural experiences, or educators with 'informed intercultural orientation', are likely to empower language-minority children to succeed in school learning (Cummins, 1996, pp. 72–6; 2000).

This is supported by the evidence from the National Writing Project, that bilinguals see themselves as writers when they 'work in classrooms which take their voice as the primary learning resource' (Savva, 1990). Writing about deep personal experiences offers them opportunities to understand the importance of selecting and ordering memories of experiences and events or thoughts and ideas; in short, it enables them to make wider connections with the demands of writing. This means power and control (Rosen, 1989, p. 24). The affirmation of these resources as valid for writing affects their motivation and writing ability deeply, showing 'a growing ability to construct and convey meaning . . . matching style to audience and purpose' (Cox, 1989, 17.23). They use their personal 'voice' as a primary reservoir in many forms of writing. Language use at word, phrase, sentence or episode level is carefully considered to carry the voice of the writer, and the process allows bilinguals to use their entire repertoire of meaning experiences in both languages and cultures as was suggested by the Bullock Report (1975). Learning must be a two-way process for every child. Separating bilingual children's learning worlds creates blocks in their cognitive and language development, as well as conflicts in their identities.

Bilinguality and intercultural literate community

> [M]ost learning in most settings is a communal activity, a sharing of the culture. It is not just that the child must make his knowledge his own, but that he must make it his own in a community of those who share his sense of belonging to a culture. It is this that leads me to emphasize . . . the importance of negotiating and sharing – in a word, of joint culture creating. (Bruner, 1986, p. 127)

For young bilinguals such sharing communities are essential to fully activate, understand and construct deep meaning at a personal level in the second language, as well as to feel free to use the first language to articulate thoughts and feelings.

Once children are respected for what they know about language and literacy, classroom learning can be a liberating experience for bilinguals to make choices to express themselves freely in their first language whenever appropriate. The following (uncorrected) examples show writing in Lithuanian and Russian. Along with writing by different children in English these were displayed in school to promote language awareness (see opposite page).

Literacy learning is an interactive social activity; it is 'not a set of skills but the result of conditions that allow children to be part of a literate community, doing the things that literate people do' (Hickman and Cullinan, 1989). This 'joint culture creating' in the company of literate people is an empowering model of learning for bilinguals. Writing has its roots in speech, 'It is the voice in speech that is carried over into writing' (Graves, 1983, p. 162). In the following account, children's writing began with contexts for talk across a variety of topics and ended with talking to share and evaluate one another's writing and ideas. This helped the children to enhance their understanding about writing and internalize by looking, listening, talking, reflecting and taking risks in multi-ability settings.

Aš gimes Leatavoie aš gёvenau Leatavoie
Aš iš važawau į angleia aš gevenu angleia tris metus man dašim metū aš gevenū su mama ir tete aš žaizdavor su draugaie pre namu aš oražinejau su dviradchais su draugais

Eivinas Jarala in Year 6 speaks to his mum and dad in Lithuanian and is helping his mum improve her English. In his article he tells that he has lived in England for three years. He remembers playing with his friends in Lithuania, riding their bikes outside his home.

Oleg Ozaling   22nd October, 1998

How I spent my weekend in Kazakstan.

На некоторые выходные мы выезжали на дачу. Дача у нас была в горах, поэтому мы купались в речке рядом с дачей.
А зимой мы ночивали там одну или две ночи но не больше потому что делать там больше.
Я расскажу вам как я проводил лето на даче с моей двоюродней сестрой и бабушкей.
Мы приезжали на дачу на один месяц мы купались, играли в карты и спали

Oleg Ozaling in Year 6 has lived in England for eighteen months. He speaks and writes confidently in Russian. In his article he tells of visits to the family villa in the mountains of Kazakstan. In summer they would stay for nearly a month, walking and swimming in the river. In winter they would stay for only a day or two.

In the children's writing below we see examples of significant meanings or images that bilinguals 'carry' in their head, and when afforded equal opportunity using meanings from *both* their worlds to write fluidly, they demonstrate deeper understanding of writing skills and literary language. The intercultural process offers an equitable assessment of children's writing skills. We begin with following the writing behaviour of one child over a seven-month period.

Paramjeet's emerging writing skills

Paramjeet was a rising seven-year-old Punjabi-English bilingual child and was at an early stage of her development as a writer. However, her interest in and knowledge of written language far exceeded her ability to transcribe. Even in her developmental stages her writing was deeply personal, in that the fear of 'loss' seemed to be a recurring theme in her writing. Paramjeet lost her father when she was four years of age and seemed to carry the experience in her memory. It became a significant resource at the early stages of her writing. We also come to learn about her relationship with her mother and her older sister, her 'teacher at home', through her writing.

Developmentally, Paramjeet began to recognize word boundaries, namely that a string of letters arranged in a certain order symbolized a certain word and meaning. She became aware of spellings. Interestingly, at this stage Paramjeet's writing became quite short and repetitive. Perhaps she felt secure and confident in using the stock of words she had under her control.

Shortly after this intense technical development Paramjeet ventured again into narrative-making. The context for writing was talking about the story they had heard in the morning assembly. *'How about making up a story today?'* I said. The children were delighted at the prospect. The story of 'The Lost Boy' was one such venture of *composing* a story. I helped out the group whenever they felt they were stuck by revising the work with them and asking a few guiding open-ended questions. Help with spelling was given whenever it was sought; the objective was to enable them to engage in cognitive and communicative demands of writing. Paramjeet was very absorbed in her writing, and at one point I noticed she had digressed from the story line. I asked her to read her story to me to see if she could identify any lack of coherence in her text. Paramjeet began to read:

Taking control: **'The Lost Boy'**

'One day I saw a boy and he didn't have a mummy or a daddy and he went away and I went to the shop and I saw my friends Sasha and Vicky . . ..'

onebpp/ m~ nobie tioPm
misrtoi bnrnsig
he ris kis WPys prsh
mis rkisev p
Prepbksit The isr k the
rut Pis i$ Potk pe kvaui
PiskrMiliskkw
Chmbme pipisrkkili
anb prpkisithe teme
Pise is Pisisipvr$roo
bisreeivitr Theotirtop
prsPw the Le tp to bou
ropwr t hoLvn~

'One day my mummy bought me a toy and I lost it. Then I found it and then I was lucky. I put it back where it was and then my mummy said that was good. Then I had my didder and then I went to bed. Paramjeet.'

Onebee IWPs eong to
tThe pakr Anb I 'Wse p pora
Iwate IC Pore up
(wpmjoeh) I Wiher to TheShop

'One day I was going to the park and I was playing. I had a sweet and I ate it all up. I went to the shop.'

Paramjeet stopped reading and fell about with laughter; she said, '*Oh Miss, I writ about Sasha and Vicky when I was writing about the Lost Boy!*' She wanted to erase her mistakes, she had never attempted that before. Was this the controlling interest of a writer asserting her ownership? However, her audience was gripped and wanted to know what happened to the lost boy in the end. Paramjeet was visibly overwhelmed by the peer reaction to her story. Enthused by this, Paramjeet carried on writing vigorously. She stopped from time to time and revised her text before continuing. When she had finished the group wanted her to read the story to them. The story is presented below with original errors.

'The Lost Boy'

'One day I saw a boy and he didn't have a mummy or a daddy and he went away and he was 10 years old. He went in a dark place in the forest and he said I wish I didn't come to here. And he saw his friend and [who] said to him I am going to see my auntie and the [lost] boy said shall I go with you and he said NO! and he went. and the boy stayed and he walked until he was in his house and he was happy.'

Developing a writing voice

The impact of Paramjeet's story on her listeners was deep. Everyone heaved a sigh of relief listening to the end of her story. As a story-maker we see that Paramjeet writes in a simple and lucid style and her voice accompanies her writing. It contains many voice elements – her fear, her feelings, her ideas – yet in this simplicity she has provided us with narrative descriptions that would grip a young audience. The quality of learning in a small interactive group far outweighs 'prescribed' methods of writing. The human voice underlies the whole process. The dramatic 'NO!' was her own punctuation. We reread the story and put in more punctuation for clarity of meaning. We also looked at some connectives that could replace her repetition of '*and*' to make the story more interesting. Following this we read the text again with tone and intonation, and Paramjeet was visibly impressed by the changes. '*The Lost Boy*' was a crucial turning point in her development as a writer; here we see her moving from writing about self or dialoguing with herself to *composing* an objective form of writing in that the composition and the style of writing are aimed at a wider audience. Enthused by her writing and the positive response from her peers and teacher, Paramjeet began to experiment with other forms of writing – poems, comic strips, recipes and menus, cards and letters, among others.

'Summer'

The flowers come up
I like the colours – yellow, red, mauve, green, blue, pink or orange

I like them
I picked one up and gave it to my mum

Paramjeet regularly took her writing home and always talked about it with her sister and mother. At home she wrote a menu for her birthday party that included a range of Indian and English dishes and brought in a recipe for her teacher who had mentioned how much she liked samosas. Here she was guided by her mother and sister. Her mother recited the recipe in Punjabi and her eight-year-old sister helped her to write in English. The recipe makes an interesting read, and reflects a six-year-old child's perception of cooking, including some detailed instructions such as *'First you get a pan then you put the pan on the cooker.'*

How to make Samosas (Recipe for Miss Thompson)
What you need for the dough:
For 6 people you will need
Flour – ½ kg of atta
Water – 1 jug of water
Oil – 1 bottle of oil
Salt – ½ teaspoon of salt

What you need for the stuffing:
Carrot
Peas
Potatoes
Onions
Chillies
Salt
Haldi (turmeric)
Garam masala

How to make the dough:
First you will need some water. Then you pour the water in a bowl and you put some flour and you mix it up with your hands and you must make it firm.

How to prepare the vegetables:
First you need some carrots and chop them up into little bits. Then you wash them and get some onion and you chop them too and you wash them. Then you get some peas. Then you get ready to cook them in a pan with a little oil, haldi, garam masala, chillies and salt.

How to fry the samosas:
First you get a pan then you put the pan on the cooker. Then you get some oil and put it in the pan and let it get very hot. And when the oil is bubbling you put the samosas in the pan and it will take about 20 minutes to be cooked.

With tea you can have lovely samosas.

Paramjeet did not seem to have any problem with the objective style of information writing.

'No my dear, there ain't any little Indian girl here'

We begin with looking at how play-writing began in a class of six- to seven-year-old children. The school project was designing and creating a school garden, and the children were expected to do some writing on any aspect of the project. Two competent writers in the class initiated the idea of writing a play with fruit as characters. The class routine was that they read their play everyday to the class as they were writing. The play was performed on the stage for the whole school after going through the whole process of selecting actors, costumes, music, etc.

Collaborative looking, listening and talking seemed to affect the imagination of many children. Inspired by their peers, Paramjeet and her friend Sasha wanted to write a play based on the story of 'Jack and the Beanstalk' which she eventually called *Rani and the Beanstalk*. Paramjeet's confidence was growing. The discussion of how she created the title of the play is discussed in Chapter 2. She chose to be Rani, the brave protagonist in the play, and her friend wanted to be Andrianna as the Greek she-giant. The teacher helped them with visual representation of a format for play-writing and talked about the importance of stage directions, 'acting without talking'. She also started them off with the process, and after a while the children were seen talking (role-playing) to each other and the dialogues seemed to flow. They carried on writing and were already on the fourth act by the end of the morning. They auditioned actors from the class for different parts, musicians to accompany the moods of the play, and rehearsed the cast before successfully performing for the others. The young playwrights were very happy to have achieved their goals.

Rani and the Beanstalk

A play by Paramjeet and Sasha
With music by Sasha and Paramjeet
CHARACTERS
Rani a little girl
Andrianna the mummy giant
Michael the daddy giant
Rupert the Beanstalk

ACT 1
Rani: I'll sow this seed. And I'll water it every day and I'll look after it
[She goes to bed. In the morning she looks out of the window and she sees a big, big beanstalk]

ACT 2
Rani: Oh dear, my seed has grown into a beanstalk. A ginormous one!
[She climbs out of the window and she starts climbing up the beanstalk]
Beanstalk: Oof it hurts. It prickles. Hurry up and climb up
Rani: OK I'll climb it as fast as I can

Beanstalk: *Careful you're nearly falling off. Go onto the other branch*
Rani: *I've reached the top of the beanstalk. I can see a castle there. It has a big, big gate*
Beanstalk: *Go and knock on the door*
[Rani goes and knocks on the door. The door opens by itself. Mummy Giant appears]
Mummy Giant: *Hello little girl. Come in*
Rani: *I'm starving. Can I have something to eat?*
Mummy Giant: *Eat these eggs and cakes*
Rani: *Thank you*
Mummy Giant: *Eat up quickly my husband will be coming home soon and he might eat you up*
Rani: *Oh, what am I going to do?*
Mummy Giant: *Hide in the cupboard. Quick. Before my husband comes back*

Act 3
Daddy Giant: *Fi fo fum, I can smell the blood of a little Indian girl*
Mummy Giant: *No my dear, there ain't any little Indian girl here*
Daddy Giant: *Are you lying to me?*
Mummy Giant: *No my dear*
Daddy Giant: *I am hungry. I want my dinner*
[Mummy Giant gets 10 plates for dinner, 10 mugs of beer. Daddy Giant gobbles it all up and he falls asleep]

(Paramjeet's own script is in Chapter 2, p. 48)

Act 4

… and so the play goes on

We may conclude that writing for young writers needs to be *purposeful, fun and personal*. The phenomenal development of this young bilingual writer over a period of nearly seven months was due to some specific factors. For example, as her confidence in her ability to communicate in written language grew she began to take more and more control of her writing, which was greatly helped by teacher knowledge of Paramjeet as a bilingual learner, her needs, and some significant personal history. This was essential to understand the inner voice of a writer whose topics for stories revolved round 'losses' of toys and people. She seemed to be negotiating that loss through writing. Her voice seemed to free up after writing 'The Lost Boy', and in writing the play with her friend Sasha she was able to assert her identity as an Indian girl in the play. We see very clearly that Paramjeet's knowledge of written language, including spellings, punctuation and grammar, developed strongly from writing about her personal history and life.

Chomsky tells us that as humans we show a 'creative propensity' for generating language in any given culture; this happens within sociocultural contexts. Young children learning to write demonstrate the same learning behaviour if they meet with an 'enabling environment', 'one that possesses certain characteristics and presents us with certain opportunities' (Chomsky, cited in Emig, 1981, p. 22).

It is 'safe, structured, private, unobtrusive, and literate' (ibid.). The example below affords a glimpse of what a safe, interactive literate community might look like.

Teacher as a knowledgeable guide

Writing should be energizing and fun for children. In this study we share a glimpse of an interculturally and linguistically aware teacher as a 'significant other' in the role of 'loan of consciousness' (Bruner, 1986) to the newly arrived minority-language children from a tropical country in his class. For many of the children it was their first opportunity to actively play with language and cultural images of snow in England. Learning a new language (English in this instance) means learning about new cultural meanings, new images, and new ways of saying things. Developing a meaningful awareness of how cultural artifacts are used in English literature at a higher level, in a *shared* learning environment, helps bilingual children to learn how to infer meaning from images, metaphors and complex literary structures (Britton, 1972) in English literature (see also Chapter 7). Fluent reading and understanding of English literature requires a good understanding of cultural meanings and images.

However, it is crucial that renegotiation of meanings *must be developed as a shared knowledge* rather than taught as an academic exercise. It must include intercultural classroom talk about children's different experiences, for example comparing the experience below with soaring heat in tropical countries, and images and cultural ways of describing these, for example Namita's poem on a hot summer day in India in Chapter 2. Bilinguals must be encouraged to situate themselves in 'simultaneous worlds', as this is their natural world.

The account below describes the work of Chris East (2000), an advisor in the Bilingual Support service in a North London borough:

> One day in early December it snowed – too good an opportunity to miss! We abandoned the intended work programme in order to create a class poem. I had been looking out for some way of carrying forward and extending our group poetry writing skills, following earlier work based around the local market.
>
> On that snowy morning the initial discussions with the children were wide ranging, providing a basis from which I could draw a web of starting points – how excited we felt; memories of previous snowfall; what we can do with snow – throw snowballs, make snow people and slides; what snow looks like as it falls, settles on the ground or melts; what it feels like, how cold it is and what we can do to keep warm. The children were sitting on the carpet and I ensured that early bilingual children were involved as listeners and encouraged them to become possible contributors in the class and whole group discussion. The discussions were animated.

I moved the discussion on to some of the language that we might use to describe their ideas, stressing the value of images and meanings. The children quickly caught on and ideas flowed thick and fast and my role as scribe became quite taxing! I recorded everything and later we collaboratively sifted through the crop of ideas, matching snippets of this with bits of that, trying them out for sound, flow, rhythm, rhyme, alliteration. My role as a model, joining in, enjoying the process of composition was crucial here until we felt satisfied with the following elements:

The snowflakes fall from the cloudy sky

Wrap up well, wrap up tight, make sure you keep warm tonight
Like ballerinas dancing
Like white flowers falling
Swirling, falling, zig-zagging down
Slipping, sliding, splashing through the slush
Like crystal teardrops melting [my input]
Woolly hats, wellingtons, winter coats
Quiet as a baby sleeping

We revisited the structure and with some collaborative, though teacher-led, editing, we re-assembled the ideas and added more. We looked at how we could present clusters of ideas and sounds to structure our poem and also agreed on why 'Quiet as a baby sleeping' should be our starting line.

The First Snow of Spring

Quiet as a baby sleeping
The snowflakes fall
From the cloudy grey sky.
Swirling, falling, zig-zagging down,
Like ballerinas dancing,
Like white flowers falling,
Like crystal teardrops melting.

Slipping, sliding,
Splashing through the slush.
    Wrap up well, wrap up tight,
    Make sure you keep warm tonight.
    Woolly hats,
    Wellingtons,
And winter coats,
Gloves and ear-muffs too,
Scarves wound round
Just an eye peeping through

Slipping, sliding,
Splashing through the slush.

The children were delighted with the result and so was I! We spent some time comparing in detail the finished article with their original ideas, individual children keen to note the parts they had contributed. They were impressed to see the poem in print and note how their ideas, generated in a sense as word-play, could take on the status of a poem.

Young bilinguals learn the new language enactively. They need to visualize the new language and learn how it works. They learn by 'doing' language and literacy (Datta and Pomphrey, 2004, pp. 44–53), and develop an emotional relationship with learning and make it their own. Poetry plays an important role in bilinguals' development of language and literacy. It helps them to tune into the new language and enables them to experience the whole shape and rhythm of the language. Chapters 4 and 7 discuss how poetry is used to develop fluency in literary language.

Peer collaboration: planning a visit and learning to write

A class of nine-year-old children was to visit the Commonwealth Institute, a multicultural gallery in London. The class teacher saw this as an opportunity to develop literacy in a real, purposeful context addressing the requirements of the language and literacy curriculum in English. She consciously chose a small group of multi-ability children to plan the visit. The group consisted of two confident writers, Anna and Michelle, and two others, Caglar and Mahinder, who seldom enjoyed writing. There was a strong collaborative ethos in the classroom and the teacher knew the children would cooperate to respond to a challenging task. The children understood the task clearly as it was based on their previous experience of many such visits, and they were also used to enquiry-based learning.

Of the two boys, Mahinder's 'voice' was peripheral in the classroom and he rarely participated in whole-class discussions and his friend Caglar liked talking but not writing. I chose to focus on Mahinder and Caglar's development through the process of planning the visit, as it seemed to have awakened in them an urge to write. They collaborated strongly throughout the process and Mahinder seemed to be quietly taking the lead.

Planning the visit was a multi-competence task with many things to consider. The children brainstormed the whole process at various levels. *First*, they considered what the whole visit entailed. Here is an extract from discussion in the preliminary stage from the audio-tape.

> *Anna*: [announces] Our visit to the Commonwealth Institute. How can we organize it and everything? Now what do we have to do?
> *Michelle*: We have to cancel a few things . . .
> *Anna*: We have to cancel all our playtimes.
> *Michelle*: No . . . don't have to cancel . . .
> *Caglar*: Yes, you've got to cancel playtime. We do.
> *Anna*: Yes, because we'd be at the Commonwealth Institute.
> *Michelle*: Such a silly thing. If you don't want to go to playtime, you don't have to go to playtime.
> *Mahinder*: We have to cancel dinners and bring packed lunch.

Mahinder did not enter into the debate either to agree or disagree with anyone in the group. However, it was interesting to note his contribution to the plan of action (see sample below). He proudly claimed ownership of his work by signifying its international membership, drawing flags from group members' root countries as well as clarifying ideas and presentation. We can see that Adam, who was not in the group, represented the Union Flag; he was Mahinder's best friend. Mahinder was eager to take his work to the class conference where children discussed their plan and gave useful suggestions to writers at different stages of writing. *Second*, the group brainstormed each aspect of the visit (for example, transport), and considered achievable targets to produce a plan of action. *Third*, they needed to consider points of organization for each aspect. At every stage the group had to bring their plan and the result of discussions to the whole class for collaborative feedback.

The class teacher's role was significant in organizing the learning environment, providing resources, including dictionaries, asking helpful questions about aspects of planning, improving aspects of the children's writing, and chairing whole-class discussions. The children worked collaboratively and cooperatively. In an established 'literate community' one never fails to be impressed by the patience and understanding children show towards each other. At every stage of planning the children were engaged in developing critical literacy skills (Cox, 1998), they were challenged to justify their comments, arguments or responses and thereby become aware of their own writing. Mahinder's successful achievement in stage one of the plan gave him the confidence to participate, albeit in a small way, and he took part confidently in later discussions. In the following extract we see his calm persistence to assert a point.

> *Michelle*: What do you think we should travel in – train, bus, coach?
> *Caglar*: I think tube.
> *Anna*: No, no. I think a train will be nice. If it's far away then – a train, because in a coach most people get sick. We don't want to be . . .
> *Michelle*: Let's find out where the place is [looking at map to locate].
> *Mahinder*: I know where it is.
> *Michelle*: No you don't!
> *Mahinder*: A bus takes you straight there.
> *Caglar*: I think we should go by bus because it's cheaper and everything.
> *Anna*: No – it's quite noisy and everything. But in the train you can sit down and be comfortable. Anyway how do you know [to Mahinder] it's a straight journey?
> *Mahinder*: I know a bus takes you straight there, I've been . . . [his voice trails off].
> *Michelle*: Well how do we know?

Mahinder knew it was a straight journey, he had been past the Commonwealth Institute before on a bus and remembered it well. He remembered some of the flags 'waving' outside the building, which may have accounted for the

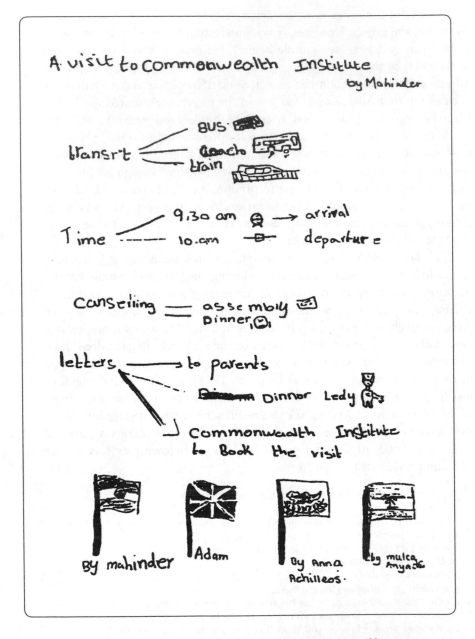

Mahinder's plan of action for organizing the class visit to the Commonwealth Institute

Dear Parents

We are going on a trip to
the Commonwealth Institute we
are leaving at 9.30 pm and we
will be coming back at 3.30 pm
you child would need a
packed lanch (no glass please).
your child can breing up to £2.00
the reason why we are going
is to see the   story about
to the Commonwealth   story about
man. to See How man developed
form a Single Cell to Human
bengs.

yours sincereluy

mahinder

if you allow your child to go
Please tick

yes   or   no   • • • • • • • • • •

Signature

Mahinder's draft of a letter to parents

flags on his action plan. After the session, Mahinder went with Caglar to the school secretary to get a bus map. They sifted through the Commonwealth Institute information leaflet and Mahinder highlighted the route on the map to prove to the group that it was a straight bus journey. They were very pleased and pleasantly surprised by Mahinder's effort and agreed to travel by bus, and took his plan to discuss at the class conference.

When the plan was accepted, final *preparation* for the journey began. The children started writing a variety of letters to various places and people. When it came to writing letters to parents, Mahinder's voice had grown strong. He knew what he wanted to write, he showed editorial skills to revise and redraft his letter, and he worked hard to overcome difficulties with spelling and transcription to produce his first piece of sustained writing, which he valued so much.

Once again his creative presentation had his hallmark. Alongside his letter to parents he drew the evolutionary process, ending with a representation of himself at the end of the process, identified with an M. It was a very moving learning experience for Mahinder to be recognized by his friends. He was no longer at the periphery of learning in the classroom and became an important member of the learning classroom. His parents were very pleased and proudly showed their letter to all their relatives.

Peer learning and *peer assessment* is essential in literacy learning development. Mahinder and Caglar's development within four weeks was possible in a peer-learning context, and in these contexts teacher time becomes quality time. The experience seemed to free up the learners in their own ways. Following a visit to the seaside, Mahinder made a scrapbook of the shells he collected from the beach. He went to the library to find books on shells to identify his collection and wrote a detailed description of each shell. Many others followed his lead. Mahinder started taking a 'controlling interest' in writing; he was interested in 'information-based' writing and reading, and developed adequate researching skills to support his future mini-projects. Soon Adam, a confident writer, was seen working with him; through collaborative learning he was able to assert his membership in his class. Mahinder encouraged Caglar to stay in the group, and Caglar began to develop an interest in information books as well.

Writing a running commentary travelling on a bus

The visit was planned and the class was on the bus going to the Commonwealth Institute. Mukasolu presents a detailed commentary on the journey which was written while travelling on the bus.

'We passed the Kings Cross underground and the Kings Cross Snooker Club and we even passed the big view of Kings Cross Station. There was [were] lots of people there, maybe they were going on holiday or to see their friends coming back from a country.

Anna and Michelle was [were] talking too much like chatterboxes.

We passed the trickshop with legs dangling about from the ceiling. It looked really funny.

We passed lots of fashion shops and a Japanese bank and an Arab bank. Linda and Reetha saw a naked statue and they were laughing. We passed the Scottish house. That was at Knightsbridge Green, W1.

We went passed Kensington High Street. We are nearly there.

We are at the Commonwealth Institute.'

Mukasolu's account has all the ingredients of a running commentary: the style, the details, the pace, and her distinct voice. In an interactive literate community teachers can have a view of children's intelligences about life and literacy and provide space, support and a safe environment in which to develop these. Most importantly, it helps young writers to make choices about 'best topics'. This is essential for bilinguals' development of writing in English.

Children's talk and memorable personal histories

In the following section we will explore further how bilinguals negotiate their 'best topics' at a personal level through small group talk and learn to form a 'strong link between voice and subject' (Graves, 1983) or 'how to mean'. As noted above, young bilinguals have a deep desire to share personal experiences, anecdotes, feelings, fears and delights, in short, their personal histories.

Lurking beneath the surface of anecdotes, the telling of moments of disasters or delight, recollections of childhood crisis, . . . are the great themes of memory, identity and the making of meaning. (Rosen, 1994, p. 11)

Given below are some such memorable episodes from bilingual children's personal histories arising out of 'verbal communication' (ibid.) with peers and an adult in the role of an *active participant listener*, who also identified possibilities of best topics for writing in their talk.

The wind of words takes me

The children were talking about books. Ten-year-old Zakiya talked endlessly about the books she had enjoyed reading recently. On my suggestion that she write a poem to share her love of books with other children in the class, she went away to a private corner to compose a poem. In a previous session we had read some poems and looked closely at ways of structuring them. Zakiya went through two drafts to produce her final poem, entitled 'Books Glorious Books'. She was happy to read to the group and this set off a craze for poetry-writing.

Books Glorious Books

They give me courage
They give me feelings
I am never alone in a book
I'm always in my own world.

The wind of words takes me to
Mole's burrow when he was spring-cleaning
I was there when Rat gave Fieldmouse a cup of tea.
I met Harry Potter in the Dursley's house
I met Skellig in his bit of corner.

I like Roald Dahl, Charles Dickens
And Jacqueline Wilson

You just need your imagination
To bring the books alive.

Mitesh, whom we met in Chapter 2 was a reluctant writer. Working in a collaborative group he caught the 'poetry-writing bug' and words seemed to flow from his pen. The group looked at Michael Rosen's poems 'After Dark' and 'What if . . .' which he and his friends enjoyed reading. They talked about how poets shape meanings using poetic structures such as poetic refrains, rhyme and rhythm. They also talked about how the poems use rhythm and sounds in language to express feeling or meaning. All of Mitesh's poems were autobiographical and that gave him the confidence to write fluently. His first draft of 'About Football' read like poetic prose. Following that, I chose a line from Mitesh's initial attempt as a starting point and Mitesh wrote the rest of his poem in response to it. We see how Mitesh used a very simple structure to communicate his love of football; the only guidance given to him was to use new lines for new thoughts.

'About Football' by Mitesh

I love football
When I score they shout 'yeh yeh'
But when I miss they say something . . .
I'm not allowed to say
But I love football

I just play
Sometimes we win
Sometimes we lose
But I love football

And when it's time to go
The fun starts to go.

Another context for writing poems occurred when the children were talking about spellings. I asked Mitesh to monitor his spellings carefully, to which he replied, *'I know my spellings are not good, yesterday I asked my sister to learn me my spellings'*, but she said, *'No – do it yourself'*. Mitesh added, *'She's horrible'*. His friend Yew joined in to sympathize with him, saying that his sister was horrible too: *'She makes me do chores in the house.'* The rest of his thoughts are in the children's poems. Following our last session on how meaning can be shaped in a poem, I saw them helping each other by reading and rereading their poems to arrive at the structures below. It is interesting to see how both the writers have woven family culture into their poems, for example *'Because my uncle said . . . NEVER HIT A GIRL'; 'She loves reading romances … Even my mum doesn't want her to read them'*.

'My Sister Neela' by Mitesh

My sister Neela is a pain in the neck
but sometimes she is nice
When we had one TV
we used to fight for the remote control
She has a TV in her bedroom now
I've got a TV downstairs
But we need a new TV wire

I don't like her
she has to wake me in the morning
But she does not
and I am late for school
Yesterday I asked her to learn me my spellings
and she said 'NO'
When we have a fight
she always wins
Because my uncle said . . .
NEVER HIT A GIRL!

But sometimes she is nice
She buys me my favourite drinks
And at Diwali and Christmas
She gives me nice presents.

'My Sister Sui Ying' by Yew

My sister Sui Ying
Is a pain in the neck
Whenever I want to go to the park
She stirs up trouble for me
She tells my mum that I can't go
Because I haven't done my chores
She bosses me around
Always

But sometimes she is nice and kind to me
She helps me with my homework
And whenever I want to buy an alien
She takes me to Toy City in Wood Green

But I'll tell you a secret
She's a real bookworm
She loves reading romances
All about love stories
I think she shouldn't be reading these kinds of books
Even my mum doesn't want her to read them
Because there are some rude parts in them
Like snogging in the swimming pool
That's what she told me
Just before I went swimming.

Recounting journeys

Journeys are significant personal experiences for bilingual children. It is more than the experience of travelling. Making cultural connections with their root countries can provide rich topics for writing. In the following poem Yew recalls his experience of a hot summer day in Malaysia:

'Light Rain'
One hot summer day
When I was in Malaysia
I could see the copper sky
Over my head
Then
Little drops of rain fell on the street
Dropping swiftly through the air
Water dropping on my face
Little puddles starting to form on the street
All running down hill
Like some kind of waves.

This is another example of the importance of listening to children's shared talk to identify 'best topics' for their writing development. Seven-year-old Nimesh's writing can be termed a travelogue and shows how experience of distant places can provide a rich source for literary inspiration. Nimesh had just returned from his trip to India. He talked very excitedly about it in great detail, using many voices. The suggestion of writing came following this talk and he was told he could read his story to two parallel classes. Nimesh began his writing in school but took it home to finish. He was highly motivated and set his own high standards for writing. Nimesh's account conveys the excitement and pace of his journey, telling his readers about his enjoyment of different activities as well as warning them about mosquitoes, or at least not to put one's foot outside the blanket!

'My Trip to India': *Mosquitoes are like Dracula*

Six weeks ago I went to India to attend my Aunty's wedding. I flew Air India. The flight number was AI 132. The plane took off at 6.00pm. As soon as the plane took off my ears were blocked. I could not eat anything because I felt sick.

When we got to India we saw my Uncle Mahindra. He came to collect us from Bombay Airport. It was air conditioned inside the airport. There were lots and lots of people. The porters came and helped us carry our luggage and we gave the porters 25 rupees each.

We had our dinner at my uncle's friend's house in Bombay. Then we went to Pipulug. It took one day in the car to get there. I met nani and two aunties. It was then I came screaming in and said 'a mosquito has bitten me'. Mosquitoes like human blood. When they bite you they leave big red blotches. When they bite you at night you don't feel it. In the morning you start to itch. Mosquitoes have sharp needles and the mosquito sucks blood with its needle like Dracula.

Two days after we went to my aunty's wedding. We had lots of food. I liked drinking nimbo pani. I went for a ride on my uncle's motor bike. That's what I enjoyed best.

The next day we went on a train to Ahmedabad. We stayed there for six days. Then we went to Sanojiya. We stayed there for two days. Then we went back home to Pipulug. We travelled a lot.

I played cricket at the cricket ground. I had lots of fun. I bowled very well and got Brigesh out. He is my uncle's son. Every morning I went to God's Temple. There the swami-ji gave me a holy necklace to wear. I have stopped eating meat like the rest of my family.

One day a letter came from Calcutta it was from masiji (mother's sister). She asked us to come to Calcutta. Two days passed and then my mum's jiji (older sister) came with us to Calcutta. It was fun in the aeroplane.

I played with my cousin Chirag in Calcutta. We stayed in calcutta for four days. I watched Star Wars and we played cricket. At night I put my foot outside of the blanket and a mosquito came and bit me. Chirag had a little computer game. I played with it. Chirag gave it to me and I have brought it here. When it was time to go back my masiji gave me 501 rupees.

The flight number was AI 115. When we got to London we landed at Heathrow Airport.

Similarly, Mitesh, who 'struggled with writing' (Ofsted, in 2003), wrote a deeply personal, reflective and a very rich account of his feelings visiting an Indian village. His experience gave him a powerful context to write about and he was able to move into abstract level thoughts with ease (Mitesh's poem 'Run Away' Chapter 2, p. 43), shows the bilingual potential for doing even better (Ofsted, 2005) with appropriate guidance and choice of best topics.

Conclusion

In a typical 'intercultural literate community' children engage fluidly in all aspects of language, using all modes of learning – speaking, listening, reading, writing – feeling free to switch between both their language and learning worlds to make meaning. Structured times are given to such activities, for children in the community to exchange notes on journeys they made and personal narratives of memorable experiences, books they read, and their favourite authors, discuss authorship and style and declare future reading interests. Teachers share their enthusiasm for reading with children, and have a comprehensive knowledge of children's literature. They interact with readers to extend understanding or listen 'actively' to suggest further reading or identify topics for writing possibilities in their literary talk. Everyone shares a 'sense of belonging to a culture' (Bruner, 1986).

The children's author Berlie Doherty (1994) said that 'the idea for a story comes in sensations and feelings and they eventually take their form in language', and that 'writing is a mixture of "I remember" and "let's pretend"'. For bilingual children savouring past experiences, *'I remember'* is of significant importance. Words in the second language make more sense to them at a personal level, embedded in personal 'sensations and feelings' in their development stages. 'When the writing concerned is personal it has the potential of putting the writer at centre stage' (Rosen, 1989, p. 24).

Writing about their memorable experiences gives children a sense of purpose, interest and honesty, and enables them to present writing coherently, using a range of vocabulary and meaning structures and phrases in some unique combinations. This also deeply validates their cultural, linguistic and personal identities in the classroom, and *equalizes learning and writing potential*. I believe this is one of the most important aspects of 'inclusive classrooms' to allow and encourage children from minority cultures to express themselves equally strongly in English. Language, culture and cognition are intimately related (see Chapter 2). Without these opportunities most of their writing experiences become an exercise in 'rehearsals' (Rosen, 1989, p. 14). Children's voices are strong in an intercultural literate community, they feel safe to evaluate and synthesize their 'cultural capital' in their writing and become active meaning-seekers and meaning-makers. Beginning with *personal narratives* in many forms and many styles is an essential foundation for their future development as writers to construct meaning and text objectively and confidently in English.

Moreover, visual texts should be encouraged strongly in multilingual classrooms in all years as these open up many 'silent' voices in class; Zubair's animated visual text in Chapter 4 signifies his future development as a writer. This also solves the problem of less-confident writers being confused about 'how to mean' in English; constructing a storyboard gives them time to think and develop ideas coherently.

Teachers in intercultural literate communities work collaboratively with learners in many roles – as knowledgeable others, teachers, instructors, organizers, monitors and assessors of children's work and planners for future possibilities of development.

Teacher–learner relationship is strong in this environment, listening carefully to children's talk about personal experiences, helping young writers to select best topics and possible best form, style, and ways to go about it. This is an invaluable support that underpins bilinguals' identities as writers. The environment makes it possible to invest in every child's identity and enables creating a strong link between 'voice and subject' (Graves, 1983). It also offers teachers opportunities for *true assessment* of children's ability that informs their future development. As educators we need to work towards 'inclusive' classroom learning to situate every learner positively and actively; 'mono' cultural classrooms handicap the development of bilingual children, and writing remains a 'struggle' for them despite acquiring spoken fluency in English.

Developing English Literary Language: Imagination and Personal Learning

7

Manjula Datta

One's emotions, imagination and intellect mutually support and enrich one another. Our positive feelings strengthen our rationality. (Bettelheim, 1976, p. 4)

We encountered bilingual children's literary constructs on personal best topics in many forms, with cultural images and ways of looking at things or communicating meaning in Chapter 6. This chapter looks closely at the teaching and learning approaches that enable ten- to eleven-year-old bilingual children to engage in deep reading of English literature at a challenging level, and how this knowledge provides a valuable resource for developing their skills in composing interesting literary texts. Underpinning this is the fluid interaction between essential teacher knowledge of the wealth of literacies that bilingual children carry in their head – how the bilingual mind processes meaning mediating between *both* their language and their cultural worlds – and teacher knowledge of literature as 'cultural artifact', in that they contain the possibility of different interpretations of words, images, structure and style: these acquire life in the reader's mind in different ways (see Chapter 2). The study shows that bilingual children develop their literacy skills significantly with an *intercultural* orientation to learning which incorporates their cultural meanings as well.

Continuing on from the previous chapter, here we look closely at the strategy of *reading like a writer* and reflect on what makes it possible for bilinguals to read deeply and internalize important literacy knowledge and skills and concurrently develop the ability to write strongly in English, in personally satisfying ways. The children's comments below clearly show their ambivalence and deep anxiety about *how to use* their literacy knowledge that they acquired in classroom learning; they seem to 'struggle with writing'. The evidence from my research shows that the process of 'reading like a writer' is strongly helped by using *imagination* as an intercultural learning tool for thinking, integrating meaning from both their learning worlds for deep interaction between text and self at a personal level. It draws on my personal experience of reading literature at a higher level in what would be construed as my second language (see Chapter 1). Imagination is 'dialogic' in nature in that it helps create thinking dialogues and further associated images in the reader's mind in the process of reading. The process is further supported by step-by-step open questions, which allows bilinguals to engage in multidimensional thinking as well as connecting with how they are going to *use* this knowledge to create their own literary texts. This was demonstrated in the children's assessment of the process and the outcomes of learning in their writing in many forms in the chapter.

The immediate context for my research was based on the Reading and Writing Tests (SATs, 1999) of ten- to eleven-year-old children (Key Stage 2) for my book published in 2000. It is a matter of concern that despite gaining conceptual knowledge about literary writing bilingual children are continuing to 'struggle' with their application of literacy knowledge in writing, contrary to the evidence from my research on bilingual children's enormous capacity to read and construct literary texts at a higher level. Clearly we need to consider alternative strategies to respond to bilingual children's specific needs, which is the focus of this chapter. The chapter continues to respond to Ofsted reports (2003; 2005) as well as teaching professionals and children.

The *children's* comments made post-1999 exam seem to concur with the reports' findings. Talking to a group of bilinguals who shared Bengali, Turkish, Chinese, Arabic, Hindi and Gujarati between them, and were second-generation bilinguals in England and fluent speakers of English, it became clear that their conceptual understanding of literacy and literary constructs was clear, but they encountered great difficulty in applying this knowledge to their compositions in writing. The 'Writing Test' (1999) included choices of information-based persuasive writing in the form of a letter or a leaflet, as well as two interesting story titles for creative writing, 'If Pictures Could Speak' and 'Home At Last'. However, it seems that most of them avoided writing a story and spoke quite fluidly about their anxiety:

> 'I did a story [showing anxiety about her choice]; if I had done the letter I would have got more points.' Her friend nodded in agreement, '. . . non-fiction gets more marks than fiction that's why I did the letter.'

A competent writer chose the title 'Home At Last' because he had some *'wicked'* ideas (meaning 'excellent' in youth language in London) but was anxious: *'I don't think I put in all the story things'.* Other comments were:

> 'I did the letter, I know how it's supposed to be written . . . and all that.'
> 'I didn't do the story 'cos I keep on thinking about the main problem you see, and the resolution . . . And sometimes I forget the introduction of the characters and description and all that.'
> 'Ya, the story is difficult, you've got to think about the introduction, development and . . . I just write the story you see.'
> 'Yes, you have to think very hard [when you write a story] . . . I did the leaflet.'

These are very insightful comments from very intelligent children. It shows their clear conceptual understanding of 'story grammar' or the formula for writing good stories, but ambivalence about how the parts fit into the whole. Further, it is disturbing to know that children coming from rich literary heritage backgrounds are afraid of creative writing in English. As argued previously, bilinguals learn literacy rules or formulae quickly at conceptual level but find it difficult *how to mean* in creating the whole text. As educators we need to think about how children 'receive' teaching of knowledge and skills and consider deeply how to support them with fitting the 'parts' into the 'whole'. The evidence from my research suggests that enabling bilinguals with an interactive and integrative tool, for example 'imagination', helps them to internalize and accommodate new knowledge to their schema and use it meaningfully and fluidly in personal literary constructs. This learning is deeply *personal*. The approach helps them improve their skills in persuasive or non-fiction writing as well.

I spoke to teachers in three schools who raised similar concerns about children's writing:

> 'They seem to like information kind of writing about facts They don't seem to make the connection between reading and writing, it's very frustrating...'

Making connection with reading and writing is central to children's literacy learning and is the central thesis in this chapter. The teachers talked fluently about bilingual children's strengths and needs in reading, especially at higher levels:

At lower levels of reading age stories tend to be simplified:

However, looking closely we see texts for younger readers are not necessarily simple. The picture books of such writers as John Burningham, Janet and Allan Ahlberg, Pat Hutchins, Anthony Brown and Shirley Hughes, among others, make complex and imaginative literacy demands on children that encourage young readers to *infer* meanings at many levels. The dual narrative mode in words and images helps readers to move fluidly between the *literal and visual* text to engage in exploring layers of meaning, and should be actively promoted in multilingual classrooms, to avoid failure in later years.

- 'They do like information books, because it's real life ...'
- Older bilinguals find challenging literary texts difficult, ... They don't seem to retain it or read beyond the literal.'
- 'Their phonic skills are very advanced ... and [they] are happy to read aloud to the rest of the class [but] when they come to comprehend what they have read they find it really difficult. It's really disheartening ... because you think, well you can read, but you can't make meaning from it.'

The last comment clearly sums up bilinguals' strengths and their *real need* in reading. It also shows teacher frustration of feeling 'disheartened', which is not good for any education policy. Educators must understand that bilingual children's real needs are in their meaning-making skills; crucial to this is the knowledge and understanding of how the bilingual mind works.

Talking about their Reading Comprehension Test, the *children* reflected,

- 'I couldn't get to the hidden meanings [metaphors].' 'There were too many words ... I got lost.'
- An Arabic speaker commented poignantly, *'Why don't they write in normal language?'*, when it would seem that every third sentence in his own language contains a metaphor.
- Another child, a high flier in his teachers' eyes, commented, *'If you spend too much time on the hidden meanings you get really stressed.'*

Native speakers of English bring with them the fluidity of oral speech and many ways of making meaning – idiomatic, proverbial or metaphorical; in short, meaning is made in shared cultural and social contexts. This is true of oral speech in all cultures. In every culture, 'the mother tongue is the vehicle whereby history reached the lower mass, whereby folklore reached the upper class. Poetry, songs, proverbs, mottos, and tales ... all involve basically, language behaviours and language products ... safeguarded by recitation' (Fishman, 1989, p. 281). Bilinguals carry these cultural knowledges in their head. This chapter, as well as the previous chapter, shows the process of 'awakening' and using these learning resources to develop bilinguals' literacy learning skills in English, leading to higher and deeper learning outcomes.

In the following section we will look at the underlying knowledge that informs teaching as well as learning about literary language.

Language constructs meanings in two ways: *denotative* and *connotative*. The denotative language refers to the literal meaning of a word, the meaning is fairly static, and for bilingual children it does not seem to present any ambiguity. This makes information text more accessible, in that bilinguals seem to relate to clarity in structure. Any new vocabulary or meaning is context-related and therefore the text represents something tangible. On the other hand, connotative language demands a 'shared understanding' of linguistic and cultural meanings between the reader and the writer. Words accrue meanings from 'associations, connotations and social meanings' (Turner, 1994) or cultural signs or artifacts. Cultural understanding of meaning is crucial to connotative language. As well as varying literary styles which resonate with unique manipulation of sounds, images and metaphors, this kind of language has 'a complex structure, with internal relations, relations within the construct' (Britton, 1972, p. 76). The *connotative meaning of words varies from culture to culture*. The language is fluid and less fixed. This is further exemplified in the discussion below.

Culture and meaning formation: *'it's just an arachnid'*

The text for the reading comprehension test was 'Spinners'. The children were expected to look at spiders in three different ways: 'facts' about how spiders spin their webs; 'the mystery and beauty' of spiders in the poem 'Spinners'; the 'story' behind a familiar rhyme ('Little Miss Muffet'). The children enjoyed reading the fact-finding questions and answered these to their satisfaction. However, they felt distressed by trying to comprehend 'the mystery and beauty' of spiders. The intangible grasp of cultural meanings embedded in the poem seemed to have added to the children's reading problem considerably. The children were unable to connect with a particular cultural way of looking at spiders or the connotative meanings in the text.

Several teachers commented on the images used in the poem and their relevance to the children's lives. One teacher expressed the problem succinctly: 'it means something to me because I was brought up in the countryside . . . you know it's morning and there's the sun, the dew and the spider webs across the trees . . . you carry the images in your head'; but the landscape of the poem was alien to the children.

One of the underlying principles of education is to broaden one's horizon or mind. For bilinguals to understand the culturally embedded meanings of 'beauty and mystery' of spiders in the text meant they needed the opportunity to talk, to bring past experiences to new learning, and develop new ways of looking at things or develop different cultural perspectives. Talk is essential for making such connections, but 'tests are not forums for talk' (Datta, 1999). Yet the same group of children responded energetically to metaphorical and connotative use of language in poems with such universal themes as the sea, storm, fear, peace, and leaving home. Looking at their creative skills I asked, '*So, what was the problem with* 'Spinners'*?*' A young Hindi-English bilingual responded crisply: '*The sea has many meanings. The spider has none, it's just an arachnid.*' This was the child's cultural way of looking at spiders.

My own experience of reading English literature entailed interchange and cross-fertilization of meanings. Clearly we need to find ways of cross-fertilizing text and personal and cultural meanings in readers' heads to strengthen their literary language. In an intercultural, collaborative classroom environment bilinguals' sense of self is strong and they participate actively in the new culture.

There is wide-ranging evidence to suggest that books provide very powerful models for bilingual children's academic language and writing development. Krashen's (1993) comprehensive research in this area suggests that the ability of second-language learners to use academic language in writing is crucially dependent on the amount and variety of what they read, through reading deeply they learn how to manipulate literacy knowledge and skills for different contexts and purposes. At the heart of this strategy is a *shift in emphasis* from 'word-centred' processing of meaning or looking at words only for meaning, to an *image-centred processing of meaning*, that is to look closely at the use of images in particular episodes and the overall text to communicate meaning. This holistic strategy enable bilingual children to engage deeply in making literary inferences at a personal level.

The stategy of 'imagination and image-forming' acts as an intercultural and integrative meaning-making tool for bilinguals, enabling them to 'behold the world simultaneously' (Bruner, 1986) at word, image, text, structure or style level. Underpinning this is the strategy of 'reading like a writer', which forms the main focus for the discussion below. The process culminates with children testing their new knowledge and finding ways of applying this creatively in their written texts. This is crucial as it helps them to internalize the strategy and skills for developing literary language. Many bilinguals in my research demonstrated anxiety about *how* to apply or transform their 'taught' knowledge to create personal literary text. Teachers' collaborative talk is significant in this development. Encouraging intercultural talk helps them to integrate cultural nuances when creating texts, thus relating literacy learning to life meanings (Cochran-Smith, 1984). 'Writing gives them the tools for thought and the means of developing their understanding' (Meek, 1991, p. 16) and it is through writing that they experience the power which comes from written words. We can say a literary form is a 'verbal object' which is to be interpreted as signifying something beyond the literal (Warnock, 1976, p. 197), something that bilinguals find difficult to access in English literary language. The process of developing literary language is discussed below.

Bilinguality, imagination and literature

Imagination is a complex concept as it means different things to different people. It is not a well-researched subject in education although it has been on the periphery of education for a long time.

Writing about imagination in education, Warnock (1976, pp. 206–7) suggests 'Imagination is that which ascribes meanings . . . This is the way we render the world familiar and therefore manageable.' In their everyday experience children use imagination to learn about life and the environment and relate it to their developing schema. In early years settings children's interactions with imaginary situations are an integral part of representing meaning and organizing experiences. A child's identity or 'I' is central to making meaning of life and the surrounding environment. All experiences are wrapped up with feelings and emotions, whether building the tallest tower possible and seeing it collapsing (in fact in most cases enacting the collapse), or going through a tunnel to negotiate fear or danger. 'Whatever else imagination may be it involves the simultaneous experience of thought and feeling, cognition and affect' (Meek, 1988, p. 44). To an imaginative child a bench can symbolize a boat or a horse and is accordingly supported with the necessary details in words and action to make personal journeys reliving past experience or imaginative possible worlds.

For young bilinguals the imagination acts as the *unifying force* in a linguistically and culturally unfamiliar world, and without imagination this world could appear quite chaotic or fearful to a young mind. Through play of many kinds in many contexts, the child understands and accommodates the unfamiliar world by 'constructing and composing' (Bruner, 1986) a personal world linking the past and the present in his or her schema. The availability of diverse cultural artifacts in early years settings makes play more meaningful for bilinguals.

'The art of listening to stories is a basic training for the imagination' (Frye, 1963, cited in Egan, 1992, p. 563). The story-teller's tone, intonation, gesture and facial expressions enable bilinguals to 'imagine' the story and make important connections with meanings in their head. Most importantly, through these stories and play, bilinguals develop a personal and emotional relationship with English which I believe is crucial to language learning. For example, we see three-year-old Nitya (see Chapter 2) trying to make sense of her new language in her imaginative monologue. We met Zubair in Chapters 4 and 6 weaving an imaginative story integrating meanings from all his story worlds, and in May Wei, Anwar and Raki we saw the power of images to signify meanings in the early years setting. In Chapter 5, we saw Nadia energetically pursuing her vision of becoming a fluent reader taking both her worlds with her. It would seem that the imagination acts as a driving and unifying force to render the world familiar and therefore manageable for bilinguals, and encourages further image-forming and meaning-making:

> The word imagination usually denotes not much more than the faculty of creating a picture of something in our heads and holding it there while we think about it. (Hughes, 1976, p. 38)

A strategy of imagination and image-forming allows bilinguals to 'hold the picture in their heads', to think deeply about possibilities of meanings and to listen carefully to verbal constructs and the significance of the image or metaphor in relation to meaning in an episode, characterization or text. We saw in the children's comments above how the use of imagination or 'the faculty of creating a picture' (ibid.) freed them to 'read beyond the literal' and internalize knowledge.

The *'imaginative emotion in which an idea when vividly conceived, excites us'* (John Stuart Mill, cited in Warnock, 1976, p. 206) was very evident in the bilinguals' learning. *'We didn't do any work, we just imagined'* commented Uzma, who worked diligently in class to achieve a good level in English, but found 'literary texts' difficult. Imagination and intellect are mutually supportive to one another (Bettelheim, 1976). Using imagination as a tool for learning was exciting for the children: they were all keen to write and to share their work with fellow writers.

Moreover, 'imagination and image-forming' as an interactive thinking tool has no language boundaries and seems to liberate bilinguals from the pernicious effects of 'second-language anxiety', and enables them to become deeply receptive to new learning. 'Visual thinking was [is] an alternative to verbal thinking' (Paivio, in Egan and Nadaner, 1988, p. 200). A strategy of 'imagination and imaging' energizes thinking and past images gradually begin to merge with the present, thus enriching understanding and encouraging formation of concepts underpinning English literary language. It was also evident that the process of imaging acted as a powerful tool to retain the complexity of structures in literary text in the children's memory and enabled them not to 'lose the plot' (teacher comment above).

However, we must note that the process is *holistic*; without a feeling of the whole the parts lose their significance, as was evident in bilinguals' anxiety about narrative structure above. The entire process of reading, talking, image-forming and rereading allows them to situate themselves imaginatively in the mood and mode of text to appreciate the significance of literary meanings. Rereading text and making written responses to test new knowledge enables them to make learning *personal*. Teaching and learning become mutual and collaborative and learning outcomes are high. It helps establish a strong relationship between their reading experiences and writing.

Children's creative responses to 'imagination and image-forming' as a strategy

In this section some significant episodes from my work with groups of ten- and eleven-year-old bilinguals in London schools are presented to highlight the use of 'imagination and image-forming' as a strategy to enable pupils to '*read beyond the literal*'. The group consisted mostly of 'below average' categorization in class.

Ten-year-old Abidur was literate in Bengali and had been in England for two years. He lived in Kuwait for several years before coming to England. He was highly motivated and imaginative although he made a few grammatical mistakes. Rabab, aged eleven, was also literate in Bengali and had lived in Kuwait before joining the school two years ago. She responded to tasks 'intelligently and imaginatively'. She was very keen to succeed and was in the process of catching up with the top group in her class. Her parents were keen readers of Bengali literature. Uzma was a ten-year-old Urdu-English bilingual. She was a fluent reader, and although she lacked a deep understanding to enjoy literature fully, she was very keen to succeed. She was learning Urdu and Arabic in her community school. Jaswinder was a ten-year-old English-Punjabi bilingual who needed support to raise his performance and develop self-confidence. His friendship with Abidur, also from the 'low ability' setting in class, and their support of one another, helped him pursue reading at a good level. I found Jaswinder to be very thoughtful and humorous, and Abidur, witty. Hanadi, also ten years of age, was an English-Arabic bilingual, and was the only learner at above average level. She was an excellent reader and virtually 'lived' in books and could talk incessantly about them. She was an immediate model for Uzma. The boys were impressed by her high standard, but I suspect a little envious of her performance. Hanadi was learning to read and write in Arabic. All the children came from similar socio-economic backgrounds.

Assessment of reading and literary talk

It was necessary to assess the children's reading to observe closely their interaction with text. Abidur's reading typified many in the group. He read the first four pages quite fluently, hesitating at some words, but with his good grasp of phonic skills he was able to read on. At 'word level' reading in the given extract, he hesitated when encountering the following words:

page 28: draught
page 29: bewildered, Llewelyn
page 30: reassuring, portruded
page 31: stove

At a semantic level, although he guessed the gist of the text with the help of a few cue words, his voice did not reflect the 'tune on the page' (Meek, 1982, p. 22). However, there were moments in his reading when Abidur could engage with the literary language of the book, and at such times his eyes lit up. This trait seems to be very common in bilinguals. These glimpses proved to me that Abidur had the potential or imagination to engage with literary language. Talking to Abidur I found out that he loved reading, but he was not sure that he was very good at it.

As a part of my teaching I assessed their skills in and understanding of literary language. It appeared that all the children were reading books appropriate to their level, but they were only able to talk very 'sketchily' about their reading. The lack of appropriate narrative or literary language was very evident, and I suspect the children knew that too.

Abidur's narrating skill in retelling the story of *Emlyn's Moon* was typical of many:

'There's this kid [Nia] who goes into this chapel and then they don't go. And that kid she didn't want to go [move house] and then the family moved house. And when they was [were] going the road was bumpy and that kid nearly flew up and she screamed.'

It would seem that Abidur had understood the gist of the story but was unable to sustain it in narrative speech. The anxiety of having an inadequate range of vocabulary and meaning structures was evident (see Chapters 4 and 5). Also, when prompted with helpful questions Abidur found it difficult to recall details and names of characters. Hanadi's was the only confident voice in the group to assert herself as a good reader, even better than her big brother, she told me!

Setting the context and strategy

I shared with the group my profound experience of listening to 'The Solitary Reaper' (see Chapter 1) and how the metaphor of the poem and its imagery had remained with me. I also shared my enjoyment of reading poems from different cultures, as well as my love for Tagore's poems. I had taken some poetry books to show to the group: Abdul Wahab Al-Bayati, Tagore, Wislawa Szymborska, Seamus Heaney and Paz. The children urged me to read a poem from one of the books. I read an extract from 'People on a Bridge' by Szymborska. Before reading I drew their attention to the cover picture from a painting *Squall at Ohashi* by Hiroshige on which the poem is based. I felt it was important for them to see some familiar images in the poem, 'You see a bridge over the water and people on the bridge' to communicate deep meaning, and to create an atmosphere for reading literature.

The children thought the poem *was* the painting and it was *'easy to write poems when you can see pictures'*. They were excited to talk about what might have happened next or what went on before the downpour. *'There are lots of things happening in the poem'*, *'I like how it said "lashing sharply from a dark cloud"'* said Rabab, and everyone nodded. They were very excited to have heard an adult poem. I wanted the bilingual children to understand that all languages in all cultures use metaphors, imagery, rhythm and other literary devices to make meaning (Datta, 1998). This seemed to have 'awakened' a deep interest in learning and relaxed them into negotiating metaphorical language in English, without the anxiety of having to learn a new concept in English. The children talked about their own experiences of poetry; Hanadi told us how her father read poems in Arabic, Rabab talked about her parents' recitation of Tagore, while Abidur said they had read 'The Lady of Shalott' (Tennyson) in class. Shaan commented that he had read funny poems like 'Quick, Let's Get Out of Here', but he had not read poems like this. Children's responses to poetry are presented later in the chapter. However, to draw their attention to the significance of metaphor I further read an excerpt from Antonio Skarmeta's *Burning Patient* (1988) to help elucidate this point poignantly. In one of many encounters with Neruda the poet, Mario the postman wants to know what makes poems:

> 'Metaphors . . .
> 'What's that?'. . .
> 'To be more or less imprecise, we could say that it is a way of describing something by comparing it to something else.'
> 'Give me an example' [Mario says].
> 'Well when you say the sky is weeping, what do you mean?'

'That's easy – that it's raining.'
'So you see that's a metaphor.'

Later on Mario wants the poet to tell him how to invent metaphors for the movement of the sea. Neruda continues:

'My name is sea, it repeats, striking a stone but not convincing it. Then with the seven green tongues, of seven green tigers, of seven green seas, it caresses it, kisses it, wets it, and pounds on its chest, repeating its own name.'

The images seemed to create an overwhelming sense of power of words in the children. Mario's response was that he felt dizzy, because

'I was like a boat tossing upon your words.'
'You've invented a metaphor!'
'But that was an accident' said Mario.

The children were amused by Mario's response.

Reading like a writer: teacher's guiding questions

There are many underlying factors that affect the success of the strategy:

Choosing literary text

I chose a range of classical poems with 'universal themes' and significant images to work with the group (Datta, 1999), following the children's disappointment with their inability to understand the cultural significance of meanings in the poem on spiders, as discussed above. Also, the book *Emlyn's Moon* was collectively chosen as an interesting fantasy story, written by the well-known writer, Jenny Nimmo. I thought the book provided a good context for raising literary language awareness for ten- to eleven-year-olds. I chose some significant episodes to raise children's awareness of literary language using 'imagination and image-forming' as tools for thinking in the application of the above strategy. This is followed by children's creative responses in their own stories and poems, using literary language.

The session began with the children talking about *Emlyn's Moon*, the author and their love for fantasy stories.

'How do you know it's a fantasy story?'
'From the blurb in the back,' said Abidur.
'It's scary . . . you know something's going to happen,' said Uzma.
'How can you tell from the first page that it's a fantasy story? Can you find some words, phrases or actions to suggest it's a fantasy story?'

The children scoured the page to find words, phrases or expressions that would reveal the particular genre:

'Don't go into Llewelyn's chapel – the opening line of the book', said Hanadi.
'But Nia disobeyed,' said Abidur. *'You know something's going to happen.'*
'The flower pot was lifted by unseen hands,' said Uzma.
'What about the title of the chapter "The Boy from the Chapel" – the author does not tell us his name, can you think why? And the expression "unnatural stillness", what does it mean?' I asked.

Talk was important to engage their minds and focus on language and style within the constraints of a genre.

'What makes good stories?' I asked.
'Lots of descriptive words . . . adjectives' was almost an unequivocal response.
'Is it just adjectives, what else makes writing interesting?' The children looked confused.
'Shall we find out?' I said.

Developing English literary language and intercultural learning

The process involved reading, talking, imagining, image-forming and rereading to develop literary language skills for reading and future writing potential. One important feature of this was to continuously reread text at every stage of discussion, the purpose was to enable children to 'tune into literary language' and memorize some significant lines from text. This is very important for second-language learning. My experience shows that bilinguals carry the images and the sounds of words in their heads and use these resources to create personal narrative or poems. Also at every stage the children were encouraged to imagine and think about how the identified literary feature influenced composition and communication of meaning, or the writer's intended meaning. They also talked about how different use of images and style of writing communicated meaning in different episodes in relation to the whole text. The children then wrote their own creative responses in narrative and poetic forms. It was important for the children to work collaboratively in a 'stress-free environment' (see Chapter 2) to learn deeply. The learning proceeded in stages.

The first reading was aimed at developing a feel for the narrative and style of writing. I read the first few pages of the first chapter with voice, pitch and tone to encourage active listening and to engage in meaning-making, '... task of recreating the meaning and intentions of the author behind the text' (Whitehead, 1990, p. 117).

The second reading consisted of collaborative talk on identified contexts to raise the children's awareness of significant aspects of literary language. The identified contexts for talk and interpretations were based on their observed needs as discussed above. The discussion primarily focused on the writer's intentions to create meaning at a variety of levels:

- Literary style and meaning.
- Significance of metaphorical language, imagery and other literary devices.
- Pace and pitch in style.
- The role of specificity in language.
- The relationship between literary text and genre, style, setting, episodes, plot, characterization, etc. The children were asked to follow the image of Nia's character as it unfolded in words in the first chapter. It was important for them to understand the relationship between words and images.

The third reading was to revisit the text and consolidate knowledge and to read in phrases with tone and intonation, followed by children's written responses.

> I began reading the opening paragraph of *Emlyn's Moon*:
>
> *'Don't go into Llewelyn's chapel!' they told Nia. 'No good will come of it. Something happened there!' But Nia disobeyed. If she hadn't, nothing would have changed. She'd still be plain Nia, dull Nia, Nia who couldn't do anything!*
>
> *'Is it just adjectives?'* I repeated.
> *'No'*, they all agreed very thoughtfully. *'It's also the way you say things . . .'*
> *'Why do you think the writer has repeated "plain Nia, dull Nia . . ."?'*
> *'Because it's more interesting than saying Nia wasn't very clever,'* said Uzma.
> *'It sort of rhymes as well . . . '* said Rabab.
> *'"But Nia disobeyed" tells you that something was going to happen, and you want to read on . . . it's the plot'* added Abidur.
> *'I think it also says that Nia wasn't plain, dull or who couldn't do anything . . . she was going to do something',* commented Hanadi.
> *'So what else makes it interesting?'* I repeated.
> *'How you say things . . . the way you say things makes it interesting',* said Hanadi. They all nodded in agreement.

Mood, mode and metaphor

The children were encouraged to listen and imagine how creating a story atmosphere contributes to meaning. We read on:

> It all began on the day they left Ty Llyr. The children, tucked between boxes in the back of the Landrover, were waiting for their mother to lock up. Nia was propped on a rolled mattress at the open end of the car. She was gazing at a red geranium in the kitchen window, the only bright thing left. And then the flower was lifted out of the dark window by unseen hands. It reappeared in the doorway, perched upon a pile of towels in her mother's arms. (p. 11)
>
> *'Do you find anything interesting here?'* I asked.
> Uzma thought the expression, *'the flower was lifted out of the dark window by unseen hands'* funny. *'It's scary as well like a ghost story!'*
> *'It's full of suspense'* said Hanadi.

Jaswinder, who had been quiet before, entered into the dialogue from a different angle – it was very personal. He found the children *'tucked between boxes'* very funny, and went on to add that when he went to India, he and his brother had to sit on his aunt's lap when they were driving home from Delhi airport. *'I didn't want to 'cos I was 9 . . . but I had to . . . the jeep was full with aunts, uncles, and us and boxes!'*

Before I read the following paragraph the children were asked to visualize the images in the passage and think about their significance in communicating meaning. I paused after reading *'a stray feather drifted in the sunlight'*, to see if the children were able to 'infer' the meaning from the metaphor and relate it to the text.

> Nia wished she had forgotten the flower; just for a day or two. At least there would
> have been something left alive in Ty Llyr. If a house could look forlorn, then that's how
> Ty Llyr seemed to her: curtains gone from the windows, the farmyard bare and tidy,
> and a stillness so unnatural it almost hurt. A stray feather drifted in the sunlight, the
> only reminder that chickens had once inhabited the yard. It was May but the ewes and
> their lambs had gone, and the only sounds came from bees in the giant sycamore tree.
> (pp. 11–12)

A lot of discussion followed around *'if a house could look forlorn'*. They looked in the dictionary to ensure the meaning of forlorn. *'It's a very lonely picture'*, said Abidur. *'It's a different way of saying everything was sad'*, said Uzma. A kind of word-play ensued. They looked at Roget's *Thesaurus* to find associated words, and the children were asked to consider whether changing the word 'forlorn' would take away the feeling from the image. We talked about how a sad (or happy) experience is *suggested* rather than expressed directly in words. The children talked about and imagined *'a stillness so unnatural'*, and thought about its significance in the episode or the genre. *'It feels scary!'* said Uzma. *'It can be very cold as well . . . there's no life left in the farm'*, added Hanadi. They also reflected on personal images and expressions they could use to communicate feelings in similar situations. The children found the process of imagining, image-forming and listening to the words that created the images very energizing; it inspired them to create more images, which were very personal.

> *'What kind of images did the writer use in this paragraph and why?'* I asked.
> The responses varied, but they were mostly personal. *'It's sad images . . . it's about leaving
> your best home . . . and it's very sad thoughts'*, said Uzma. *'It's very quiet images'*, said
> Rabab. Abidur talked about his sadness at leaving his home and friends in Kuwait: *'I still
> remember it.'* Hanadi talked about how lonely she would feel if she were to move: *'I'll
> probably feel like Nia.'*
> *'"A stray feather drifted in the sunlight", what does it mean?'*
> *'It tells you it was a farm'*, said Jaswinder.
> *'And so?'*
> *'There's nothing there now, it's all empty'*, said Rabab.

The children looked visibly moved, it was an emotional experience for them. The process of imagination seemed to work at two levels. *First*, it would seem they were able to infer the metaphorical significance in relation to the story as they deeply empathized with Nia's sadness, contrary to the situation in 'The Spinner' as noted above. This shows the importance of cultural significance in learning. *Second*, holding the images in their heads freed them from 'word anxiety' or abstract level thinking in English, and allowed them to think deeply about how language is used to create meanings in literature. In other words, it was a simultaneous experience of thought and feeling. They seemed to be able to 'read beyond the literal' with ease as the strategy allowed them to situate themselves confidently in the text. Jaswinder offered a personal interpretation of the metaphorical significance of a drifting stray feather, *'perhaps the chickens sent the feather to say goodbye!'* They were motivated to read the passage again and again to enjoy the meaning. As we read on I drew their attention to another extract to show the relationship between style and its significance in constructing meaning and how it relates to the whole text, or the genre:

> They walked on in silence until they reached the pink and gold railings of the chapel and all at once Nia began to feel afraid . . .
> It was too bright: the painted door, the coloured curtains; it was like the house of gingerbread that had tempted Hansel and Gretel. (p. 27)

The children talked about how an atmosphere of tension was created with words and how intertextuality created a meaning in a few words, and the significance of story metaphors to create deep meanings. We talked about how the story was unfolding with an underlying meaning structure.

Pace and pitch in style

Bilingual children need to read, rehearse and enact pace and pitch in writing to enable them to experience how the fluidity and pace of written language can communicate meaning. Native English speakers acquire this with little effort, but bilinguals need to tune into the style and pace of words through reading, rereading and rehearsing as well as creating their own.

> Alun leant over his sister, accidentally knocking the sheep dog's nose with his elbow. Fly yelped, the Landrover lurched round a bend and Alun was flung backwards on top of his twin brothers. Sion and Gareth were too happy to grumble.
> Gwyn Griffiths disappeared from sight.
> The Landrover rattled on, down the mountain gathering speed as the lane became steeper, and the chatter in the back increased to a hysterical crescendo of excitement; Catrin even broke into song. (p. 12)

I read the above passage with pace and pitching my voice high and low, accenting the verbs that accentuated speed. I asked the children to take turns in reading the passage fluently with pitch and tone; they were very keen to talk about how it felt to read fast. They were encouraged to use the

Thesaurus to find associated words. They also talked about their experiences in car or jeep journeys, for example, in Jaswinder's case in India. Following this I asked them to identify words that signified the car journey, to listen to the sounds of words and talk about why these words were used. Abidur said, *'the sounds of the words – lurched, rattled, yelped, hysterical – are very harsh!'* Hanadi, who seemed very emotionally involved with Nia's feelings at leaving Ty Llyr, added, *'The words tell you it wasn't a happy journey . . . 'Cos they were leaving Ty Llyr'*. They enjoyed the expression, *'a hysterical crescendo of excitement'*. They discussed what 'crescendo' could mean. They also looked in the dictionary for its precise meaning. Uzma thought the children *'laughed like hyenas, 'cos hyenas laugh hysterically'*. The pace in style was further strengthened by another passage in the chapter:

> Nia [was] jerked backwards, her heel caught in the hem of the violet dress and she tumbled to the floor, followed by a pile of cans. Suddenly the whole top shelf became possessed. Cans and bottles tottered and clinked and began to roll towards her. There was nothing Nia could do to stop that dreadful and inexorable shower of cans. (p. 24)

The children thought the description was hilarious. There was a lot of talk about how things like that happened to them. The shelf being *possessed* was a culturally difficult expression for them; however, talking about ghosts and haunted houses clarified the meaning. They read and reread the section to enjoy the language and the image of Nia collapsing in the middle of it.

The role of specificity in language

I talked about the importance of specificity in writing and how it carries the writer's voice. The use of specific detail is a gap I have noticed in many bilinguals' writing; this indicates their insecurity with 'what to say' and makes 'how to say' difficult. Their writing mostly lacks the vividness or the enthusiasm of a voice: *'their ideas are good . . . but they can't develop them'* (teacher comment above). I underlined elements of specificity in the following passage in order for them to reflect on how to claim 'ownership' of writing with a distinct voice or bring the text alive.

> Sunshine flooded the High Street. The trees were in blossom and Saturday shoppers in bright spring clothes bustled in and out of the narrow grey tiled houses . . .
>   The Lloyds parked outside a tall black and white building at the furthest end of the town. There was a huge blue van in front of them, with removal men in grey overalls munching sandwiches in the cabin . . .
>   There were two entrances: one that led into a shop furbished with red carcasses and neat trays of sliced meat: the other, a very private-looking black door with a brass number 6 on it. (p. 16)
> *'It's like real pictures on the TV, you can see everything'*, said Uzma.
> *'You can see the pictures in your head'*, added Hanadi.

The imagination makes *thought more personal* [my emphasis] and gives the individual a more authentic kind of participation. (Nadener, 1988, p. 206)

[Imagination helps] form further images . . . related to the image we first thought of in relation to the word which we are using or seeking to understand. (Warnock, 1976, p. 18)

The children's images were personal and wrapped up in personal voices, and the strategy encouraged them to cross linguistic and cultural boundaries, and take risks with their second language. This was evident in the children's written responses. Their learning experience was very deep, and drafting, composing, reading, rereading and sharing outcomes with peers formed an important aspect of their learning.

Assessment of the process

Self-evaluation and peer assessment was central to children's personal development. Uzma commented on how the process helped her:

'We have been trying to imagine how things happened [how language was used], we were not doing any work, we were just imagining.'
Jaswinder added, *'You kept on reading and my mind just carried on imagining the pictures in my mind. I tried to think of words which would describe the pictures.'*
Abidur said, *'I concentrated hard in my head and followed the words and created pictures and I got some interesting words that go with the pictures.'*

Abidur's comment *'I got some interesting words that go with the pictures'* is significant, and we see examples of this in his writing. As discussed above, a divided world of home and school learning creates a feeling of anguish and confusion in the bilingual mind. A strategy of 'imagination and image-forming' breaks up that division, energizing bilinguals' thinking to integrate both their worlds and learning outcomes are high.

A very close reading of literary text is crucial for bilinguals to relate to a deeper significance of meaning. Following the reading of the first chapter of *Emlyn's Moon* the children were asked to identify similar passages in the next chapter. They were encouraged to read in pairs to enable talk around personal interpretations of meaning. This I consider is the best pathway to becoming independent readers. Writing their personal responses helped internalize literary language, skills and creativity.

Children's creative responses

It was interesting to note that with their deep experience of literary language and literature the children looked for a quiet place to create their *personal responses*. An enabling environment is 'safe, structured, private, unobtrusive and literate' (Emig, 1981, p. 25). This is evident in their responses. As can be seen, the children responded in a variety of ways and styles but their personal voice is very clear.

> If imagination is creative in all its uses, then children will be creating their own meanings and interpretations of things as much by looking at them as by making them. (Warnock, 1976, p. 207)

Their responses clearly demonstrate that bilingual children had the *ability* to *'use their reading experiences in writing'* (see teachers' comments above), provided the teaching instructions and the learning process are appropriate to address their strengths and needs and relate to their intercultural identities. *'Why don't they write in normal language?'* no longer seemed to apply. The strategy of 'imagination and image-forming' provided a stress-free, enjoyable and strong meaning-making facilitator that incorporated children's bilinguality to respond to literature.

The title 'Leaving Home' was collectively chosen by the children as their first 'best topic' following their reading of Nia's experience above. We see many interpretations of leaving home from their personal experiences. Only Hanadi (high-achiever) kept close to Nia's leaving home. The children's samples presented were the beginnings of their stories; they had intended to write in chapters. We see below Jaswinder's personal choice of responding to the literary style in the opening paragraph of the book: '. . . *plain Nia, dull Nia, Nia!'* He was moved by the style, that *'simple words'* could produce such *'fantastic'* style.

Given below are samples of children's writing. Peer and teacher assessments were carried out collaboratively in children's learning, and proved to be significant in their learning. This included revisiting and evaluating learning, and listening actively to others' views. The children were deeply affected by peer assessment.

'A Poem' by Jaswinder

Plain Imrul, poor Imrul, still a baby Imrul
Plain Nimesh still the same Nimesh
Small silent Suresh as small as a seven-year-old

I was as small as a grape when I was small
Now I am as tall as a giraffe reaching for a leaf to eat
My brother is as tall as a skyscraper
Reaching for the sky.

'Leaving Home' by Jaswinder (first draft)

I was seeing good memories going through my head. I was born in this house and grew up with my brother here. We played lots of games. We had lots of fights, lots of laughs. Suddenly my mum called out, 'Come on hurry up we've got to go to the airport now'.
I got in the car feeling sad. I had a dream about what Toronto would be like. It was a big city with lots and lots of tall buildings. I was leaving England.

Jaswinder demonstrates a capacity to play with sounds and images and style to communicate meaning. The children enjoyed his sense of humour expressed in the poem. The process of imagination and image-making seemed to have liberated his thinking and he demonstrated his potential as a writer with a distinct voice. We will recall he was very insecure at the beginning of the study.

'Leaving Home' by Abidur (first draft)

I left the house that I used to live in. The house was empty, just standing there. The house was full of the spider web especially the attic, which was very dark. There were no more beautiful colours in the house, no flowers that were planted there. There was no black smoke that flew across the sky coming out of the chimney pots.

The car engine started with a louder grumble than ever, and we started off. The road was bumpy and my head was jumping up and down with the car. I nearly fell out of my seat and screamed like a cat being attacked. My brothers and sisters in the back seat were singing hysterically because they were scared. My dad was driving as normal and my mum was afraid, as normal.

We arrived in Wales, the streets were full of people wearing summer clothes.

Abidur's first draft is presented to show how his account resonates with sounds in the text and for Uzma's analysis of his plot. We can see personal images of leaving home and a dramatic use of language demonstrating future possibilities of his development as a writer. Uzma identified a flaw in the structure of his text: '*Abidur had already brought us outside the house, and he can't take us back in to describe the attic*', she said. Jaswinder noted that he '*doesn't say anything about going to the car*'. I believe this was the direct outcome of belonging to an intercultural community of writers and the process of imagination and image-forming that proved to be an empowering anchor for coherence at many levels. The children were very impressed by Abidur's metaphor for a deserted house and how he suggested a feeling of nothingness. This *upset* is carried into the second paragraph in an inferential style of writing, 'suggesting' upset rather than describing it. They were delighted at his sense of humour. There are many voice features in Abidur's writing. My contribution to the discussion was to add the expression *as normal* at the end to add to his humourous style. He told me with a glint in his eye that this was really the case!

Alex Furginson, a character (first draft)

Abidur begins again with a few dramatic lines that set the tone of his writing: '*His name was Alex Furginson. Alex was a loner. He didn't have any friends, not true friends anyway.*' 'Authors know that, to catch a reader, they must switch them into a compelling discourse straight away' (Meek, 1982, p. 55). However, the development of his character seemed to 'jump about' from school to his home life and back to school again with no linking meanings or sentences. Abidur had also mixed his tenses in the process. He became aware of this as we talked about it, and was asked to read back continuously for grammatical and structural cohesiveness. He was also asked to 'stay with his images' a little longer to allow his readers to enjoy his writing, and to use the *Thesaurus* to look at possibilities of using synonyms for common vocabulary.

> **'Alex' (second draft)**
>
> His name was Alex Furginson. Alex was a loner. He didn't have any friends, not true friends anyway. Every morning when he got ready for school he didn't comb his hair or brush his teeth. He wore cool baggy clothes that were too long for him. He looked lazy in them. His boots were as long as a giraffe's neck. He wore a leather jacket that stank like he never had a bath for weeks and weeks. Alex wore CK shades even when it wasn't sunny. He liked telling jokes. His jokes were so funny that you will laugh for a minute or two. When he walked to school he swung his shoulders from side to side thinking he was special.
>
> At home time he didn't act cool unless it was sunny. Instead he walked in a normal sort of way. His mum and dad bought him good presents like a robot which can light up. When he went out with them he acted normal and walked normal.

We can hear the distinctive voice of a young writer. Abidur was a very observant and thoughtful boy by nature and had a quirky sense of humour. He used images effectively to create tension in his character – Alex leads a dual life, which opens up possibilities for further development. The children were very impressed with his character. Uzma said, '*It's like someone on TV!*'

'The Pink Girl' by Uzma

Uzma's *first draft* showed her potential as a writer. There were many 'sparks' in her writing. Her first few lines grab the reader's attention and she also used an interesting style to write about her character. Her character resonates with Nia's characteristics, but she developed it with excellent creativity.

> Nia had found a violet dress, patterned with pink and white flowers . . . and a pair of pink shoes with stars on them. (*Emlyn's Moon*, p. 20)

Like Abidur, Uzma seemed to be rushing with her ideas. Many features of her character or plot were not developed. She was advised to visualize the situation, characters and plot and to use specificity in her descriptions as discussed above (for example, *pink-ness, clever-clogs-ness*) to present a vivid picture that is fun to read.

> **Second draft of 'The Pink Girl'**
> Her response shows a carefully 'crafted' story.

Last Saturday a new girl moved into my street. A new girl who is roughly my age. She always wears pretty shoes and pretty pink dresses – pink with yellow flowers, pink with black polka dots, pink with blue stripes, pink with green checks. Dark pink, light pink, medium pink. She ALWAYS wears pink. She also knows how to tap dance. The people on our street call her 'clever clogs'. She's the only girl on the street who knows her tables up to twenty-seven.

Her father is a full time worker in a shoe shop called 'Impressive Shoes'. Her mother is a housewife who dusts and cleans and cooks massive meals for her family every day.

One afternoon the extraordinary 'pink girl' was surrounded by people on my street.

'I can say my 26 times table' she said and rattled off her 26 times table without breathing.

Sharif came up and said 'What is four-hundred-thousand and fifty plus six-thousand and three?'

The pink girl snapped '406,053' as quick as lightning.

Everyone gasped. Mrs Rockbottom who was standing outside the crowd of people pushed her way in and said 'My dear you are the cleverest girl I have ever seen on this street'. She gave her a big grin very proudly.

In school the next day I was shocked to find her in my class. Whenever Miss Locket asked questions like 545 + 756 her hand shoots up like a full speed rocket. No-one gets a chance to answer. Miss Locket always chooses her. I found out her name when she answered the register. Her name is Sarah James.

Uzma used her imagination and thought profoundly to fill in the 'gaps' left in her first draft. She is a dramatic writer with a great sense of humour and has a fluid style. The children found her character interesting and funny, commenting on the image of the pink girl's '*hand shooting up like a full speed rocket*' and Mrs Rockbottom's '*pushy*' nature. Uzma's writing clearly shows that she is *able to transfer* reading experiences to writing. When asked how she wanted to develop her story, she said promptly, '*It's going to be a funny story and we become friends in the end.*'

'Leaving Home' by Rabab (third draft)

Rabab was immersed in composing her story. She went through three drafts to refine her story, this was her own choice. The second and third drafts were word processed on the computer at home. Rabab said very little during discussion about her story but seemed to be deeply immersed in her thoughts throughout. A collaborative learning environment allows learners to negotiate their own style of learning. Children learn in different ways, and intelligent listening is a rich resource for imagination and meaning-making. In Rabab's story we see a skilful blending of stories from different sources, the melodrama of Bollywood films which she loved watching, indication of her classroom learning about the poor orphan children in Victorian times, as well as self-identity, i.e. situating her identity in the face of adversity. In a supportive environment she felt free to create her story from her experiences of different cultural worlds. This was evident in her story. She took away from the discussion literary skills and devices to tell her own story of 'Leaving Home'.

It was Saturday afternoon. The sky was filled with clouds, sooty clouds. This meant a heavy shower. That means soaked for me, I have no umbrellas. Soaked to the skin.

It was mid-December. The streets were full of crowds – crowds with many faces of all colours, shapes and sizes. Talking, chatting, laughing, shouting, babies crying and children squealing for toys they were longing to have. The shopkeepers had satisfied looks on their faces and said 'Merry Christmas' to every customer. Everyone was buying gifts for their dear and near ones. Some were trying to catch the last Christmas mail for different destinations.

I wish I had someone loving and caring in this world, abroad or local it didn't matter at least somebody to communicate with. I didn't have anybody in the world from whom I could receive or give presents to, except for that mean, old Uncle Tim and his forever-confused wife.

It was last Friday. Uncle and Auntie Tim were leaving to shop in the mall but before that they gave me a whole lot of work that I had to do.

'Clean the mess in my room, scrub the bathroom and make the beds. And don't forget to change the water and food in the pigsty. And also remember to post the letter for me, will you?' he asked in his brutal way.

'Yes I will', I said, the only thing I could say and was expected from me.

'And I want it done within an hour and a half, do you understand Miss Ann?' he said in a sarcastic voice.

'Yes I do', I said softly.

'Good. And don't take too long if you don't want burnt supper', he shouted and left. As soon as they left I started to work.

'The mess is cleaned, the pig-sty refreshed and the beds are made' I thought, 'only the scrubbing and the posting are left'. While cleaning I made sure there was nothing left for that mean uncle to scowl at. Then, as a lightning flash, something struck into my head. 'Did I scrub the lime-scale around the taps?' I hurried to check in the bathroom.

Then it happened. I tore off my apron, washed my rough hands and ran to my tiny, little room. I got my bag out and stuffed some of my clothes in it as quick as lightning. 'Is everything in there? My brush, clothes and oh my shoes.' Then I wore my trainers and ran out of the house as fast as my legs could carry me, looking back every minute to make sure no one's after me. Only five minutes for them to get back. I ran out like a horse running a Derby race. The faces of the people swept passed me like wind. It was becoming very difficult to cope with my breath. Then I came to a deserted station. I stopped there to catch my breath. There were cobwebs in most places and dust on everything. I then saw a glimpse of something moving. A pigeon! It flew and landed on something. It was a notice board! I could hardly read it. I dusted it with my fingers. It read 'North Lowdon Station closed', I panicked. My hope for escape melted into fear, because I'd always heard Uncle Tim say 'oh no, the car isn't working and the nearest station is about five miles away.'

Five miles! Now I had no other choice but to run five miles to the station if I wanted to be free.

Rabab's self-evaluation was significant in that she identified content and stylistic gaps in her story as she was reading it to me. She realized that she needed more vivid images and the pace of writing needed to match the climax of her story. Talking to peers and a knowledgeable adult, along an energizing strategy, helped her to internalize knowledge.

We can see that Rabab writes in a fluent narrative language. She had been in England for only two years and prior to her arrival her English language experience came mostly from books. The children were visibly moved by her story. Rabab was also advised to stay with her story metaphor and develop it, using images and an appropriate style. I gave her the expression 'then it happened' (at the start of the penultimate paragraph), and that seemed to set the tone and pace of her style in her final draft. Her story carries the tone of Bollywood film texts in her characterization and melodrama, and it would seem that she situated herself in the story. Rabab was a polite and thoughtful young girl but had an air of affirmation about her. Despite locating herself in the story she gave her characters English names and called herself 'Miss Ann'. When asked about this she only smiled. Perhaps not finding many non-Christian names in her books had created this block.

Leaving Home by Hanadi (first draft)

> I looked around the old house I used to share with my two sisters. It looked dank and dismal, no smiling faces, no toys or books strewn across the floor, it was just empty and dusty. I strolled around each of the rooms and the more I looked at the bare walls, bare floor and bare ceiling, the more I couldn't believe I was actually leaving the house I was brought up in. The house which to me was home. It was all I had. My life didn't stretch out further than the world outside my home.
>
> I walked outside and stared at the beautiful farmland for a while, I sat under the shade of the old oak tree, closed my eyes and started imagining how life was, when we had no intention of moving. I stood outside and took one last look at the house. Somehow I couldn't quite grasp the fact that we were moving. I mean moving was a foreign thing to me, I just couldn't take it all in. I stepped into the old rusty jeep and it took off.
>
> The ride was bumpy and at the end I felt very sick. The scenery was beautiful. We drove past daisies, marigolds, roses, geraniums and lobelias. We drove past many beautiful trees, silver birches, evergreens and magnolia and conifers. My mind was occupied with the thoughts of my old home and how I missed it. I was trying strongly to imagine how my new home would be like. I found myself standing outside the new house and saying, 'this will never replace my old home'.

The children were very impressed by Hanadi's style and images suggesting 'emptiness'. They were moved by her image of sitting under the oak tree as a lone figure. Others thought she had a good knowledge of the names of flowers and trees. We can see in Hanadi's writing that her style carries her voice well. She writes intimately about her feelings, using some poignant images. She was asked to take her readers along as she developed her story.

Reading like a writer is a strong strategy, however it needs to be situated in children's personal or cultural experiences to relate to text meaning as well as how the bilingual child's mind works. Cognitive understanding must be developed at a personal level. Therefore, experimenting with construction of literary texts by situating themselves imaginatively in a variety of situations encourages appropriate use of language, images and meaning structures and helps *internalize* learning. This is supported by the teacher's knowledge and understanding at many levels, as discussed above.

Poetry and writing development

In this section we will look at how poetry as models can be used to develop literary language awareness. Poetry helps people to connect with their inner feelings, 'telling them things they didn't know (or had forgotten they knew), and making them feel things they didn't know they felt (or had forgotten to feel)' (Motion, 1999). We are moved by the significance which poetry brings to our lives and we make deep personal meanings (see Chapter 1). However, as educators of young children in a culturally diverse society we must be sensitive to experiences of children coming from different cultural backgrounds (Datta, 1999). Reading resources and cultural significance in meaning-making are of significant importance. I believe locating children's wider experiences of life and the environment – for example, the selection of universal themes in poetry for experimenting with creative self-expression – help them to engage deeply with literary language experience. We will recall the children's experience and talk about reading poetry presented earlier in this chapter.

Here we include some significant episodes from groups of ten- and eleven-year-old bilinguals on appreciating and experimenting with writing personal responses to poems. Sitara was a ten-year-old Gujarati-English bilingual, her twin sister was Zakiya. Both loved reading. Shaan was an eleven-year-old English-Gujarati bilingual, who loved maths and writing detective stories. He was a high-flyer in his teachers' eyes. His mother was a parent governor in the school and had high expectations of him. Dawood was a ten-year-old Arabic-English bilingual who had been in Britain for two years. Vipul was an eleven-year-old Gujarati-English bilingual who had very low self-esteem. His grammatical structures in written English were insecure. He enjoyed watching Bombay films. I found him thoughtful and keen to learn. The other children from the *Emlyn's Moon* group were in this group as well. All the children regularly bought books from the school 'book fair'.

Shared poetry reading

The children engaged in close reading of John Masefield's poem 'Sea Fever' with a process of identified talking points. Reading, talking, rereading, imagining and image-forming and thinking constituted a substantial aspect of this process. Selected extracts from English literature (my own favourites as a student) were read with the knowledge that the familiar images and the rhythm of the poems will create rhythmic thinking in the children (as we saw in other chapters) in making personal responses. We read extracts from Coleridge's 'The Rime of the Ancient Mariner' and Arnold's 'Dover Beach', to give the children a flavour of different images of the sea and different styles of writing. They also read extracts from Wordsworth's 'Morning After a Storm' and Shelley's 'Away, Away'. The poems were chosen for their universal appeal. The children talked about their sea and storm experiences, consciously activating past experiences to connect with current learning. Looking at some difficult words which were considered to hinder their enjoyment of the poem followed this. For example, in John Masefield's poem, such words as *yarn, rover, vagrant, whetted knife* were discussed. From their experience of reading *Emlyn's Moon* the children were prepared to look at the use of imagery in poems and their thematic significance in meaning-making.

The overall process of learning was similar to reading *Emlyn's Moon*.

The first reading allowed the children to tune into the rhythm and metaphor of the poem. The children talked about some images and offered their own interpretation in relation to the poem.

The second reading was deep, and entailed talking about identified contexts planned around their needs. I read Masefield's 'Sea Fever' one verse at a time, encouraging the children to imagine and visualize the significance of poetic images and how they relate to the poet's 'sea fever'. We looked at particular images, for example, *'a grey mist on the sea's face, and a grey dawn breaking'* and the children were invited to offer personal interpretations, to think about the images in their heads. The children seemed to be moved by the image. Some used 'mist' images in their poems as well.

'"To the gull's way and the whale's way where the wind's like a whetted knife"' Why did Masefield choose to use these images?' I asked. Children's responses were free and personal and they were keen to form further images. There was much talk around imagery as a literary device. As before, the process was accompanied by continuous reading and rereading of verses to enable the children to actively listen to the poetic language and rhythm. Jaswinder said, *'you kept on reading and I kept on feeling the rhythm in my head'*. The children talked about how the images were in tune with the mood and tenor of the poems. They talked about the significance of refrain and how it contributes to meaning and rhythmic structure. The children were encouraged to read the verses with tone, intonation and rhythm, and in some cases to *practise* reading them. I believe much of the meaning is lost

if bilingual children do not hear the language and the rhythm in their inner ear and in their voice. Poetry in all cultures is meant to be heard.

The third reading was essential for children to enjoy the whole poem and to see how linguistic and structural devices were used to convey meaning. This reading was usually started by me and was given over to the children to take turns in reading out to the group. Reading, rehearsing and revisiting poems help bilinguals to see how meaning is communicated in literature. Identified extracts from other poems were read to strengthen understanding and develop an awareness of different ways of looking at the same object – different voice, different imagery, different rhythm and different atmosphere – to give them a feeling of freedom and choice in their own creative self-expressions. The children were encouraged to memorize significant verses from the poems. Memorization is an important literary skill, along with literacy techniques and interpretations of meanings at different levels (Spiro, cited in Zyngier, 1994, p. 105).

Writing is a cognitive process and an integral part of learning. For children, the most difficult aspect of writing poems seems to be the structure. The strategy of using the first line or first two lines of poems proved effective in developing bilinguals' composition skills. It set the mood and rhythm of the poem and gave them the freedom as well as structural constraints to articulate their thoughts, feelings and ideas.

Once again shared reading of own compositions and peer responses proved to be invaluable in their learning development. Being listened to and praised by peers played a key role in this development.

Some *significant extracts* from the selected poems are given below which enabled talk around images and encouraged thinking at personal level.

From 'Sea Fever' by John Masefield

I must go down to the seas again, to the lonely sea and the sky,
To the gull's way and the whale's way . . .

From 'Dover Beach' by Matthew Arnold

The sea is calm to-night.
The tide is full, the moon lies fair
Upon the straits; – on the French coast the light
Gleams and is gone; the cliffs of England stand,
Glimmering and vast, out in the tranquil bay.

From 'The Rime of the Ancient Mariner' by Samuel Taylor Coleridge

Day after day, day after day,
We stuck, nor breath nor motion;
As idle as a painted ship
Upon a painted ocean.

Water, water, everywhere,
Nor any drop to drink.

***'Morning After a Storm'* by William Wordsworth. *From* Resolution and Independence**

There was a roaring in the wind all night;
The rain came heavily and fell in floods.

***'Away, Away'* by Percy Bysshe Shelley. *From* The Invitation**

Away, away from men and towns,
To the wild wood and the downs.

Children's personal responses

The children's responses were very personal, very profound. 'Children cannot be taught to feel deeply; but they can be taught to look and listen in such a way that the imaginative emotion flows' (Warnock, 1976, p. 206). This was true of the bilinguals in my study. Imagination and image-forming had an invigorating effect on their learning process. Here are some of the responses to Masefield's 'Sea Fever'.

Uzma created a romantic image of the sea mermaids in her favourite colour:

'The Mermaids' by Uzma

I want to go down to the seas again
To the lonely seas and the sky
To the Dolphins dancing merrily
With the sounds of the sea

I want to go down to the mermaids in the sea
In scales of shiny green,
To be like one of them
Shining in pure green.

I want to hear the mermaids singing
A sweet serenade to me
To hear the wind whistling
And blowing back my hair.

'Going to the Sea' by Abidur

I want to go to the seas again
Riding on the waves
To see the thunder breaking the sea apart
To see my mother resting
Under the deep deep sea

I want to go to the seas again
To hear the whales' song
To see the whales rising up in the air
And falling down crashing back into the sea

I want to go to the seas again
In the ship sailing away from England.
To go to the distant land
To be with the sea.

Jaswinder used images from Hindu mythology to write his very personal poem:

'Solid Air' by Jaswinder

I want to go down to the seas again
To the lonely seas and the sky
To the mermaids' land
Which lead to solid air in heaven
Where they amuse themselves
Watching the ships go by
On the shiny seas
Reflecting like a mirror.

'What's solid air?' I asked. *'Thick mist'* he answered. This reminded me of Indian films where the heaven is depicted as full of thick mist.

Hanadi created a very personal poem blending ideas from the poems she read:

'The Sea and I' by Hanadi

I want to go down to the seas again
To the lonely seas and the sky
To the sounds of the seagulls crying
Flying in the distant sky
To hear the dolphins' song
Echo through the sky
To be at one with the sea
Just it and I

I want to go down to the seas again
To the lonely seas and the sky
To be showered by the flinging foam
Tossing low and high
To stand upon the cliff's peak
To feel the mist upon my cheek
To feel the soft breeze through my hair
Just standing there
It and I.

Hanadi's powerful image of standing on the 'cliff's peak' came from Arnold's 'Dover Beach' which she blended beautifully with Masefield's 'mist' to locate herself strongly within the poem. This could have led to the use of 'It and I', showing potential to use language at an abstract level. In composing her poem Hanadi paced up and down the library floor, struggling with what she wanted to say and how she wanted to say it.

Sitara's response to 'Away, Away' is very personal; she vividly expresses her fear of the sea and told me she enjoyed creating the fearful images of the sea.

'Take Me Away' by Sitara

Take me away for a day
From the sea
Why I will say
The cries of the seagulls as loud as traffic
The gushing of the foam from high distant seas
The waves crashing on the rocks of scary ghosts

The black cold night as cold as winter frost
The cries that echo through the mountains
The serpent's eyes as fierce as the night

That's what I want to run away from
Just for a day
I will return to my wilderness
I will come back again.

'Rain Rain Everywhere': Vipul and personal learning

Vipul's development within the group was very interesting. As noted above he had a very low self-esteem and was considered to perform below average in the class. Vipul was present with the group from the beginning, he was silent throughout. He seemed to be on the periphery of the group, learning silently by looking and listening. Although 'silent', I observed him listening *actively* to make sense of literary language in various group talks. He was surrounded by very rich contextualized talk and children's creative responses, which were read out to the group, and perhaps was silently making connections with his personal images. Significantly, he declined to share his first attempt at writing a poem, saying plainly, *'I don't have any hidden meanings [the phrase used for metaphor by the group] in my poem!'* This was a first major step in Vipul's learning development, i.e. an awareness of metaphorical use of language. The collaborative process provided rich listening input and understanding, which was important for him and strengthened his motivation to learn and to take risks with self-confidence and self-expression in his poem. The rhythmic and repetitive structure of Coleridge's *'water, water, everywhere . . .'* seemed to trigger rhythmic thinking and a way with words – it enabled him to imagine and create images based on his own personal experiences.

Drip drip drip drip
All night
Rain rain rain
All day
No sun to be seen
Then lightning struck
Like a tiger stripe
Going down down
On the tree
On the ground

> Drip drip drip
> Pitter patter pitter patter
> On my car
> On my door
> On my window
> Pitter patter everywhere
> Will it ever stop?

Vipul was energized to use all his available resources, rhythm, images and a simple stock of words to write his poem, which was much appreciated by the group.

'Last Monday's Storm' by Dawood

Dawood took Wordsworth's title and Coleridge's images to create his own poem. We may recall Dawood's comment on the use of literary language: *'Why can't they write in normal language?'* He did not seem to have any problem with metaphors, with imagination as a tool for learning he understood how language can be manipulated in literary texts.

> Rain rain rain day and night
> Thunder roaring
> Lightning zigzagging
> Like a shining knife

> Rain rain rain day and night
> I stayed in bed
> Feeling safe and warm
> Looking at the rain
> Dripping on my window pane
> Dark clouds covering the sun
> Water drops covering the earth
> Drip drop drip drop
> Like a slow beat of the drum.

'Morning After a Storm' by Shaan

Shaan enjoyed writing this poem. After reading Wordsworth's poem he talked about a tornado he had seen on television. His poem 'Morning After a Storm' was influenced by the images he had seen. The concluding stanza was his imaginative response to personal crises. '[Imagination] is a faculty that embraces both [the inner and the outer] worlds simultaneously' (Hughes, 1976, p. 77). He was delighted and visibly moved: *'I've not written poems like this before.'*

> There was a roaring in the wind last night
> Lightning decorated the sky with flashing stripes
> Thunder roared and boomed like bombs exploding
> And from the sky came a spinning demon
> That sucked up everything in its way

In the morning
As the sun pierced through the darkness
The damage was clear
Homes ripped apart like houses made of cards
Trees uprooted and lying across roads

People came out
Of whatever was left of their homes
With sad faces and tears in their eyes
Ready for another day.

Conclusion

The evidence from children's work suggests that the strategy of 'imagination and image-forming' and the process of intercultural and collaborative learning liberated them from second-language anxiety: 'feeling energises the cognitive process' (Meek, 1988, p. 43). Imagination is 'dialogic' in nature. Repeated reading, collaborative talk and imagining enabled the bilinguals to 'hold pictures in their heads' and think deeply about how language is used in literature. Continuous listening to literary text is an important aspect of this process. As Egan (1992, p. 41) points out, 'once imagined it [imagination] seems to serve as an identifier, evoker and retriever of a range of images'.

The 'image forming aspect of the imagination' (Warnock, 1976, p. 203) allowed the children to form further images. These images were very personal and wrapped up in personal voices.

Working with the children, it became clear that images and meanings from both their learning worlds are an integral aspect of bilinguals' meaning-making process. The children seemed to take away significant phrases, images, metaphors and different sounds of words from poems and prose and blend them into personal constructs: 'if imagination is creative in all its uses, then children will be creating their own meanings and interpretations of things' (Warnock, 1976, p. 207). This helped them to develop 'knowledge of the language itself' (Cummins, 1996, p. 58).

Sharing understanding of text with peers as well as making written responses proved to be of significant importance in a multi-ability setting. They needed to test/play with their new knowledge to internalize it. Everyone's learning experience was significant and personal. Listening to different meanings, different perspectives, different sounds, broadened their horizon of thinking and making-meaning in English literary language.

All the children went through two or three drafts to give a final shape and voice to their poems and stories. Making them aware of producing the desired effect on their readers or audience helped them to concentrate on developing their meaning and style of writing. The adult role was supportive, collaborative, knowledgeable, giving specific instructions to guide individuals to develop learning in the 'zone of proximal development' (Vygotsky, 1962/1986). For a strategy to be effective it must relate deeply to learners' available learning resources as well as have an awareness of their specific needs. This is crucial teacher knowledge. The power of imagination creates this relationship and creative dialogues in bilinguals' heads, as the evidence from children's talk suggests.

The strategy and the process of learning enabled the bilinguals to develop a deep relationship with literature and a desire to read more. They were all visibly moved by the experience. Abidur and Jaswinder selected a new text, *The Other Side of Silence*, by Margaret Mahy, to show to the group in the following session. Jaswinder said *'this is going to be good'* and read the blurb on the back cover: *'the line between fantasy and reality becomes very blurred.'*

We may further evaluate children's learning in both the chapters on writing and development and conclude that developing a sense of 'intercultural community of learners' created fluid peer learning and talk. Using imagination as an interactive tool for thinking allowed them to evaluate and *synthesize* meanings freely from all their cultural and learning worlds and apply them creatively to their advantage, creating 'unique blends' (Grosjean, 1982). In an intercultural learning community bilinguals feel free to *borrow* and blend different cultural ways of thinking: *'To be at one with the sea/Just it and I'*; or ways with words, for example, *'seeing good memories in my head'*; or cultural [artifacts] ways of thinking or expressing an experience, *'it makes me feel calm and beautiful'*; or cultural use of colour, *'I could see the copper sky'*; and ideas, *'listen to the music in your head'*. These examples bear testimony to the potential richness of meanings and images that bilinguals carry in their head and how they use it confidently and creatively in the company of a knowledgeable adult and peers, as well as the use of a supportive and creative strategy.

Bilingual Children and Whole-School Policy

Peter Cunningham

Chapter Outline

Britain is a multicultural society, and with growing migration in response to the opportunities and challenges of globalization, along with free movement within the European Union, it is likely to become increasingly so. Schools need to be responsive to change, and policy cannot remain static. The National Curriculum for England sets out an entitlement to learning for all pupils, with equality of opportunity stressed as 'one of a broad set of common values and purposes which underpin the school curriculum and the work of schools' (Foreword: National Curriculum, QCA/DfEE, 1999). Making a curriculum available to all children without recourse to the cultural resources they bring to it does not 'ensure access to the curriculum and to assessment' (ibid., p37), and is likely to lead to differential educational outcomes as evidenced by the underachievement of certain minority groups (Ofsted, 2003). There is clear need for school policy to facilitate specific action to address potential underachievement and to articulate high expectations for all children regardless of their heritage culture or language.

Many schools have developed good practice and this chapter draws on the experience of different schools to exemplify possible ways in which the strengths and needs of bilingual pupils can be addressed as part of policies at a whole-school level. No single model is advocated, as this would be inappropriate given the range of possible contexts; rather principles and possibilities for developing policy and practice in any setting are suggested. To this end, three overarching and interrelated imperatives are discussed, namely the need to:

1. Develop an informed ethos and policy that respects, includes and activates the linguistic and cultural resources that children bring to school learning.
2. Plan and deliver policy that aims to support and develop bilingual children's literacy and language learning through a practice embedded in shared understanding, interactive talk and cognitively demanding work across the curriculum.
3. Work in partnership with parents and the wider community.

Developing an informed ethos

A person's language is an inherent part of their identity. Let us consider the impact of not recognizing this identity in a positive light. Gloria Anzaldua (1990, p. 76) expresses it passionately:

'if you really want to hurt me, talk badly about my language'

She goes on to explain 'Ethnic identity is twin skin to cultural identity – I am my language. Until I can take pride in my language I cannot take pride in myself.' The link between self-esteem, motivation and academic success is now widely acknowledged. Important to this is the argument that: 'when students' language, culture and experience are ignored or excluded in classroom interaction, students are immediately starting from a disadvantage . . . [and] they resist further devaluation of their identities by mentally withdrawing from participation in the life of the school' (Cummins, 1996, pp. 2–3). In the past, too many of our children have been made to feel ashamed of their language and identity. As primary school teacher Yasmin Ali recalls:

'As a child in school I wasn't allowed to use my first language. I was not allowed to talk in my first language in the playground. Because of my lack of English I was put in the lowest ability group [at primary school], even for maths I was in the lowest group. In secondary school I was put in the lowest group. I had to do everything after leaving school so I could become a teacher.

As I grew up I refused to use my own language within the home because I was ashamed, I wanted to be like my friends at school. Language is not just a way of communicating but it's you as a person. So you've got to understand what you are doing to that person. It's not just about learning English – it's about a whole identity.'

We learn by making connections and Yasmin was denied opportunity to connect school learning with that of her home, first-language and culture. *School had failed her.*

In more positive contexts, when children's cultures and languages are activated in school learning they can achieve to a high level. This is also important to them taking pride in their own cultural and linguistic heritage. It can help strengthen family relationships as well as relationships between home and school. In addition, in a globalized economy, maintaining knowledge and understanding of two languages and cultures can bring economic and social benefits later in life, which in turn benefit the whole of society. Baker (2006, p. 434) argues that the 'new economy requires the crossing of linguistic boundaries' and that 'bilinguals can become the pivotal bridge makers and go-betweens in global economic operations'.

Having an informed ethos and policy requires informational knowledge about bilingualism and bilingual education on the part of educators; it encourages an attitude that views bilingualism positively. Research evidence shows that educators with an intercultural orientation actively seek out information to promote minority students' academic and personal development while those with an Anglo-conformity orientation reject information that challenges their socio-political attitude (Cummins, 1988, p. 136). Informed policy provides more than technologies and structures that allow access to the curriculum, it recognizes *cultural and emotional dimensions of learning* and actively encourages membership of a learning community, where children are helped to make sense of new learning from their own and others' perspectives. In this respect ethos and policy inform practice, and practice informs policy and ethos; it is a dynamic process, 'whoever teaches learns in the act of teaching, and whoever learns teaches in the act of learning' (Freire, 1998, p. 31).

Schools also learn from parents and the wider communities. A positive attitude to working in partnership with parents is crucial. Parents from all cultures strongly desire to contribute to their children's education, but if ability to speak English and knowledge of majority or dominant cultural conventions are made prerequisites then many of these parents feel disempowered and remain uninvolved with school (Cummins, 1996, pp. 8–9). Close collaboration with parents, recognizing families and their communities as 'funds of knowledge' (Moll et al., 1992) with cultural practices that support learning, helps develop intercultural understanding. Mutual respect and a sense of common purpose are crucial if children are to achieve to their full potential. However, this collaboration should be located within the professional role of the teacher and the senior management of the school: expertise that reflects deep understanding of how children learn, of government legislation, policy and guidance, and of principles that underpin bilingual education, must be central to the development of policy and practice.

In recent years, increased awareness of differential achievement, with underachievement of children from certain minority language backgrounds, has positively affected monitoring and recording procedures. In fact the Race Relations (Amendment) Act (2000) requires schools and LEAs (Local Education Authorities in the UK) to make sure that all pupils from minority ethnic backgrounds are given equality of opportunity to succeed and to meet their potential with a duty on schools to 'monitor and assess how their policies affect ethnic minority pupils, staff and parents; the emphasis here is on pupils' achievements' (cited in Standards Site, DfES: accessed November 2006). On an annual basis schools report ethnicity data to the DfES, who along with Ofsted and other agencies see its use as a key factor in raising standards. Other initiatives include QCA guidance on working with minority-language groups at curriculum level, particularly in the National Literacy Strategy; and Standards for the Award of Qualified Teacher Status that reflect knowledge and understanding in teaching children with English as an Additional Language. However, despite recent improvements in initial teacher education, many newly qualified teachers do not feel adequately prepared to teach pupils with English as an additional language (TTA, 2006), as discussed in Chapter 2 of this book. There is patent need for continuing professional development that critically reflects on research findings and positive practice from other settings in order to develop informed policy and practice.

Planning and delivering a policy

Developing informed ethos and policy is a dynamic and ongoing process. Such a vision must be grounded in sound principles and is best realized when shared by all involved in the teaching and learning process. Leadership is important to this process: it must build on existing strengths; facilitate, encourage and support professional development; and, while allowing flexibility, set out a realistic timetable with achievable goals.

Stating principles

Several schools have found making a general statement on bilingualism a useful starting point in presenting a vision that reflects and helps inform the ethos of the school, as a foundation on which to build policy and as a benchmark against which to review practice. An east London primary school included the following in their statement (see Cunningham, 2000):

- Bilingualism should be seen as a positive ability, bringing a richness of language to children's learning.
- Children should be given wide scope to talk, read and write in both languages – the two languages are mutually supportive.
- Children should be encouraged to share their social, cultural and language experiences in school. These experiences should feed into learning in all areas of the curriculum.
- Teachers should not equate children's cognitive development with their developing knowledge of English. A child's cognitive ability should not be underestimated because of a limited vocabulary in English.

These statements not only send important messages to children and parents that their culture and language are valued in school but also provide the bedrock from which to develop policy and practice to give children opportunity to achieve to their highest potential. To this end, the importance of collaborative learning that provides children with appropriate cognitively demanding learning opportunities across the curriculum is stressed; as is talk that sees code-switching as a necessary tool for bilinguals' learning in a new language.

We recall how Yasmin Ali was made to feel ashamed of her home language and how in school she was put in the 'lowest group' even in maths. Yasmin had always felt confident in maths and still finds it difficult to understand why her higher conceptual knowledge was not perceived as qualifying for higher status or group in class. Her assessment was based on her English language proficiency alone, disregarding her understanding or potential for development across the curriculum. Once assigned to an ability group, academic expectations were based on that assignation and she was given work that did not match her cognitive ability. She was not only deprived of learning within subject domains but also of learning English at a good level across the curriculum. Unfortunately many bilingual children still fall within this category in today's classrooms, regardless of their ability in other curriculum subjects.

What is the practice for multilingual classrooms? The importance of a sociocultural and intercultural approach to teaching and literacy learning is stressed in Chapter 2. In Vygotskian terms learning development takes place in the 'zone of proximal development' (ZPD) which refers to the gap between what children can do unaided and what they can do with adult support and guidance or in collaboration with more able peers (see Vygotsky, 1978). Clearly, teacher knowledge of what the child can do unaided and the proximal development possibilities within the ZPD is important. The fundamental question is how could the child be supported to achieve their learning potential? Vygotsky argues (1978, p. 104) that, 'The only good kind of instruction is that which marches ahead of development and leads it: it must not be aimed so much at the ripe as the *ripening* fruit [my emphasis].' We can say that a prime aim of assessment is for it to be *formative*, which looks closely at the process of how a child is 'negotiating' a task; the child's strengths and needs inform future teaching support and learning development of the child, as many of the examples of children's work demonstrate in this book. Formative assessment should therefore be integral to any teaching and learning or curriculum policy: it assesses specific learning strengths and needs.

Assessment is most effective when it actively involves the child in target setting in their continuum of development as learners. This helps provide focus for progression and encourages reflection on their own work as part of the learning process. Several schools also involve peer-assessment as a strategy. This both helps children develop understanding of their own learning and provides a tool to aid the teacher in assessment information gathering. A teacher of seven- to eight-year-olds explains with respect to 'setting' in story: 'The children talk to each other about their work but this talk has to be structured. For example, they discuss "was that successful as an introduction to the story?" This is important, because the focus is on content and the children don't feel threatened and are confident to say "I don't like that" or "I think you could improve that by doing this." Children are allowed to use their community language in these shared talks. The children are in control of their own learning. As a teacher you can see that a child has met the objectives, or needs to do more work on it.'

Making accurate assessment of any child's learning achievement and potential is difficult but may be more so with bilingual children whose proficiency in English may prevent them from demonstrating their full understanding in language-based assessments. There are of course many assessment opportunities that are not language based, including, for example, observations of enactive modes of learning (see Chapter 4), or evidence from children's model making, map-reading, drawing, number work, etc. As exemplified in the National Curriculum (QCA/DfEE, p. 37), policy might also seek to provide opportunity for children to demonstrate understanding and achievement in their home language. This can be useful even for assessing fluent bilinguals since they might be able to express greater understanding if their other language is stronger than their English. Also, involving parents can be particularly helpful in providing a fuller profile of a bilingual learner. Some schools make home visits to inform baseline assessments for example, in the belief that observations made in the home setting tend to give a more accurate picture of capability than if the child is assessed in an alien environment on first starting school.

However, making assessments in the child's first language is not always practicable; parents' assessments are unlikely to be based on the same criteria as the school's, and English language activity is embedded in the teaching and learning process across the curriculum. All children will need to be given opportunity to use English language to demonstrate their achievement. In order to help children demonstrate higher-order cognitive skills (such as evaluating, classifying, inferring, comparing and contrasting) demanded by higher level descriptors in the National Curriculum, teaching, learning and assessment based on context embedded tasks can be usefully employed (see discussion on CALP in Chapter 2). For example, in science, demonstrating understanding of the relative hardness of different substances and how this may be used as a criterion to classify them requires higher order skills. Asking a child to explain this in the abstract through discussion or writing demands high-level language proficiency. Asking a child to give a commentary in the context of actually doing the activity demands a lower level of language proficiency. Both assessments would allow the child to demonstrate their conceptual understanding. 'Sensitivity to the need for contextual support and the cognitive demands of the classroom are important if an individual is to maximize learning in the curriculum' (Baker, 2006, p. 185). This sensitivity needs to be set within a policy framework that recognizes that the child's English language proficiency is continually evolving through activity across the curriculum, that it can take up to seven years for children to develop academic language proficiency (Cummins, 1996) and that ongoing contextual support and guidance for deep-level language and literacy development is necessary throughout the teaching–learning process.

Case study
Developing and implementing policy in context

Located in one of the least prosperous schools in Bradford with nearly 40 per cent of pupils entitled to free school meals. Approximately 90% of the children are of Pakistani origin with Punjabi/Urdu being the majority home language; in all, 95 per cent of the children come from homes where English is not the first language. An Ofsted inspection report noted 'an effective bilingual policy is well implemented, promoting an appreciation and respect for pupils' own language'.

Policy becomes more meaningful when all those involved in its implementation (teachers, classroom assistants, mentors, parent helpers, lunchtime supervisors, etc.) develop a shared understanding. Successful policy is rarely imposed: it needs space and time to develop and this is best built into school development plans with identified training and evaluation sessions.

A summary of how one school in Bradford developed its policy over a five-year period is presented. It helps illustrate that a long-term vision and time to work towards and develop a policy are crucial.

The first step was to identify the need for the policy. The school felt that many children were not achieving to their full potential. A visit to a school in Amsterdam that had a similar pupil intake with a large percentage of bilingual children, but higher levels of achievement, convinced the headteacher that a more rigorous policy would help raise standards. In analysing policy from the Dutch school, he felt that in his own school language policy 'talk was sometimes viewed superficially, tokenistically in the classroom'.

Through input in staff meetings awareness and understanding of bilingualism was raised and the headteacher and his staff agreed that talk should be central to children's learning.

A working group was set up who fed back to the staff at INSET meetings where teachers and support staff had opportunity to look at resources and discuss how they would use them. 'We wanted it to be supportive of teachers, it was important that we raised awareness and carried everybody with us, but at the same time we realized that staff will always be at different stages of their professional development and that they would take policy on board at different rates' (headteacher's comment).

They started by providing a few keywords in the children's home languages, days of the week, months of the year. They then looked at subject vocabulary in topics. 'From this it developed further because the staff said it was good to have materials they could use. The teachers felt confident and said "we'd like to try this or try that". We got the whole school involved.' Monolingual and bilingual staff worked closely together to produce dual language resources. Things took off because of 'enthusiasm fuelled by the children's positive responses ... there was a buzz around the school. The excitement created was an important part of the staff development' (headteacher's comment).

Teachers in each year team were given time away from their class in order to develop policy detail. So, for example, for each year group aims and objectives were identified and supported by a scheme of work that prescribes opportunities for talk across the curriculum.

As an ongoing process, plans and evaluations were shared in staff meetings and curriculum leaders monitored the effectiveness of policy implementation. Summative end of term assessments were used as part of this monitoring process to help identify general progress against targets, as well as to monitor the progress of particular groups. This data not only proved a useful measure of success but also helped identify areas for further development.

Intercultural awareness, parents and the community

Working in partnership with parents and the wider community is considered good educational practice in all contexts. For example, the DfES consider 'engaging and working with parents ... one of the most vital parts of providing children with an excellent education' (Standards Site, DfES: accessed November 2006). However, there can be particular challenges in engaging and working with diverse communities. Involving parents, especially non-English-speaking parents, and other family members in educational activity at home and in the school can be challenging. There are language matters to consider as well as the various ways that parents in different cultures and communities view their role and the school's role in educating their children (Faltis, 1995, p. 245). A Russian parent recently commented that she was 'worried about her daughter's progress in school' and was waiting for the school to contact her: she saw this as their 'professional responsibility' and did not think it appropriate to contact the school herself. In her cultural experience such an approach would be considered impolite and may be seen as a challenge to the teacher's professionalism.

We as educators working with different communities, including the English community, know that partnership to a large extent depends on mutual trust and understanding. There is a great anxiety amongst minority-language parents to understand the British education system; facilitating this would go a long way towards involving these parents. This would also encourage interchange of knowledge: schools must also know where the children are coming from. Parents want to know the ways of teaching and learning in the school and how their collaboration with the school can positively enhance their children's learning. It is a two-way process: it is equally important that schools know how parents contribute to their children's learning at home and are open to understanding how parents can positively contribute to the development of school policy and practice. Parental participation in the life of the school can enrich the curriculum, providing supplementary knowledge and skill, and evidence shows this helps children develop and affirm their identity as learners. In this collaborative process parents can develop a sense of belonging to the school community, while the school can develop a sense of being at the heart of a wider community. Such a relationship can only be built up over time and will involve many initiatives and ongoing practices that aim to sustain and develop fuller parental participation in multiple ways. To help illustrate this, some examples of policy in practice that proved successful in involving parents in a multicultural, inner-city London school are presented.

Case study

Involving parents in the life of the school

Located in inner London, children from over 25 different language backgrounds represent the school population. Three-quarters of the pupils have English as an additional language. The majority of the other children are black African-Caribbean. Approximately 70 per cent are entitled to free school meals. Ofsted noted 'good links with the community have been developed and these enrich the work of the school'.

Many parents had no previous contact with the English education system, while for those who had attended school in Britain, changes in school curriculum, pedagogic practice and school management structures rendered the system barely recognizable. The school saw a need to 'demystify school' and hoped that sharing information and consulting over matters that concerned parents would be a positive starting point to encourage and enable fuller parental participation. This in turn they believed would have a positive impact on attitudes towards school and also help give parents confidence to support their children's education both at home and in school. To facilitate consultation a series of meetings in parents' first language, or in community groups, were set up to raise awareness and understanding of the educational system, the school and the curriculum as well as the specific needs of particular community groups, and to provide a forum in which parents had a role in informing school policy. Mutual exchange of information and discussion around issues helped increase parental confidence and trust in the school. The meetings were not just about communicating in a different language, but concerned with providing a secure environment for information exchange. Sometimes the school 'heard things we didn't necessarily want to hear – but we needed to hear them' (headteacher) and were then able to consider how to address concerns through policy development. Significantly these meetings were well attended: 'I suppose this shows that if you approach people in a way that says "you have an interest and we are interested in what you have to say" they turn up willingly because it concerns them and because they feel that their contribution is valued' (headteacher).

The school celebrated religious and cultural festivals such as Diwali, Carnival, Eid, Hanuka, Turkish Children's Day, Chinese New Year, etc., to enable children to take pride in aspects of their own culture and to learn about other cultural practices. Such celebrations provide good opportunities to invite parents and community groups into school, to participate in collaborative work that draws on their particular expertise and help bring home and school closer together. When children see their parents or members of their community working positively with school it adds to their status as learners, and helps give meaning to and motivation for their school learning. It is important that celebration also includes traditional British and Christian festivals; all children and their families should be made to feel included with no group presented as the 'exotic other'. The school also encouraged children to do further research into these festivals using books, websites, cultural artifacts, photographs and other resources as well as through interviews and visits: this also provided great opportunity for active parental involvement at home. These initiatives not only made different cultures and languages visible but also gave them an academic status with parental involvement seen as expert and invaluable.

For many years, greetings displayed in different languages had welcomed visitors. An extension to this was to develop *language awareness* among children, parents and staff by displaying a world map in the entrance hall with labels providing information about the languages spoken in the school. The display actively invited contributions and stimulated interest from a diverse range of parents form European, Asian, American and African backgrounds all keen to make corrections, clarify points and add information. It also generated debate around 'when is a language a language?' in relation to various creoles, patois, and accents of English. In this way the profile and status of different languages was raised in school and learning about languages transcended the boundaries of the school, and there was a flow of information and ideas between parents, children, teachers and other school staff. With such activity it is important to include English language and culture: multicultural education is not just about 'other' cultures, but about getting to know our own language and culture (Datta and Pomphrey, 2004, p.1), with new understandings often generated by intercultural exchange. Donmall (1985, cited in Baker, 1996, p. 379) outlines some aims for language awareness activity:

- To make explicit a student's implicit knowledge of his or her first or other language.
- To develop a perception and understanding of the nature and functions of language.
- To develop an understanding among students of the richness of language variety within the class, school, community, region, nation and world. This may include a variety of spoken and written forms.
- To foster better relations between ethnic groups by arousing students' awareness of the origins and characteristics of their own language and its place in the world.
- To help students overcome any feeling of dislocation between the language of the home, the language of the school and the language of textbooks.
- To impart an understanding of the value of language as a crucial part of human life.
- To develop an understanding of bilingualism and biculturalism and the wider world.

The school also established a toy library in the parents' room, which was initially run by a Turkish-speaking parent. This proved to be popular and another parent, who could speak several South Asian languages, then helped to coordinate a weekly drop-in session. Library use was never exclusive to a particular language group but open to all parents: parent volunteers from a range of backgrounds soon became involved in helping to run the library. Two main factors contributed to the popularity of this scheme. Firstly, the library was useful for the parents and enjoyed by their children. Secondly, it provided a non-threatening context in which parents could participate in the life of the school. Such schemes help to break down potential barriers to communication between school and parents, and between parents from different ethnic backgrounds. They allow for informal chat and exchange of ideas and help foster a sense of mutual trust and respect. This provides opportunity for the school to positively draw on the resources that parents can provide and for parents from diverse backgrounds to have a sense of membership of the school community and the status that can bring.

Following successful involvement with the toy library, some parents went on to join the Parent Teachers Association, one became a Parent Governor and others were encouraged and felt confident enough to work alongside teachers in the nursery and other classes in the school. In some cases they assisted with teacher-directed activity, while in others they utilized their knowledge or skills (including language) to bring an added dimension to curricular activity or in support of individual children. Although parental assistance in the classroom can only involve a small number of parents, it has wider significance in that it gives important messages about school ethos, policy and culture. Making visible the multicultural nature of the school population and the wider community, and among teaching and non-teaching staff, managers and governors, helps parents from minority communities to feel empowered to participate in the life of the school.

The school also provided a location for community-run 'Saturday schools' that aimed to promote mother tongue and/or cultural maintenance. One of the major concerns ethnic minority communities have is how to help their British-born children to learn and maintain their mother tongue for familial or social identity and harmony (Li Wei, 2000). Support from the school for mother tongue and cultural maintenance activities helps place the school at the heart of the local community. This sense of community helps bridge gaps between home and school and sends out a pivotal message that the school cares about, respects and trusts its diverse communities; that it understands that there is a relationship between culture and learning; that it sees these communities as funds of knowledge; and that collaboration with families and their communities can positively support children's learning.

Summary

Developing effective policy to support bilingual learners is not easy or unproblematic. It requires vision based on knowledge and understanding of bilingualism and bilingual education and an intercultural attitude that actively strives for the success of all children. This vision is informed by research evidence, shared successful classroom practice in school, collaboration with parents and the wider school community, and most importantly by the academic and personal achievements of the children. Developing policy is a dynamic process and is best when understood by all those involved with the child's education. It needs commitment and an investment in resources and time.

Refugee Children in Primary Schools

Peter Cunningham, Ian Menter and Azar Sheibani

In this chapter we first seek to define what the term *refugee* means, then look at the educational needs that refugee children have when they arrive in school and at some of the challenges that they, their parents and schools are set. In describing these matters we seek to avoid making generalizations about the experiences and needs of such children, given the diversity and complexity of the contexts and backgrounds involved. In part we do this through drawing on the experiences of a number of particular cases recounted to us from a variety of sources, including children, parents, teachers and refugee community workers.

An overview of the refugee context

> 'We don't want to be refugees, we want to be in our own country . . . It is not my choice to be a refugee.' (Giang from South Vietnam – Channel 4, 1999)

Refugees do not leave their country as a matter of choice; they are forced to flee out of fear for their lives and the values they believe in. They often give up everything they value: their homeland, family and friends, social status, belongings and whatever they fought for, and come to a strange environment facing an uncertain future.

In recent decades there has been a rise in the number of refugees. Political instability, civil wars and conflicts, violation of human rights, and extreme religious tensions, have all contributed to this increase. At the beginning of 2005, there were more than nine million refugees and

800,000 asylum seekers in the world (UNHCR, 2006) and it is estimated that children represent over half the refugee population (Anderson, 2004). The majority of refugees just manage to leave their own country and reside in the neighbouring countries, which often have insufficient resources to support them. Only a small minority manages to overcome the numerous hurdles and 'touch the Western soil'.

In this chapter, the term *refugee* is used in its broad sense and might refer to the following categories in the UK:

- *Convention refugees*: Convention refugees are those who obtained refugee status under the 1951 Geneva Convention. Previously *refugee status* gave indefinite leave to remain in the UK, but those granted refugee status since August 2005 are given a five-year leave in the first instance. Their status is subject to review after five years and they could at that stage be faced with removal.
- *Asylum seekers*: Asylum seekers are those who have applied for refugee status and are awaiting a decision by the Home Office.
- *Humanitarian Protection* is granted where the Home Office recognizes that there is a real risk of death, torture, or other inhuman or degrading treatment, which falls outside the strict terms of the 1951 Refugee Convention but which comes within the scope of Article 3 of the European Convention for Human Rights (ECHR).
- *Discretionary leave* is normally granted for a period of three years but, as with humanitarian protection, it can be granted for shorter periods. For example, when an unaccompanied child under 18 has their asylum claim refused, a period of discretionary leave would be granted for the period up until their 18th birthday.

Refugee agencies are concerned that the shift towards more temporary and insecure forms of protection exacerbates feelings of uncertainty and trauma, and frustrates the integration process. This is particularly true of the removal of automatic Indefinite Leave to Remain on the granting of refugee status which undermines the government's own integration strategy (Refugee Council, May 2006), and the uncertainty this generates has further long-term implications for refugees' educational, training and employment prospects.

Refugee children

Refugees flee their country for various reasons, and those reasons will profoundly influence the way they will choose to settle and conduct their lives in the receiving society (for a detailed account see Rutter, 2006). For example, refugees who have escaped as a result of ethnic conflicts will have different experiences to those who have suffered long-term political repression and persecution. Refugees represent a wide spectrum even if they come from the same country, so their needs and expectations would vary enormously. Refugee children are not homogeneous either. Important factors that will influence their experiences, needs and future development include:

- their experience of their country: traumas caused by civil wars, atrocities, witnessing their parents' persecution, etc.;
- the length of disruption to their education prior to their departure;
- mother tongue and its proximity to the language of the receiving country;
- age when they arrive in the receiving country;
- different educational experience (which in some cases may have been extremely repressive);
- possible loss of their parents/carers;
- experience of fleeing as an unaccompanied child;
- home culture and parent–child relationship;
- tension between 'home' and 'school' culture;
- access to appropriate accommodation in the receiving country;
- tension between some refugee communities/fighting factions.

One important consideration in responding to the needs of refugee children is to avoid assuming these needs are the same as those of children from more established ethnic minority communities, most of whom now belong to second or third generations. Although there might be some common issues, the differences are very significant. Refugee children share with their parents an extreme sense of loss and bewilderment. All of them will have experienced serious disruption to their daily lives before leaving their homeland and uncertainty will not disappear when they arrive in this country. The lack of stability and security will be experienced for some time.

They learn from their parents that it was not their choice to come to the UK, and some are told they will return back home as soon as the situation changes. This may further perpetuate feelings of displacement. Children from communities where an early return is envisaged are likely to develop a very different outlook from those who do not hold out such expectations. Alvaro, a support teacher from Colombia working in a London primary school, tells how refugee children often say 'I don't belong here'. Other parents are aware that they will be 'here' for the foreseeable future and that however long they remain it will be a significant period of time for their children. Mushtak, an Iraqi refugee, notes the dual cultures which many children experience and points out, 'this will be their homeland'.

Children from families that have left their homes at very short notice can arrive in school feeling deeply disorientated and sometimes traumatized by their experience. Some children have seen family members being removed from their homes, beaten up, tortured or even murdered. Whatever the circumstances on leaving, feelings of displacement are inevitable. Usually children are not told about departure until the last possible minute. As Mushtak explains:

'It's not easy to talk with adults about our situation in our own country, you have to imagine it is very dangerous talking with children . . . because of the war they know there is some problem but they didn't know we were coming from one country to another . . . there is no way to clear everything first, the situation is too dangerous.'

His seventeen-year-old daughter Zia said: '*[on arrival] we were very excited about the country – a new country, but uncomfortable because of new people, new language*'. Zia's mother, Intalak, recalls: '*the children cried every night for two months. They came home from school and cried. They miss their friends, their cousins, relations, everything.*' Zia found it best to deal with her trauma privately: '*it is better to keep it [the upset/trauma] private. You might find [for] somebody else it's good to tell everybody but I don't think so for me.*'

Such experiences can leave children deeply traumatized and may lead to their having a deep mistrust of adults, especially adults whom they do not know. Again we stress that this is not necessarily true of all refugee children and that different children will respond differently to their situation and experiences. The majority of refugee children show great capacity to manage huge change and in general adapt to their new country with greater ease than adults (Alhern and Athey, 1991). While showing sensitivity to their possible needs it is important for educators not to assume extreme disadvantage and develop low expectations for refugee children in terms of their academic capabilities or in terms of the nature of their future goals (Hamilton and Moore, 2004, p. 93).

In common with other minority groups, refugee children may have English as an additional language. It is clearly essential that newly arrived children learn English as quickly as possible. However, as emphasized throughout this book, this should not be associated with the denial of their home language. Indeed, maintaining that language and being given opportunities to use it in school could be a key factor in facilitating the learning of English and the maintenance of identity.

Children, parents and teachers with whom we have spoken have stressed the use of the mother tongue. Sorani, a Kurdish language, is spoken in Shayan's home. Shayan's parents are acutely aware of the importance of language. They left Iran out of fear of persecution for cultural activity and, as Shayan's mother explains, '*a very simple thing like writing in our own language is banned in our own country*'.

The children attend a Saturday Kurdish school which promotes both mother-tongue learning and cultural activities. As Shayan, who has never lived in 'Kurdistan', proudly says, '*we have our own language, our religion, our traditional songs and dresses*', before adding, '*I like being English as well*'.

As can be seen from Shayan's comment, language is clearly closely related to culture and identity. Children have to negotiate their identity, their culture and their language with regard to their new situation and education. Close liaison between mainstream and 'supplementary' schools can help bring different worlds together, to bridge a gap between perceived cultural values and educational expectations.

Refugee parents

Experience shows that invariably refugee parents want the best for their children. As Mushtak put it: *'[our children] are the only possession we have left'*. Sahela, a Kurdish refugee, said: *'[we] want children to do well for back home as well'*. In other words, there is a sense that many parents want their children to have benefited from their forced migration, both as a form of compensation for the disruption or trauma and because of a commitment to bringing about social development in their home country.

Families arriving in this country as refugees can face a labyrinth of bureaucracy in settling down. This can be particularly true of the housing experience. Many refugees are allocated temporary housing until decisions are made about longer-term plans. This may or may not be in areas where there are local schools which have places available. A study into the links between homelessness of refugees and asylum seekers and their schooling (Power et al., 1998) found that large numbers of children were not attending school on a regular basis. The elaborate and systematic steps taken by Mushtak in finding a school are exceptional:

> 'when we reach here first of all we try to assist our children and we try to find a school ... because my wife is a teacher so already we know at least we have some minimal background [about] the education system ... we wanted to start with some success ... the first thing I tried was to [go to] the local library to find a proper way to find a school. From them I got a Department of Education address ... I went there. I tried to ask [for] some background, a list of schools – which is the best according to their awarding system. The second thing, I returned back home and got a telephone book and checked all the schools around here. I had no problem with the primary school because there is one next door to my house. But the secondary school I need to find what is the best so I visit all the nearest schools around and I am talking with the teachers. Later on I returned back and checked some things on the computer website to see the school results. By the end I selected three schools and returned back to the education department just to see if there were any places for my children to start by January. We were lucky.'

Gewirtz et al. (1995) have shown how erratic the outcomes of 'parental choice' are. The reality is that most parents have very limited choice, if any, and those who are most disadvantaged in this will be those who know least about the education system in this country and who are faced simultaneously with other major challenges in their lives, such as seeking accommodation and securing a regular income. Even with an appropriate school place it can still take some time to adjust. For many children there is a world of difference between schooling they have experienced before leaving their homeland and the provision they find in Britain. This, for some, may be seen as a 'liberation' from strict and/or formal approaches experienced previously, but it can also be confusing and disorientating.

In addition to the physical and mental uprooting experienced by refugee parents and children, their relationship with each other may take strange turns. Children rapidly develop new skills, including language and communications skills. As a result, they obtain a tool that can shift the balance of power between them and their parents. The parents feel that they are no longer in control; this being because they do not know about the education system, and they do not speak the language so they cannot liaise directly with school authorities. Some of us may be familiar with situations at parents' evenings when children are interpreters in the meetings and exercise their power to choose what to interpret and what to omit!

Outside school, children act as interpreters when parents meet their solicitor, benefit or housing officer or their GP. This shows tremendous ability on the part of these refugee children but it can also be a burden on children to enter the adult realm and come across a range of complicated and worrying issues which most children are not aware of. At the same time, the parents suffer because they have to share those issues with their children and talk about, for example, their prison experience or private medical issues in the presence of their children. Acquiring language skills empowers the children but, parallel to this process, their parents feel disempowered. Children start to speak English with their siblings at home and gradually they may stop using their mother tongue, so lines of communication with parents are broken, their worlds grow further apart and a power vacuum is created.

This indicates the need to acknowledge the heterogeneity of refugees and refugee children at two separate levels. We are often confronted with sweeping generalizations about refugees and the level of their needs. When we are thinking about the children, it is not only that their experiences as refugees may be very varied, but that as children their understanding of their experience and their readiness to articulate it may vary enormously.

The parent–school relationship is not an easy one for many refugees and their children. If parents feel they cannot communicate effectively they may prefer to avoid any encounter with the school. Moreover, if schools do not have effective policies to involve all parents, refugee children may not wish their parents to come to school because they would feel embarrassed in front of the teachers and other children. This leads parents to feel that they cannot have an effective role in their children's education. It is almost inevitable that the majority of refugee parents will initially lack knowledge about the education system in general and local schools in particular. Matters such as the nature of interaction between the pupil and the teacher and the school curriculum will be new to them. They may be unable to use the usual channels of communication such as parent–school associations because they are not familiar with that part of the system or because their English-language proficiency is seen as a barrier. In short, the situation may create a wide gap between their desire to cooperate and the possibility for them to do so.

To counter this, schools need to engage in outreach work and empowering activities. Many positive examples of how this might be done are included in Chapter 8 of this book. These strategies take a proactive approach, aiming to develop between school and home clear communication channels, a sense of mutual trust, parental participation in the life of the school and shared goals for the education of children.

In our experience we have found mediation between refugee parents and school a positive way forward. To this end we established a university certificated course, which we designed with teachers and other professionals from refugee backgrounds, that has now been running in various guises for over five years at London Metropolitan University. The course is based on the principle of developing skills within the refugee community for meeting the current challenges in the area of education of refugee children and forging stronger links between refugee communities and schools. The course provides an introduction to the educational system in England: its management, curriculum and pedagogy. It includes a school placement, as well as a module on community and communication with support for English language development in professional educational contexts.

Teachers and schools

Awareness, ethos and policy

Questions of ethos, curriculum and pedagogy for the whole school are especially significant when considering refugees and can have a great impact – either positive or negative – on children. Schools experienced in receiving refugee children will have an atmosphere among staff, children and parents that welcomes new children and empathizes with their experiences. A school with an established and effective anti-racist policy is a school which will be much more likely to provide a secure learning environment for refugee children, but the ideal anti-racist policy is the one which could make refugees visible, portraying and representing them in a positive manner. Also, such schools will be able to provide translations of key documents, whether through government, Local Education Authority and EMAS (Ethnic Minority Achievement Service) services or community organizations, and may use videos or other visual explanations of their procedures. We are thinking here of such information as descriptions of the education system, curriculum and assessment policy or anti-bullying procedures.

In many situations (but not all), there will be community organizations which the newly arrived families may or may not be in touch with. Schools can achieve a great deal by encouraging parents to network through such organizations. Offering facilities for meetings and workshops, for example, can make a major contribution to securing stability for newly arrived families (Richman, 1998).

However, even where schools are responding effectively to the arrival of refugee families, children and their parents may experience very hostile reactions elsewhere in the local community. We suggest that schools not only provide a safe environment for children but also a secure setting in which such matters are acknowledged and discussed openly but sensitively. The tendency to 'shield' primary schoolchildren from the harsh realities of politics and war is likely to be avoided. School assemblies and circle time present important opportunities for establishing the appropriate ethos: getting the right balance to the approach is a highly skilled task for teachers, but can make an enormous difference to the experience of all of the children in a school. The critical point is not to marginalize refugee children's issues but to consider them as part of the mainstream issues for a school.

Induction to school

When refugee children remembered their feelings on first going to school here, or were asked by the researcher how a refugee child might feel, common responses were *'frightened'* and *'sad'*. Abduli, a Somali boy, remembered starting in Year 1: *'[it was] scary . . . I didn't know any people and I missed my dad. There were different people and I didn't know they were going to teach me.'*

The first introduction to school is particularly significant and many children can remember the very words that were said to them on that first day. Shayan, remembering when she first started in a reception class, said:

'The first week I went into Reception and was doing my piece of work and I was crying but then I tried my hardest not to, so I left my work and went to read a book. It came again and suddenly I started crying and I said "I don't like school" and then I said "I want my mummy" and said "I don't want to be here" but [the teacher] instead of just being rude like that, said "But we like you here". She actually comforted me and I felt better. I felt more comfortable in school.'

Those words were deeply significant to Shayan.

Like Shayan, other children remembered introductions to the class or the school. When Abduli was asked what he would do if he were the teacher, he suggested: *'I would get another Somali student to show them round the school.'* The first few days can certainly be difficult for any child starting a new school, but these days can be particularly significant for refugee children with fear and anxiety attached to displacement. It is important to involve children, as Abduli suggested, for an introduction to the school, but also, as Hassan remarks, *'you would feel frightened because you don't know the teachers or the children . . . at playtime I would tell people to play with you'.*

Refugee children need 'induction and orientation' programmes for a smooth transition from their previous experience to a new educational system. There is no doubt that the approach to the induction of refugee children is crucial not just to their immediate adaptation to the school, but to their long-term educational welfare and indeed to that of the school as a whole.

Coping with trauma

As David, an infant school teacher said, *'The ones that find it difficult tend to be very extreme – when it's difficult it's really difficult.'* He gave the example of Nurgin, a child in the reception class:

'he came into the class and was just so anxious about being separated from his mother he screamed the whole class down. He was impossible to teach and it was impossible to teach the lesson because he just kept screaming, so eventually my classroom assistant took him out of the classroom to play with him, that was the only way we could do it.'

Coming from situations of fear and mistrust, many refugee children need time to build trust and establish positive relationships; this will often mean planning for one-to-one sessions within normal classroom routines.

'you need to spend more time with them and find what they engage with. "Circle time" is the classic way you would introduce the children to simple language games and sharing games but it doesn't seem to work with [some] children because they are so withdrawn so you have to have one-to-one with them to bring them out and get them to work in groups. [In these one-to-one times] I play games, play with them, share things with them and give them things like apples, at circle time we share apples out, but you need to give it to them, make sure they're there.' (David)

Several teachers stressed the importance of using games and familiar stories as a means of developing confidence, a sense of belonging, and developing ability and sufficient trust to cooperate as a collaborative learning experience.

Developing an appropriate pedagogy is perhaps the most challenging aspect for teachers who are working with classes that include refugee children suffering from trauma. Given the range of factors which refugee children may have experienced, it is essential that the individuals' needs – physical, emotional and educational – are met. The teacher will need to spend some time in the early days making a detailed assessment of strengths and needs and produce an action plan in order to ensure that those needs can indeed be met and the strengths built upon. In making assessments we stress the importance of seeking expert advice from appropriate outside agencies (for example educational psychology services) and involving parents, perhaps through a mediator or 'co-educator'. Obviously this and a pedagogy that aims to address individual needs can be a major draw on the teacher's time. The challenge for the teacher therefore is to organize his or her teaching and management of support staff (specialist teacher support, classroom assistants, parent volunteers, etc.) so that these diverse needs can be met. The other key element in successful pedagogy in this context is in ensuring that the relationships between children in the classroom and beyond are productive both socially and educationally. Peer mentoring schemes have been shown to be effective (Richman, 1998, Chapter 14), but even at a very simple informal level, the support of children for each other can be a very powerful, positive influence for refugee children.

Assessing children's experiences

'It is difficult to know what circumstances the child has come from . . . Part of it is you are sensitive about asking about their background, that's something I've always held back from really. You never know how open to be about their previous experience.' (David)

Teachers do need to be sensitive to the parents' experiences and to those of the children. While it is inappropriate to ask parents to disclose their reasons for flight from their home country and thereby relive traumatic experience, it is crucial to enquire, within an atmosphere of security and trust, about the children's previous educational experiences and background. Refugee children may have very significant educational experiences already and it is important to build upon this experience in order to support their learning in the new context.

'I was good at reading [in French]. The first term in Reception I had easy work. I was like doing handwriting A, B to learn my alphabet. Then the next term they started giving me things like how to spell "cat" and "mouse". Then we were doing a topic on "Cornflakes" and our teacher brought out a pack of Special K and she said "can anyone read this?". Every hand shot up in the air and she chose a boy who said "the second's 'K'". Then I looked and I thought the word looked a bit familiar and I said "espec", "spec-ial", then the teacher said "Yes?" and I said "SPECIAL" and she was so astonished every playtime she kept asking "how did you do it?" and I was stuck for words and I just said "My mum taught me", but she didn't really believe me.' (Shayan)

Shayan's account immediately raises two issues for teachers which are not uncommon when responding to refugee children, namely potential under-assessment of the child (i.e. low expectations), and potential underestimation of the child's parents and their educational influence on the child. It is worth noting the high value placed on education in other cultures and societies and how family members in a range of contexts and through a variety of cultural practices support children. Moreover, many refugees who come to the UK are from professional backgrounds: they not only positively support their own children's learning but can enrich the curriculum through their contributions. For example, nursery teacher Ann recognizes the benefits of proactively involving parents:

'I've set up a system so parents can borrow dual language story books and tapes so the parents can hear the story as well. Parents have written translations of books and we have pooled resources between schools. Ideally it would be good to have parents in with groups listening to dual language tapes [or] telling stories in their mother tongue.'

Giving time and building relationships

We have previously noted the importance of outreach work in establishing positive relationships with parents, the need for building peer relationships and how first meetings with teachers are significant to induction to a new school. The need to give time and space to building teacher–child and peer relationships should not be underestimated, as Cummins (1996, p. 1) argues 'The interactions that take place between students and teachers and among students are more central to student success than any method for teaching literacy, or science or math. When powerful relationships are established between teachers and students, these relationships frequently can transcend the economic and social disadvantages that afflict communities and schools alike …' Zia recognizes the importance of this relationship:

'I think the most important thing is the teachers, how friendly they are . . . when you feel like the teacher is your friend you'll be more relaxed.'

Given the impact and possible trauma associated with displacement, there is also a need in teaching to allow time for explanation and the completion of work, which does not always sit easily with class routines and prescribed ways of working where children's tasks or activities need to be completed within a strict time framework.

> 'Time is crucial for them . . . many refugee children feel left out, and sometimes that shows in their behaviour, and the children say to me "I don't know what to do, I don't know what to do" . . . they like it when you can give them some time and they can do it by themselves.' (Alvaro)

Lena, an Iraqi refugee, found that homework clubs were a particularly important aspect of provision:

> 'Only the ones who want to work come to the club, so you can understand what the teacher says, ask questions, do more on the subject so you can understand it better . . . I think the club is good, but it's late time [after school] and everyone all tired, they could have them in breaktime, but it's good the club. If there wasn't the club I don't think I'd get on well. I need some club. I need some teacher to explain something for us.'

Considering the curriculum

There are opportunities too within the formal curriculum for teachers to enable all children to understand the causes and processes of migration, including enforced migration, and issues surrounding them. The obvious subjects for this will include PHSE, citizenship, geography and history, but literature is also invaluable for enabling children to explore the affective as well as the factual aspects. In order to help refugee children feel a sense of inclusion and to help them establish a connection with their new learning and environment, curriculum material should reflect a multicultural society. As discussed throughout this book, pedagogy that invites and supports children to make connection with the curriculum is of vital importance. Giving access to the curriculum in this way also helps satisfy parental desire for their children to maintain their language and culture, as well as wider societal aspirations for integration. As Mushtak says:

> 'We don't want our children to lose their culture, every day they pass through the gate into a completely different culture from their first culture. We want them to join that culture, to communicate with them, to know what people are thinking.'

Conclusions

We have highlighted some of the major issues which teachers and schools need to address when considering their provision for children from refugee communities. There are no simple solutions and all children will need to be assessed individually, but a lot depends on the ethos and culture of the school, which is a matter for all members of the school's community – teachers, other staff, parents, governors and pupils. Good schools will communicate effectively with refugee parents, have high expectations for their children, and plan and deliver a curriculum that actively recognizes and positively uses the children's cultural backgrounds and languages. However, refugee children may need very careful and sensitive teaching. Among them will be children who are traumatized and disoriented. Their first experiences in school are likely to shape their long-term experience and success. But beyond this, the ways in which schools respond to refugee children are likely to be indicative of the way in which a school relates to all its pupils – treating them as individuals, allowing them opportunity to draw on their knowledges to negotiate new meanings, recognizing their own particular needs and potential for contributing to school life.

Bilinguality and Literacy: A Conclusion

Manjula Datta

We may conclude that children's bilinguality is a strong and dynamic resource that, if and when activated in classroom learning, leads to fluent and deep learning outcomes. Learning becomes a *deep personal experience* with its own intrinsic rewards. Bilingual children bring a wealth of cognitive, linguistic and literacy skills to school learning; the evidence in this book shows that scaffolding these skills in further literacy learning in English as an additional language is a primary need that affects the educational outcomes of bilingual children. To that effect we have argued that the multilingual classroom should function as an *'intercultural literate community'*, which creates an enabling environment where most learning is collaborative, intercultural and a 'continual oscillation' (Rumelhart, 1976) between text and personal meaning to help develop literacy in English strongly.

A collaborative intercultural classroom environment creates an interpersonal space, which inspires strong peer learning motivating one another to cross linguistic, cultural and gender boundaries in their creativity, where each voice is unique in exploring its own pathway to literacy and follow it vigorously to meet the curriculum requirements and beyond. Children engage in higher level thinking skills (QCA/DfEE, 1999, p. 22) in processing, evaluating and synthesizing significant cultural resources in their interpretation or composition of texts in English. This way learning becomes highly *personalized*.

The polysemic nature of literary texts makes it possible to anchor many interpretations, and should be a common practice in diverse classrooms. It strengthens the curricular 'teaching and learning objectives ... at text, word and sentence level ... it allows [every child] to think about language more deeply and flexibly ... The main resource for learning is children's languages, and this includes English ... Multiculturalism is not just about "other" cultures, but about getting to know our own language and culture

through collaborative talk … Children have a special way with words …'
(Datta and Pomphrey, 2004). Learning becomes a social and socialization
activity for every child. Every child develops a deeper understanding of
self and culture 'to know oneself better through others and to know others
better through oneself …' (Gramsci, 1977). It creates a thinking classroom
where children develop intellectually, linguistically and socially.

It is disconcerting that in twenty-first-century classrooms in a globalized
world, too often children's binguality is seen as a *barrier* to their language
and literacy achievement in English. Labelling children linguistically
and culturally deprived, and consequent misconceptions (Chapter 2),
puts these children in low-ability settings, affecting children's self-belief.
This inevitably creates a downward spiral and unequal opportunity for
learning. Culture is not a product reduced to a set of artifacts, such as
food, costumes or festivals, but rather a meaning-making process. 'Culture
is both meaning and the process of making meaning' (Floria-Ruane, 2001,
p. 27). This theme has been explored throughout the book, and is evident
in children's literacy development in English. The studies in this book prove
conclusively that 'excluding' these rich learning resources creates a chasm
and confusion in bilinguals' continuum of learning, and learning outcomes.
Evidence from many studies shows that in second-language learning, 'the
engagement of their [learners'] emotions is seen as vital' (Johnstone, 1993,
p. 139).

As well as the above factor for maximizing bilingual children's potential
for high learning outcomes, the studies in the book demonstrate the
importance of the following *affect creating factors* in bilingual children's
learning development.

- A knowledgeable and enabling adult with 'consciousness for two' (Bruner, 1986, p. 74), who understands how the bilingual mind works and the possible cultural knowledge and skills that bilinguals carry in their head for language and literacy development in school. Bilinguals' learning will only make sense if new meanings and messages are assimilated to their existing schema and make learning a meaningful and cumulative experience and develop learning at a challenging level in a higher zone.
- Informed and empowering approaches to teaching and learning that incorporate *and enable interaction between* 'best available knowledge' from both their learning worlds. Excluding the use of children's bilingual and cultural resources from school learning would suggest that English is the only 'natural language' (Stubbs, quoted in Garcia, 1996, p. 36) for learning. This would further suggest that school learning is based on experiences through English language only, or should somehow relate only to English culture.
- A shared awareness of literacy practices and goals between school and home provides crucial underpinning for children's literacy development in school. We need to develop collaborative relationships with bilingual parents and have a shared awareness of models of teaching and learning in school and home. It is very

important that minority cultures' traditional perception and teaching of literacy are not replaced but *added* to by schools' 'research-based' approaches to literacy. This is an essential knowledge for bilingual parents in that the reading process in the second language is different from the first.

- Listening input is central to language learning and this has been emphasized throughout the book in many strategies. Listening to rhythmic patterns of language use and part memorizing prose or poems helps structure mental steps that are necessary to understand meanings in the second language and to develop an understanding of literary structures at a *personal level*. Repeated readings and listening to repetitive meaning structures is very important for literacy development of young bilinguals in English. The role of enactive and integrative strategies is crucial in this process.

- Texts, literal and visual, that invite readers to join in a linguistic and imaginative dialogue encourage fluency in reading and meaning-making. They allow readers to draw on higher level semantic and syntactic meanings and lower level grapho-phonic decoding of words (Rumelhart, 1976). In good narratives the interplay of predictable narrative conventions, structure and literary devices are held together by what may be termed the 'narrative force'. Texts with repetitive grammatical structures enable younger bilingual readers to play with and memorize some of these meaning structures, and most importantly to create their own. We have also argued that in multilingual classrooms children must be encouraged to 'take meaning' from their personal experience and perspectives. Good books nurture talk and imagination, meaning is understood at a personal level. By engaging in interactive talk about text and life experiences bilingual learners learn how to construct themselves as readers.

- Peer and friendship learning seems to trigger a learning rhythm in the intercultural literate classroom which energizes multi-ability children to find their own pathways to engage in literacy and learning development in a higher zone. Intersubjectivity is crucial. Teachers' self-knowledge of subject and children as learners – their strengths and needs – is central to learning development. Additionally, collaborative learning and peer assessment seem to create powerful motivations for learning. This is a rewarding experience for both children and teachers.

Some final thoughts

Language planning for bilinguals 'is always going to be a complex equation, a social and linguistic experiment and endlessly debated' (Baker, 1998, p. 47). However, it is clear that bilinguals have an enormous capacity to learn intelligently and imaginatively when meaning is mediated through *intercultural and collaborative strategies* that produce cognition and affect, and enable them to think using the entire repertoire of meanings from both their learning worlds. Children's bilinguality is an asset and a powerful thinking and mediating tool between home and classroom learning. The book argues for rethinking of methodological approaches to additional language teaching and learning, and asserts that it should 'aspire toward multicompetence . . . enabling learners to mediate between their languages rather than become ersatz native speakers' (Cook, in Johnstone, 1993, p. 133); we had many examples of this in children's writing. Children's bilingual identity must be recognized for their development of learning in school.

The most exciting new writing in English during the last thirty years or so has often come from non-English backgrounds: Toni Morrison, Michael Ondaatje, Margaret Atwood, Grace Nichols, Salman Rushdie, Timothy Mo, Kazuo Ishiguro, Alice Walker, Maya Angelou (Wilks, 1998, p. 144). Many more award-winning British bilingual writers in English have contributed to Britain's literary heritage since. Britain is becoming increasingly multilingual. The demography of school populations in Britain is becoming increasingly multilingual. There is a real need for reframing literacy strategy and make learning a cross-cultural process in today's classrooms, to enhance every child's learning potential and identity. This is the central thesis of this edition, and is true for all students.

Finally, 'in an era of globalization, a society that has access to multilingual and multicultural resources is advantaged in its ability to play an important social and economic role on the world stage. At a time when cross-cultural contact is at an all time high in human history, the identities of all societies are evolving ... The challenge for educators and policy-makers is to shape the evolution of national identity in such a way that the rights of all citizens (including school children) are respected, and the cultural, linguistic, and economic resources of the nation are maximized' (Cummins, www.iteachilearn.com/cummins/mothertongue).

Talking about greetings is an ideal first step in this direction. It gives children an insight into other cultures and social relationships that are beyond their everyday experiences. It promotes communicative sensitivity, which is crucial for intercultural relationships. At a deeper level it shows children as thinkers in the multilingual classroom and raises issues of moral education and citizenship. The final thought must be for all children to celebrate their languages and cultures in the learning classroom (Datta, 2004), as exemplified in the poem below:

Greetings
From ten- to eleven-year-old Ozzie, Adedoyin Stephanie, Luna, Michael, Emma, Rebecca and Ezekie

People greet each other in many ways
And in many languages...
In Turkish we say Nasilsiniz! How are you?
I say E karo *to my aunts and uncles in Yoruba*
I say Ciao! Como que tal?
In Italian
In English I wave to my friends and say Hey!
In Kiswahili I say Salaam Aleykum *and some say* Jambo
I greet my family and friends with
We say Shalom!

In French we say, Bonjour!
In Jamaican we say, Whagawan!
And clasp our hands
And hit shoulders
That makes me feel strong
Because I'm happy
And I feel welcome.

If there were no greetings
Everyone will be enemy to each other
They'll be fighting and killing each other
That's why it's good to greet each other
And live in happiness and peace.

References

Ada, F. (1988) cited in Baker, C. (1996) *Foundations of Bilingual Education and Bilingualism* (2nd edn). Clevedon: Multilingual Matters.

Ada, F. (1995) 'Creative Education in Bilingual Teachers', in Garcia, O. and Baker, C. (eds) *Policy and Practice in Bilingual Education: Extending the Foundations*. Clevedon: Multilingual Matters.

Aitchison, J. (1992) *Linguistics* (4th edn). London: Hodder and Stoughton.

Alhearn, F. L. and Athey, J. L. (1991) *Refugee Children: Theory, Research and Services*. Washington DC: MCH Bureau.

Alladina, S. and Edwards, V. (1991) *Multilingualism in the British Isles*. London: Longmans.

Alred, G., Byram, M. and Fleming, M. (2003) *Intercultural Experience and Education*. Clevedon: Multilingual Matters.

Anderson, A. (2004) 'Issues of Migration', in Hamilton, R. and Moore, D. *Educational Interventions for Refugee Children: Theoretical Perspectives and Implementing Best Practice*. London: Routledge Falmer.

Anderson, J. R. (1985) *Cognitive Psychology and its Implications*. San Francisco: Freeman.

Andersson, G. (1997) *Nordic Roads to Multilingualism: How to help minority children to become multilingual*. Helsinki: The National Board of Education Centre for Professional Development.

Anzaldua, G. (1990) 'How to Tame a Wild Tongue', in Chambers, I. (1994) *Migrancy Culture Identity*. London: Routledge.

Au, Kathryn Hu-Pei (2006) *Multicultural Issues and Literacy Achievement*. Mahwah, NJ: Lawrence Earlbaum.

Baker, C. (1996) *Foundations of Bilingual Education and Bilingualism*. Clevedon: Multilingual Matters.

Baker, C. (1998) 'Minority Languages and Education: Ruination or Revival', *Primary Teaching Studies*, **10**(1), 43–8 (Trentham Books).

Baker, C. (2000) *Cultural Studies: Theory and Practice*. London: Sage Publications.

Baker, C. (2006) *Foundations of Bilingual Education and Bilingualism* (4th edn). Clevedon: Multilingual Matters.

Baker, C. and Prys Jones, S. (1998) *Encyclopaedia of Bilingualism and Bilingual Education*. Clevedon: Multilingual Matters.

Barrs, M., Ellis, S., Hester, H. and Thomas, A. (1990) *Patterns of Learning: The Primary Language Record and the National Curriculum*. London: CLPE.

Barrs, M. and Thomas, A. (eds) (1986) *The Reading Book*. London: CLPE.

Bearne, E. (1992) 'Myth and Legend: the oldest language', in Styles, M., Bearne, E. and Watson, V. (eds) *After Alice*. London: Cassell.

Bell, A. (1994) 'Telling Stories', in Graddol, D. and Boyd-Barrett, O. *Media Texts: Authors and Readers*. Clevedon: Multilingual Matters/The Open University.

Bernstein, B. (1972) 'A critique of the concept of compensatory education', in Cazden, C. B., John, V. P. and Hymes, D. (eds) *Functions of Language in the Classroom*. New York: Teacher College Press.

Bettelheim, B. (1976) *The Uses of Enchantment: The meaning and importance of fairy tales*. London: Penguin Books.

Bhatti, G. (2004) 'Good, bad and normal teachers: the experiences of south Asian children', in Ladson-Billings, G. and Gilborn, D. (eds) *The Routledge Falmer Reader in Multicultural Education*. London: Routledge Falmer.

Bialystok, E. (ed.) (1991) *Language Processing in Bilingual Children*. Cambridge: Cambridge University Press.

Bochner, S. (1982) *Cultures in Contact: Studies in Cross Cultural Interaction*. Oxford: Pergamon Press.

Bocker, A. (1998) *Asylum Migration to the European Union: Patterns of Origin and Destination*. Luxembourg: Office for Offical Publications of the European Community.

Bourdieu, P. and Passeron, J. (1977) *Reproduction in Education, Society and Culture*. London: Sage.

Brisk, M. E. (1985) 'Using the Computer to Develop Literacy', *Equality and Choice*, **1**(1), 25–32.

Britton, J. (1972) *Language and Learning*. Harmondsworth: Penguin Books.

Bruner, J. S. (1965) 'The growth of mind', *American Psychologist*, **20**, 1007–17.

Bruner, J. S. (1966) *Towards a Theory of Instruction*. London: Harvard University Press.

Bruner, J. S. (1977a) 'Early social interaction and language development', in Schaffer, H. R. (ed.) *Studies in Mother–Child Interaction*. London: Academic Press.

Bruner, J. S. (1977b) *The Process of Education*. Cambridge, MA: Harvard University Press.

Bruner, J. S. (1986) *Actual Minds, Possible Worlds*. Cambridge, MA: Harvard University Press.

Bullock, A. (1975) *A Language for Life (Report of the Bullock Committee)*. London: HMSO.

Bussis, A., Chittenden, E., Amarel, M. and Klauser, E. (1985) *Inquiry into Meaning: An investigation into learning to read*. London: Lawrence Erlbaum/CLPE.

Carrasquillo, A. L. and Rodriguez, V. (1995) *Langauge Minority Students in the Mainstream Classroom*. Clevedon: Multilingual Matters.

Cazden, C. B., John, V. P. and Hymes, D. (eds) (1972) *Functions of Language in the Classroom*. New York: Teacher College Press.

Chambers, A. (1996) *The Reading Environment*. Stroud, UK: Thimble Press.

Channel 4 (1999) *Off Limits: Refugee Voices*. London: Channel 4.

Chomsky, N. (1957) *Syntactic Structures*. The Hague: Mouton.

Chomsky, N. (1972) *Language and Mind*. New York: Harcourt Brace Jovanovich.

Chukovsky, K. (1963) cited in Britton, J. *Language and Learning*. Harmondsworth: Penguin Books.

Clark, M. (1976) *Young Fluent Readers*. London: Heinemann Education.

Clarke, P. (1999) 'Investigation second language acquisition in pre-schools: a longitudinal study of four Vietnamese-speaking children's acquisition of English in a bi-lingual pre-school', *International Journal of Early Years Education*, **7**, 11.

Clay, M. (1976) *What did I write*. London: Heinemann.

Clay, M., (1979) *The Early Detection of Reading Difficulties: A Diagnostic Survey with Recovery Procedures* (2nd edn). Tadworth: Windmill Press.

Cline, T. and Frederichson, N. (eds) (1997) *Curriculum Realated Assessment, Cummins and Bilingual Children*. Clevedon: Multilingual Matters.

CLPE/ Barrs, M and Thomas, A (eds) (1991) *The Reading Book*. London: CLPE.

Cochran, M. and Riley, D. (1990) 'The social networks of six-year-olds: context, content, and consequence', in Cochran, M. et al. *Extending Families: The social networks of parents and their children* (pp. 154–77). Cambridge: Cambridge University Press.

Cochran, M., Lamer, M., Riley, D., Gunnarsson, L. and Henderson, C. R., Jr. (1990) *Extending Families: The social networks of parents and their children*. Cambridge: Cambridge University Press.

Cochran-Smith, M. (1984) *The Making of a Reader*. Norwood, NJ: Ablex.

Collier, V. (1997) see Thomas, W. P. and Collier, V. (1997) *School Effectiveness for Language Minority Students*. NCBE Resource Collection Series. www.ncbe.gwu.edu/ncbepubs/resource/effectiveness/thomas-collier97.pAf

Corson, D. (1994) 'Bilingual education policy and social justice', in Blackledge, A. (ed.) *Teaching Bilingual Children*. Stoke-on-Trent: Trentham Books.

Cox, B. (1989) *English for Ages 5–11*. London: HMSO.

Cox, B. (ed.) (1998) *Literacy is Not Enough: Essays on the Importance of Reading*. Manchester: Manchester University Press.

Cummins, J. (1981) in Cummins, J. (1996) *Negotiating Identities: Education for Empowerment in a Diverse Society*. Ontario: CABE.

Cummins, J. (1984) *Bilingualism and Special Education: Issues in Assessment and Pedagogy*. Clevedon: Multilingual Matters.

Cummins, J. (1988) 'From multicultural to anti-racist education', in Skutnabb-Kangas, T. and Cummins, J. (eds) *Minority Education: From Shame to Struggle*. Clevedon: Multilingual Matters.

Cummins, J. (1991) 'Inter-dependence of first- and second-language proficiency in bilingual children', in Bialystok, E. (ed.) *Language Processing in Bilingual Children*. Cambridge: Cambridge University Press.

Cummins, J. (1996) *Negotiating Identities: Education for Empowerment in a Diverse Society*. Ontario: CABE.

Cummins, J. (2000) *Language, Power, and Pedagogy. Bilingual Children in the Crossfire*. Clevedon: Multilingual Matters.

Cunningham, P. (2000) 'Bilingual Children: Whole-school Policy and Practice', in Datta, M. *Bilinguality and Literacy: Principles and Practice* (1st edn). London: Continuum.

Cunningham, V. (1998) 'Reading Now and Then', in Cox, B. (ed.) *Literacy is Not Enough: Essays on the Importance of Reading*. Manchester: Manchester University Press.

Datta, M. (1998) 'Double Speak', *Times Education Supplement*, August.

Datta M. (1999) 'Blow away the Cobwebs', *Times Education Supplement*, August.

Datta, M. (2000) *Bilinguality and Literacy: Principles and Practice*. London: Continuum.

Datta, M. (2004) 'Friendship literacy', in Gregory, E. Long, S. and Volk, D. (eds) *Many Pathways to Literacy: Young children with grandparents, peers and communities*. London: Routledge Falmer.

Datta, M. and Pomphrey, C. (2004) *A World of Languages: Developing Children's Love of Languages*. London: CILT.

DfES (2005) *Raising the Achievement of Bilingual Learners in Primary Schools*. London: HMSO.

Doherty, B. (1994) 'The Power and Magic of the Language of the Imagination', *NATE News*, Conference Special, 14–15.

Donaldson, M. (1978) *Children's Minds*. Glasgow: Fontana Collins.

Donmall, B. G. (1985), cited in Baker, C. (1996, 2001) *Foundations of Bilingual Education and Bilingualism* (2nd edn). Clevedon: Multilingual Matters.

Drury, R. (1997) 'Two Sisters at School: Issues for Educators of Young Bilingual Children', in Gregory, E. (ed.) *One Child, Many Worlds: Early Learning in Multicultural Communities*. London: David Fulton Publishers.

Drury, R. (2000) 'Bilingual children in the pre-school years: different experiences of early learning', in Drury, R., Miller, L. and Campbell, R. (eds) *Looking at Early Years Education and Care*. London: David Fulton Publishers.

Duffy, B. (1998) *Supporting Creativity and Imagination in the Early Years*. Milton Keynes: Open University Press.

Duley, H., Burt, M. and Krashen, S. (1982) *Language Two*. Oxford: Oxford University Press.

East, C. (1999) 'Episodes in a Multilingual Classroom', *Primary Teaching Studies*, **10**(1) (Trentham Books).

East, C. (2000) *Fostering the Use of Community Languages in School*. London: UNL (unpublished).

Edelsky, C. (1986) *Writing in a Bilingual Program; Habia una vez*. Norwood, NJ: Ablex.

Edwards, V. (1986) *Language in a Black Community*. Clevedon: Multilingual Matters.

Edwards, V. (1998) *The |power of Babel: Teaching and learning in multilingual classrooms*. Stoke-on-Trent: Trentham Books.

Egan, K. (1992) *Imagination in Teaching and Learning Ages 8–15*. London: Routledge.

Egan, K. and Nadaner, D. (eds) (1988) *Imagination and Education*. Milton Keynes: Open University Press

Emblen, V. (1990) 'Baby wasn't accident: the natural conversation of infant children', in Levine, J. (ed.) *Bilingual Learners in the Mainstream Curriculum*. London: Falmer Press.

Emig, J. (1981) 'Non-magical Thinking: Presenting Writing Developmentally in Schools', in Frederiksen, C. H. and Dominic, J. F. (eds) *Writing: The Nature, Development, and Teaching of Written Communication, Volume 2: Process, Development and Communication*. Hillsdale, NJ: Lawrence Erlbaum.

Faltis, C. J. (1995) 'Building Bridges Between Parents and School', in Garcia, O. and Baker, C. (eds) *Policy and Practice in Bilingual Education: Extending the Foundations*. Clevedon: Multilingual Matters.

Fishman, J. A. (1989) *Language and Ethnicity in Minority and Sociolinguistic Perspective*. Clevedon: Multilingual Matters.

Fishman J. A. (1991) *Reversing Language Shift*. Clevedon: Multilingual Matters.

Floria-Ruane, S. (2001) *Teacher Education and the Cultural Imagination: Autobiography, Conversation and Narrative*. London: Lawrence Erlbaum.

Fox, G., Hammond, G. et al. (eds) (1976) *Writers, Critics and Children: Articles from Children's Literature in Education*. London: Heinemann Education

Frederiksen, J. (ed.) (1995) *Reclaiming Our Voices: Bilingual Education, Critical Pedagogy and Praxis*. Ontario: CABE.

Frederiksen, C. H. and Dominic, J. F. (eds) (1981) *Writing: The Nature, Development, and Teaching of Written Communication, Volume 2: Process, Development and Communication*. Hillsdale, NJ: Lawrence Erlbaum.

Friere, P. (1998) (ed.) in Friere, M. A. and Macedo, D. *The Paulo Friere Reader*. London: Continuum.

Frye, N. (1963) 'The Educated Imagination', cited in Egan, K. (1992) *Imagination in Teaching and Learning Ages 8–15*. London: Routledge.

Furlong, T. (1998) 'Reading in the Primary School', in Cox, B. (ed.) *Literacy is Not Enough: Essays on the Importance of Reading*. Manchester: Manchester University Press.

Garcia, O. (1996) 'Foreword' to Baker, C. (1996) *Foundations of Bilingual Education and Bilingualism* (2nd edn). Clevedon: Multilingual Matters.

Garcia, O. and Baker, C. (eds) (1995) *Policy and Practice in Bilingual Education: Extending the Foundations*. Clevedon: Multilingual Matters.

Gardener, R. C. and MacIntyre, P. D. (1993) 'A student contribution to second language learning. Part II: Affective Variables', *Language Teaching*, **26**, 1–11.

Genesee, F. (1987) *Learning Through Two Languages*. Cambridge, MA: Newbury House.

Gewirtz, S., Ball, S. and Bowe, R. (1995) *Markets, Choice and Equity in Education*. Buckingham: Open University.

Giles, H. and Coupland, N. (1991) *Language: Context and Consequences*. Milton Keynes: Open University Press.

Goodman, K. S. (1982) *Langauge and Literacy: The selected writings of Kenneth Goodman* (Gillasch, F. V. ed.). London: Routledge.

Goswami, U. and Bryant, P. E. (1990) *Phonological Skills and Learning to Read*. Hove, East Sussex: Lawrence Earlbaum.

Graddol, D. and Boyd-Barrett, O. (1994) *Media Texts: Authors and Readers*. Clevedon: Multilingual Matters/The Open University.

Gramsci, A. (1977) *Selections from Political Writings*. London: Lawrence and Wishart.

Granovetter, M. (1982) 'The strength of weak ties: A network theory revisited', in Marsden, P. V. and Lin, N. (eds) *Social Structure and Network Analysis* (pp. 105–30). Beverly Hills CA: SAGE.

Granovetter, M. (1973) 'The strength of weak ties', *American Journal of Sociology*, **78**, 1360–80.

Graves, D. H. (1983) *Writing: Teachers and Children at Work*. Heinemann Educational.

Gray, K. (1999) 'The Story of Zaida Becoming a Reader', *Primary Teaching Studies*, **10**(2), 27–33.

Gregory, E. (1996) *Making Sense of a New World: Learning to Read in a Second Language*. London: Paul Chapman Publishing.

Gregory, E., Long, S. and Volk, D. (eds) (2004) *Many Pathways to Literacy: Young children learning with grandparents, peers and communities*. London: Routledge Falmer.

Grieg, S. (1992) *New Faces New Places: Learning about People on the Move*. London: Save the Children.

Grosjean, F. (1982) *Life with Two Languages: An introduction to bilingualism*. London: Harvard University Press.

Gumperz, J. J. (1982) 'Conversational Code-switching', in *Discourse Strategies* (pp. 55–99). Cambridge: Cambridge University Press.

Gundara, J., Jones, C. and Kimberley, K. (eds) (1986) *Racism, Diversity and Education*. London: Hodder and Stoughton.

Gundlach, R. A. (1981) 'On the Nature and Development of Children's Writing', in Frederiksen, C. H. and Dominic, J. F. (eds) *Writing: The Nature, Development, and Teaching of Written Communication. Volume 2: Process, Development and Communication*. Hillsdale, NJ: Lawrence Erlbaum.

Hall, D. (1998) 'Differentiation in the Secondary Curriculum', in Cline, T. and Frederichson, N. (eds) *Curriculum Related Assessment, Cummins and Bilingual Children*. Clevedon: Multilingual Matters.

Halliday, M. A. K. (1975) *Learning How To Mean: Explorations in the development of language*. London: Edward Arnold.

Halliday, M. A. K. (1994) 'Spoken and Written Modes of Meaning', in Graddol, D. and Boyd-Barrett, O. *Media Texts: Authors and Readers*. Clevedon: Multilingual Matters/The Open University

Hamayan, E. V. (1990) 'Preparing mainstream classroom teachers to teach potentially English proficient students', Proceedings of the First Research Symposium on Limited English Proficient Students, Washington DC, Office for Bilingual Education and Minority Language Affairs.

Hamers, J. and Blanc, M. (1989) *Bilinguality and Bilingualism*. Cambridge: Cambridge University Press.

Hamilton, R. and Moore, D. (2004) *Educational Interventions for Refugee Children: Theoretical Perspectives and Implementing Best Practice*. London: Routledge Falmer.

Hardwick, N. and Rutter, J. (1998) 'The asylum white paper – what this means for schools and local authorities', *Multicultural Teaching*, **17**(1), 6–7.

Heath, S. B. (1983) *Ways with Words: Language, life, and work in communities and classrooms*. New York: Cambridge University Press.

Hester, H. (1983) *Stories in the Multilingual Primary Classroom*. London: ILEA.

Hester, H. (1986) 'Stages of Second Language Acquisistion', in Barrs, M. and Thomas, A. (eds) *The Reading Book*. London: CLPE.

Hester, H. and Barrs, M. (1990) *Patterns and Learning: the Primary Language Record*. London: CLPE.

Hickman, J. and Cullinan, B. (eds) (1989) *Children's Literature in the Classroom: Weaving Charlotte's Web*. Needham Heights, MA: Christopher Gordon.

Hudleson, S. (1994) 'Literacy Development in Second-language Children', cited in Baker, C. (1996) *Foundations of Bilingual Education and Bilingualism* (2nd edn). Clevedon: Multilingual Matters.

Hughes, T. (1976) 'Myth and Education', in Fox, G. *Writers, Critics and Children: Articles from Children's Literature in Education*. London: Heinemann Education.

Hymes, D. (1972) 'Introduction', in Cazden, C. B., John, V. P. and Hymes, D. (eds) *Functions of Language in the Classroom*. New York: Teacher College Press.

Johnstone, R. (1993) 'Research on language and teaching: 1992', *Language Teaching* **26**, 131–43.

Joly, D. with Kelly, L. and Nettleton, C. (1997) *Refugees in Europe: The Hostile New Agenda.* London: Minority Rights Group International.

Kenner, C. (2004) *Becoming Biliterate: Young Children Learning Different Writing Systems.* Stoke-on-Trent: Trentham Books.

Kenner, C., Wells, K. and Williams, H. (1996) 'Assessing a bilingual child's talk in different classroom contexts', in Hall, N. and Martello, J. (eds) *Listening to Children Think: Exploring talk in the early years.* London: Hodder and Stoughton.

Kramsch, C. (1998) *Language and Culture.* Oxford: Oxford University Press.

Krashen, S. (1982) see Duley, H., Burt, M. and Krashen, S. (1982) *Language Two.* Oxford: Oxford University Press.

Krashen, S. (1993) *The Power of Reading.* Eaglewood, CO: Libraries Unlimited.

Kress, G. (1997) *Before Writing: Rethinking the pathway to literacy.* London: Routledge.

Kress, G. (2003) *Literacy in the New Media Age.* London: Routledge.

Lambert, W. E. (1974) 'Language and culture as factors in learning and education', in Aboud, F. E. and Mead, R. D. (eds) *Cultural Factors in Learning and Education.* Bellingham, WA: Western Washington State University.

Lambert, W. E. (1984) 'The effects of bilingual-bicultural on children's attitudes and perceptions', in Homel, P. and Paliz, M. (eds) *Childhood Bilingualism: Aspects of Cognitive, Social and Emotional Development.* Hillsdale, NJ: Lawrence Erlbaum.

Li Wei (2000) 'Extending School: Bilingual Development of Chinese Children' in Datta, M. *Bilinguality and Literacy: Principles and Practice.* London: Continuum.

Linguistic Minorities Project (1985) *The Other Languages of England.* London: Routledge.

MacCabe, C. (1998) 'Television and Literacy', in Cox, B. (ed.) (1998) *Literacy is Not Enough: Essays on the Importance of Reading.* Manchester: Manchester University Press.

McKinnon, K. (1977) *Language, Education and Social Processes in a Gaelic Community.* London: Routledge.

Malafoff, M. and Hakuta, K. (1991) 'Translation skill and metalinguistic awareness in bilinguals', in Bialystok, E. (ed.) *Language Processing in Bilingual Children.* Cambridge: Cambridge University Press.

Mas, F. (1999) 'Year 3 Bilingual Learners' Cultural and Linguistic Experiences'. B.Ed. Project, UNL (unpublished).

Meek, M. (1982) *Learning to Read.* London: The Bodley Head.

Meek, M. (1985) 'Playground Paradoxes: Some consideration of imagination and language', in Wells, G. and Nicholls, J. *Language and Learning: An international perspective.* London: The Falmer Press.

Meek, M. (1988) *How Texts Teach What Readers Learn.* Stroud, UK: Thimble Press.

Meek, M. (1991) *On Being Literate.* London: The Bodley Head.

Meek, M., Warlow, A. and Barton, G. (eds) (1977) *The Cool Web: The Pattern of Children's Reading.* London: The Bodley Head.

Milardo, R. M. (ed.) (1988) *Families and Social Networks.* Newbury Park, CA: Sage.

Miller, P. H. (2002) *Theories of Developmental Psychology* (4th edn). New York: Worth Publishers.

Milroy, L. (1980) *Language and Social Networks.* Oxford: Blackwell.

Minami, M. (2002) *Culture-specific Language Styles: The Development of Oral Narrative and Literacy.* Clevedon: Multilingual Matters.

Moffatt, S. (1990) 'Becoming Bilingual: A sociolinguistic study of the communication of young mother-tongue Punjabi-speaking children'. Unpublished Ph.D. thesis, University of Newcastle upon Tyne.

Moffet, J. (1962) cited in Britton, J. (1972) *Language and Learning.* Harmondsworth: Penguin Books.

Moll, L. C. (1992) *Bilingual Classroom Studies and Community Analysis.* Educational

Researcher 21 (20–24).

Moll, L. C., Amarti, C., Neff, D. and Gonzalez, N. (1992) 'Funds of knowledge for teaching: using a qualitative approach to connect homes and classrooms', in *Theory and Practice*, **31**, 132–41.

Motion, A. (1999) *A Book of Hours: Fourteen new poems to mark National Poetry Day.* London: BBC Radio 4.

Myers-Scotton, C. (1993) *Duelling Languages: Grammatical Structures in Codeswitching.* Oxford: OUP.

Nadaner, D. (1988) in Egan, K. and Nadaner, D. (eds) (1988) *Imagination and Education.* Milton Keynes: Open University Press.

Neisser, U. (1967) *Cognitive Psychology.* New York: Appleton-Century-Crofts.

Nieto, S. (1999) *The Light in their Eyes: Creating Multicultural Learning Communities.* Stoke-on-Trent: Trentham Books.

Nimmo, N. (1999) 'How Three Schools Responded to the Recent Conflict In Kosovo', *Primary Teaching Studies*, **11**(1), 24–9.

Nuffield Foundation (1981) *Teaching Chinese Children.* London: CLT.

Nutbrown, C. (1996) 'Wide Eyes and Open Minds – Observing, Assessing and Respecting Children's Early Achievements', in Nutbrown, C. *Respectful Educators, Capable Learners: Children's Rights and Early Education.* London: Paul Chapman Publishing.

Ofsted (2003) *More Advanced Learners of English as an Additional Language.* London: Ofsted (www.ofsted.gov.uk).

Ofsted (2005) *Better Education and Care: Could they do even better?* London: Ofsted (www.ofsted.gov.uk).

Olsen, D. R. and Torrance, N. (1981) 'Learning to Meet the Requirements of Written Text: Language Development in School Years', in Frederiksen, C. H. and Dominic, J. F. (eds) *Writing: The Nature, Development, and Teaching of Written Communication, Volume 2: Process, Development and Communication.* Hillsdale, NJ: Lawrence Erlbaum.

Pafford, F. (1999) 'Level Three and the Ringling Tingling Man: Assessing Language and Literacy', in Marsh, J. and Hallet, E. (eds) *Desirable Literacies: Approaches to Language and Literacy in the Early Years.* London: Paul Chapman Publishing.

Parker, J. (1999) 'In safe hands', *Guardian Unlimited*, 10 November.

Phillips, S. U. (1972) 'Participant Structures and Communicative Competence: Warm Springs Children in Community Classrooms', in Cazden, C. B., John, V. P. and Hymes, D. (eds) *Functions of Language in the Classroom.* New York: Teacher College Press.

Power, S., Whitty, G. and Youdell, D. (1998) 'Refugees, asylum seekers and the housing crisis: no place to learn', in Rutter, J. and Jones, C. (eds) *Refugee Education: Mapping the Field.* Stoke-on-Trent: Trentham Books.

Propp, V. (1968) *Morphology of the Folktale.* Texas: University of Texas Press.

QAA (2002) *Assessment for Learning.* London: QCA.

QCA/DfEE (1999) *The National Curriculum: Handbook for Primary Teachers in England.* London: HMSO/QCA.

Rajagopalachari, C. (1958) *Mahabharata.* Mumbai: Bharatatiya Vidya Bhavan.

Richman, N. (1998) *In the Midst of the Whirlwind: A manual for helping refugee children.* Stoke-on-Trent: Trentham Books.

Richmond, J. (ed.) (1985) *Writing.* London: ILEA English Centre.

Risager, K. (2006) *Langauage and Culture: Global Flows and Local Complexity.* Clevedon: Multilingual Matters.

Rogers, E. M. and Shoemaker, F. F. (1971) *Communication of Innovations* (2nd edn). New York: Free Press.

Rogoff, B. (1990) *Apprenticeship in Thinking: Cognitive development in social context.* New York: Oxford University Press.

Romaine, S. (1989) *Bilingualism.* Oxford: Blackwell.

Rosen, H. (1994) 'The Whole Story', *NATE News*, Conference Special, 9–13.

Rosen, M. (1989) *Did I Hear You Write?* London: Andre Deutsch.

Rumelhart, D. E. (1976) 'Toward an interactive model of reading', in Dorric, S. (ed.) *Attention and Performance VI*. Stockholm: Halsted Press.

Rutter, J. (2006) *Refugee Children in the UK*. Maidenhead: Open University Press.

Rutter, J. and Jones, C. (eds) (1998) *Refugee Education: Mapping the Field*. Stoke-on-Trent: Trentham Books.

Saava, H. (1990) *National Writing Project*. Windsor: NFER-Nelson.

Siraj-Blatchford, I. and Clarke, P. (2000) *Supporting Identity, Diversity and Language in the Early Years*. Buckingham: Open University Press.

Skutnabb-Kangas, T. (1981) *Bilingualism or Not: The education of minorities*. Clevedon: Multilingual Matters.

Skutnabb-Kangas, T. (1986) 'Who wants to change what and why: conflicting paradigms in minority education research', in Spolsky, B. (ed.) *Language and Education in Multilingual Settings*. Clevedon: Multilingual Matters.

Skutnabb-Kangas, T. and Cummins, J. (eds) (1988) *Minority Education: From Shame to Struggle*. Clevedon: Multilingual Matters.

Smith, F. (1978) *Writing and the Writer*. London: Heinemann Educational.

Swain, M. and Wesche, M. (1973) 'Linguistic interaction: a case study of a bilingual child', *Working Papers on Bilingualism*, **1**, 10–34.

Taylor, I. (1998) 'Case Studies of Bilingual Readers', *Primary Teaching* Studies, **10**(1), Trentham Books.

Taylor, M. and Hegerty, S. (1985) *The Best of Both Worlds? A Review of Research into the Education of Pupils of Chinese Origin*. Windsor: NFER-Nelson.

Thomas, W. P. and Collier, V. (1997) *School Effectiveness for Language Minority Students*. NCBE Resource Collection Series. www.ncbe.gwu.edu/ncbepubs/resource/effectiveness/thomas-collier97.pAf

TTA (2004) *Results of the Newly Qualified Teacher Survey 2004: Sector Level Report*. London: Teacher Training Agency.

TTA (2006) *Results of the Newly Qualified Teacher Survey 2006: Sector Level Report*. London: Teacher Training Agency.

Turner, G. (1994) 'Film Language', in Graddol, D. and Boyd-Barrett, O. *Media Texts: Authors and Readers*. Clevedon: Multilingual Matters/The Open University.

United Nations High Commission for Refugees (UNHCR) (1993) *Report*. New York: UNHCR.

Verhoeven, L. T. (1991) 'Predicting minority children's bilingual proficiency: child, family and institutional factors', *Language Learning*, **41**(2), 205–33.

Verhoeven, L. T. (1994) 'Transfer in bilingual development: The linguistic interdependence hypothesis revisited', *Language Learning*, **44**(3), 381–415.

Vernon, M. D. (1971) *Reading and its Difficulties*. Cambridge: Cambridge University Press.

Vygotsky, L. (1962/1986) *Thought and Language*. Revised and edited by Kozulin, A. Cambridge, MA: Massachusetts Institute of Technology.

Vygotsky, L. (1978) *Mind in Society: The development of higher psychological processes* (Cole, M. et al. eds). Cambridge, MA: Harvard University Press.

Warnock, M. (1976) *Imagination*. London: Faber and Faber.

Wells, G. and Nicholls, J. (1985) *Language and Learning: An international perspective*. London: Falmer Press.

White, A. R. (1990) *The Language of Imagination*. London: Blackwell.

Whitehead, M. R. (1990) *Language and Literacy in the Early Years: An approach for education students*. London: Paul Chapman Publishing.

Whitehead, M. R. (1997) *Language and Literacy in the Early Years: An approach for education students* (2nd edn). London: Paul Chapman Publishing.

Wilks, J. (1998) 'Reading for Pupils aged 11–14', in Cox, B. (ed.) *Literacy is Not Enough: Essays on the Importance of Reading*. Manchester: Manchester University Press.

Williams, G. (ed.) (1987) 'The sociology of Welsh', *International Journal of the Sociology of Language*, **66**.

Wong-Filmore, L. Y. (1991) 'Second Language Learning in Children: A model of language learning in social context', in Bialystok, E. (ed.) *Language Processing in Bilingual Children*. Cambridge: Cambridge University Press.

Wong-Filmore, L. Y. (1992) *Education of Chinese Children in Britain and the USA*. Clevedon: Multilingual Matters.

Wood, R. (1999) 'ICT Lecture Notes', UNL (unpublished).

Zyngier, S. (1994) 'Introducing Literacy Awareness'. *Language Awareness*.

Index